"An excellent collection of texts in this noble tradition, carefully chosen and edited from ancients to moderns."

—Harvey Mansfield, Harvard University

"This inspired assemblage offers a far better primer to any would-be leader than all the current handlers, talking points, and contemporary conventional wisdom combined."

—Victor Davis Hanson, Hoover Institution

"If the world seems to lack the kinds of statesmen that once arose to meet the crises of their age, a likely reason is that the leaders we need today—unlike those of yesteryear—are no longer reading the words that have been carefully gathered in this book. John Burtka has given us all an immensely valuable gift, not as a collection of antiquarian ideas, but vital inspiration that is desperately needed for the formation of tomorrow's statesmen."

—Patrick J. Deneen, University of Notre Dame

"For too long, the modern West has imagined that we can substitute well-designed systems for wise statesmen, that we should trust in technocratic reason rather than hard-earned virtue. Today's political distempers are a sign that this fantasy of governance without largeness of soul has reached a dead end. Which is why this well-selected collection of classic texts comes at just the right moment. May it fall into the hands of the rising generation of leaders!"

—Dr. R. R. Reno, *First Things*

"Statesmanship is in short supply in our time, in no small part because the study of statesmanship is all too rare. In this rich collection, John Burtka draws on history, biography, and philosophy to fill that gap, and the result is both engaging and important."

—Dr. Yuval Levin, American Enterprise Institute

"Johnny Burtka's book turns our attention to an ancient and more venerable model of education, whose concern is the subtle art of statesmanship. Here is a book that is sorely needed in our troubled age."

—Dr. Joshua Mitchell, Georgetown University

"In an increasingly dangerous time that requires wise and vigorous leadership, Johnny Burtka performs an important service in publishing this fascinating selection of classic 'mirrors-for-princes.' Together these selections span a wide variety of different perspectives and cultures, but, as Burtka lays out in his penetrating and incisive introduction, they are bound together in thinking seriously about what leadership means in challenging times."

—Elbridge Colby, former Deputy Assistant Secretary of Defense for Strategy and Force Development

"This collection offers profound insights on political leadership that have stood the test of time. It's required reading for any aspiring statesman."

—Ambassador Robert Lighthizer, former United States Trade Representative

"In this book, Burtka continues to advance his own education while helping us with ours. The form of the book is a tour of many of the great writers who have written on statesmanship. I urge you to read it."

—Dr. Larry P. Arnn, Hillsdale College

"The modern West is the only civilization in history that has proceeded on the assumption that God or gods do not exist. Spoiler alert: It doesn't work. Johnny Burtka's book demonstrates why great leaders and civilizations take religion seriously."

—Tucker Carlson

Gateway to Statesmanship

Gateway *to* Statesmanship

Selections from Xenophon
to Churchill

Edited by John A.
Burtka IV

REGNERY GATEWAY
Washington, D.C.

Regnery Gateway™ is a trademark of Salem Communications Holding Corporation
Regnery® is a registered trademark and its colophon is a trademark of Salem Communications Holding Corporation

Cataloging-in-Publication data on file with the Library of Congress

ISBN: 978-1-68451-543-1
eISBN: 978-1-68451-699-5
Library of Congress Control Number: 2023945380

Published in the United States by
Regnery Gateway, an Imprint of
Regnery Publishing
A Division of Salem Media Group
Washington, D.C.
www.Regnery.com

Manufactured in the United States of America

10 9 8 7 6 5 4 3 2 1

Books are available in quantity for promotional or premium use. For information on discounts and terms, please visit our website: www.RegneryGateway.com.

To my wife and best friend, Amanda; my parents and role models, John and Denise; my sister, Jessica, who cares about education more than anyone I know; and to the entire Moulton family. May we strive valiantly for what is beautiful, know great enthusiasms and devotions, and spend ourselves in pursuit of a worthy cause.

For the forty-seventh president of the United States upon your inauguration, and to all leaders in any and every domain, may you govern courageously, justly, and mercifully.

Contents

Foreword

A reasonable person may think that John Burtka is very young to be giving advice to statesmen. That person would be correct. On the other hand, I knew Johnny (as we call him) when he was in college, much younger than now, and he manifested two qualities that are essential to a life of statesmanship, the archetype of the life of practical judgment.

In character, Johnny was earnest and high-minded. In intellect, he was curious. He was a *tireless* student, seeking to grow.

In this book, Johnny continues to advance his own education while helping us with ours. The book is a tour of many of the great writers who have written on statesmanship.

The study of statesmanship is the study of the whole human being in thought and action. It is not a subject for leaders in politics alone. The classics teach us that it concerns choosing, the activity by which we guide our lives and also form our characters. This requires a kind of dual-mindedness. We must focus upon the shifting details that affect every course of action we pursue. What is right to do in one circumstance might be disastrous in another. Even the goal of action itself can be altered by the necessities that arise in events. People who are good at grasping what is happening around them and speculating what might happen next make the best generals, entrepreneurs, and (most difficult of all) statesmen. At the same time, everyone deploys this capacity in guiding his daily life, and those who do it better shine.

But it is not all about the circumstances. There is something outside of them and even outside of us that the classics describe as our sense of the good or of rightness. Amidst the turbulence of action and reaction through which practical wisdom must navigate, the right path through is a form of the "truth," as Aristotle calls it. It is not the eternal truth that is the object of philosophy, but it is the truth nonetheless, the right thing to do in these circumstances. That truth may not be the most convenient thing for us. It may even be dangerous for us. It is not simply a calculation of advantage. That is why finding that truth is one of the forms of beauty by which Aristotle says we are capable. It points up toward the ultimate forms of wisdom concerned with the eternal.

The development of this capacity is the very work that produces maturity. Johnny demonstrates his maturity in this book. He has risen to the headship of a serious organization, venerable and distinguished, and its purpose is to help the young form their intellects and characters. Johnny is qualified to lead that organization because he has worked so hard. The same thing qualifies him to write this book. I urge you to read it.

Dr. Larry P. Arnn
Hillsdale, Michigan
June 2023

Introduction

Mirrors-for-Princes: A Survival Manual for an Embattled Statesman

A mericans no longer have faith in their leaders. The past thirty years have laid the foundation for the crisis facing America today. The "end of history" prophets of the early post–Cold War period that promised economic globalization, democratic expansion, and liberal individualism under the banner of American hegemony were, to steal a phrase, "mugged by reality." The world revolted against their utopian attempts to create heaven on earth by remaking human nature. A cascading series of disasters followed: China's entry into the World Trade Organization, the September 11 terrorist attacks, the War on Terror, the Great Recession, the deindustrialization of the American heartland, the opioid epidemic, pandemic lockdowns, social unrest, economic stagnation, and the war in Ukraine.

No wonder Americans have lost faith in their leaders. Examples of elite failures are so ubiquitous that there is no need to chronicle them all here. As such, the purpose of this book is to rediscover time-tested principles of political leadership that a new generation of Americans can implement in their daily lives to become leaders and to renew the nation.

It's important to remember that we're not the first people to complain about our leaders. Without proper education and mentorship, most individuals in leadership positions in most countries for most of time have been quite mediocre or even terrible. Only rarely do virtue and fate combine to elevate a person of exceptional talent who is also beloved by the people.

However, that doesn't mean we need to relegate ourselves to the role of passive observers, waiting complacently for a hero to save us. There is an almost entirely forgotten literary tradition that was designed to raise up new leaders. Called "mirrors-for-princes," its essential writings—usually short books or letters—are described as mirrors because they served as self-help manuals for political leaders to examine their conduct and appearances. The term first came into use during the High Middle Ages, but the concept underlying it dates back to antiquity.

This tradition has often helped to rectify the problem of bad leadership over the past two millennia. The texts come from peoples of all cultures, creeds, and political systems, and they have helped to inspire and instill courage, prudence, and charisma in countless leaders who have heeded their counsels. Not every admonition in this book is worthy of imitation—some of the advice is downright evil. Nevertheless, it's important for discerning readers to understand the tactics and treachery that will be used against them if they aspire to positions of leadership in the real world.

Some of the most famous authors include Xenophon, Cicero, Han Fei, al-Farabi, Thomas Aquinas, Machiavelli, Erasmus, and Thomas More, among others. Over the course of centuries, these thinkers have influenced statesmen (Alexander the Great, Julius Caesar, Justinian the Great, and Elizabeth I), theologians and poets (Ambrose, Jerome, Augustine, and Dante), and philosophers (Montesquieu, Voltaire, Hume, and Smith). And they decisively shaped American founders like Washington, Jefferson, Hamilton, and Adams.

Despite its popularity, this tradition fell out of use for two important reasons. First, these mirrors were typically written as gifts for new monarchs at their coronations. In light of the historical shift from monarchical to representative forms of government during the modern era, there was no longer occasion to present such texts to a new king or queen. However, there's no reason why the mirrors-for-princes tradition couldn't have become a "mirrors-for-presidents" tradition, presented to elected leaders at the time of their inaugurations.

Second, the tradition disappeared because the contemporary education system is guilty of presentism, prioritizing secondary literature over primary sources, and social sciences over moral philosophy and theology. While the tradition consists of many classic texts from the Western "Great Books" canon, mirrors-for-princes is a universal phenomenon that spans all races, creeds, and geographic locations. Its message of justice, religious duty, and moral and vocational excellence has the power to inspire leaders who fight for the interests and well-being of all citizens, regardless of political party.

The best example of its enduring relevance comes from Xenophon's *The Education of Cyrus*, a handbook written around 370 BC about a model Persian ruler who conquered a kingdom through self-discipline and cunning while winning the admiration of his subjects. It begins with a profound claim about the persistent problem of bad leadership: it doesn't have to be this way. "Ruling human beings does not belong among those tasks that are impossible, or even among those that are difficult, if one does it with *knowledge*."[1] In other words, Xenophon locates, as Wayne Ambler aptly notes in a translation, "the solution for the political problem in science or knowledge."[2]

Xenophon was in the business of building future worlds. While he was telling a story about a king in the Ancient Near East for his fellow Athenians, he was also painting a portrait of a leader who would inspire other nation-makers and kingdom-builders for millennia to come, from Julius Caesar to Thomas Jefferson. He showed how the education of Cyrus empowered him to both establish and rule the Persian Empire, creating order, prosperity, and peace throughout his expansive kingdom. If Cyrus could do what appeared to be impossible in his day, we too can overcome our civilizational crisis by educating a new generation with the knowledge needed to govern wisely in twenty-first-century America.

The mirrors-for-princes tradition, though representing a range of positions informed by historical and cultural context, is universal because it fundamentally forms a coherent body of wisdom that can be applied—with careful study and discernment—in nearly any place and at any time. What's needed today is a fourfold process of rediscovery and redeployment: first, we must remind ourselves that previous generations gave careful thought to the virtues needed for political leadership and paid special attention to the education required to cultivate such qualities; second, we must read widely and carefully from the works in this distinguished tradition; third, we must prudentially identify the core principles that remain applicable today; and fourth, we should not hesitate to write our own mirrors-for-presidents that draw from our unique American tradition and elevate the standards for contemporary leaders.

For the sake of better understanding the contours of this tradition, I will divide the texts into four periods: ancient, medieval, renaissance, and modern.

Ancient

From the vantage point of the twenty-first century, it's tempting to view conditions in the ancient world as "nasty, brutish, and short," echoing Thomas Hobbes's famous description of the "state of nature." While it's undoubtedly true that healthcare, technology, and agriculture lagged far behind contemporary Western standards, it's unfair to conclude that people were any less civilized, educated, or generally content with the quality of their lives than they are today.

As historian Francis Oakley has aptly noted, "Despite the seeming freshness of their vision, the world was already old when Plato and Aristotle came to write."[3] What was this world like? I hesitate to make overly broad generalizations, but there are at least two realities worth noting.

First, the religious cult was the foundation for political regimes, and kings were seen as divine or saintly beings who linked heaven and earth together in their very persons and mediated the presence of the sacred to the people through cultic actions, specifically in temples or other holy places. With slight shades of difference, the religious and monarchical foundations of politics were nearly ubiquitous across all peoples and continents in the ancient world, and the relatively brief periods of the Hebrew Judges, the Greek polis, and the Roman Republic were aberrations from this larger pattern. The merits of such a worldview aside, it's important to remember that the primary audience for the mirrors-for-princes tradition was rulers with this particular conception of their role and responsibilities.

Second, there was a tremendous degree of instability and churn as nomadic peoples settled in new regions and developed domestic agriculture. Cities emerged as focal points of religious, political, and commercial life, and empires expanded and contracted across ethnic groups. In this context of boundaries constantly being drawn and redrawn and regimes being founded and conquered, the primary political concern was maintaining order, which could be understood as a precondition for justice.

Princes, or aspiring princes, faced the constant threat of anarchy and mutiny from within and conquest from without. This should come as no surprise to anyone familiar with King

David in ancient Israel, whose main petition to God in the Psalms was for deliverance from his enemies. Beset by foes on all sides, ancient rulers often deployed brutal means to advance their interests and establish the security needed to govern their territories.

Judged in light of contemporary Western standards, many of these violent tactics shock the conscience, but they were then commonplace tools for maintaining order. Lest we be too quick to judge them in light of contemporary standards, it's important to remind ourselves that the twentieth century was the bloodiest period in the history of mankind and that many aspects of modern life would appear positively inhumane to the ancients.

As relates to the ancient Greeks and Romans, the three mirrors-for-princes of greatest relevance today are Xenophon's *Education of Cyrus*, selections from Aristotle's *Nicomachean Ethics*, and Cicero's *On Moral Duties*.

The portrait of Cyrus has endured the test of time because Xenophon was an excellent storyteller who captured the imagination of his readers. Sir Philip Sidney, a renowned English poet of the Elizabethan age, testified to this when he wrote that *The Education* has the potential to "make many Cyruses, if they will learn aright why and how [his] maker made" them.[4] At the most foundational level, the story of Cyrus persuasively demonstrates that when educational standards are raised, teaching restraint and piety, a civilization prospers, and when they are debased, men become soft and even the greatest regimes fall.

Cyrus the Great was born in the sixth century BC in what is today Iran. His father was the king of Persia and his maternal grandfather the king of Media. From a young age he learned to restrain his base desires for greater pleasures, such as glory and honor. Eventually, Cyrus would dethrone his grandfather and take his kingdom. He mastered the art of using cunning, gift-giving, competition, rewards, and punishments to first conquer extensive territory and then rule his kingdom. Ever pious toward the gods and beloved by his people until his dying day, Cyrus's last words sum up his philosophy of leadership: "Show kindness to your friends, and then shall you have it in your power to chastise your enemies."[5]

Over the course of his life, he established the largest empire known to mankind, spanning from the borders of modern-day India to Greece. When he conquered kingdoms, he was generous and merciful to his new subjects, respecting their local customs and traditions, although he commanded total obedience and left soldiers behind to police his new territories. He was often stricter with his own soldiers who disobeyed him or gave into drunkenness or lust than with his enemies—conquerors must first master their own passions, he reasoned.

One example of his benevolence as a ruler was the mercy he showed to the Hebrew people living captive in Babylon. He allowed them to return freely to Jerusalem, and the prophets considered him a kind of messiah for liberating the Jewish people from the hand of the Assyrians. The Jews held him in reverence for years to come and considered his reign to be a gift from God.

Cyrus has been revered throughout history as a strong but benevolent emperor whose advancements laid the foundation for both Western and Eastern civilizational development. He was admired by men like Alexander the Great, who devoted resources to restoring his tomb, and held in esteem by American founders such as Thomas Jefferson and Benjamin Franklin for his tolerance and liberality towards subjects of diverse religions. Xenophon, however, does not romanticize him. His portrait of Cyrus is strikingly honest about what it takes to lead and what tactics can be deployed by leaders to win men and women to themselves. With some discernment, the lessons from *The Education* can be read and profitably implemented by leaders in any era.

Aristotle's *Ethics*, compiled in ancient Greece during the fourth century BC to explore the best way to live a good life, takes a different approach. Aristotle spent more than twenty years studying at Plato's Academy. At the request of King Philip of Macedon, he served as the personal tutor to Alexander the Great, who went on to conquer the Persian Empire and Egypt by the young age of thirty. Eventually, Aristotle returned to Athens to establish his own school called the Lyceum. Towards the end of his life, he was forced into exile amid a persecution of Macedonians in Athens.

His book on ethics is largely a treatise on the nature of contemplation, friendship, and the life of virtue. The chapter on the magnanimous man reveals Aristotle's portrait of an ideal prince, who embodies the perfection of the moral virtues. The magnanimous man seeks honor because it is the reward for virtue and the highest gift the community can bestow upon one of its citizens. But being self-sufficient in every respect, he's ultimately indifferent to the prize. He's magnificent in expenditures that benefit the public, whether civil or religious, and he only speaks ill of his enemies to insult them; otherwise, he couldn't care less what others think of him. The magnanimous man looks down on others justly. His countenance is elevated, he moves slowly and deliberately, and he has mastered the virtues of courage and temperance. Above all, he practices what is fitting for the occasion and refrains from all base desires, which he has learned to master and reform.

Aristotle's magnanimous man often gets criticized for his arrogance, but it's important to understand the public nature and function of his pride. The chapter on magnanimity in *The Ethics* is situated between discourses on generosity and honor—two qualities frequently used by political leaders to maintain their regimes. This indicates that the magnanimous man is not merely a private individual, but a public figure: Aristotle's statesman. When the statesman is acting on behalf of the public or the national interest, the Churchillian qualities described by Aristotle can serve to command respect and inspire others toward greatness.

Moving from ancient Greece to Rome, the statesman and philosopher Cicero wrote the most famous mirror-for-princes text from the ancient world, *On Moral Duties*. Cicero was a Roman senator and served as consul in 63 BC. He was the political foe of "dictator-for-life" Julius Caesar. When Caesar was murdered on March 15, 44 BC, the name of Cicero was invoked by the perpetrators as a rallying cry to restore the Roman Republic, of which Cicero was the foremost champion.

Cicero's fortunes did not improve for long, as a new triumvirate consisting of Mark Antony, Octavian (Caesar's heir), and Marcus Lepidus took power. Cicero was named an enemy of the state and was killed at the order of Mark Antony, who had Cicero's head and hands cut off and displayed on the Rostra, a prominent platform for public speaking in front of the Senate building. Years later, Octavian would consolidate power and reign as the first Roman emperor, Caesar Augustus, ushering in the Pax Romana, which was a two-hundred-year period marked by general peace and prosperity.

According to classicist P. G. Walsh, Cicero's last and most famous work, *On Moral Duties*, was "addressed to a whole generation which would outlive the political corruption of Mark Antony, and might bend to the task of restoring the republic."[6] Looking beyond his impending demise, Cicero wrote the book to his son, staking his hopes on future generations that might heed his advice on manners and morals.

Yet unlike, for instance, Xenophon's tract, *On Moral Duties* is written for the righteous mind, not for those solely seeking worldly wisdom. Writing hastily yet eloquently, with a sense of prudential realism, Cicero asserts that the active life of politics is morally superior to the academic life of the mind. Reflecting on his own career preceding his exile, he rejects the notion of a tension between honorable and useful actions and maintains that the honorable course is always useful, and that the interests of individuals always align with those of the community and nation. He is an ardent defender of private property and loathes demagogues seeking to despoil the rich. For example, he laments the rise of populist politicians like Lucius Marcius Philippus, who proposed an agrarian law around 100 BC to promote the equalization of property and remission of debts. Cicero says such ideas undermine "the foundations of the state, which depends first and foremost on the harmony between classes."[7]

There is something distinctive about Cicero's claims when compared to other ancient works. His sense of duty and morality is austere in ways that could be perceived as burdensome to many of the celebrated statesmen from history. He speaks as a senator, not a prince. Nevertheless, his work does contain practical guidance for how to be virtuous and rightly order one's desires. It stands the test of time and influenced countless early Christian theologians, as well as those of the Reformation and Counter-Reformation periods.

It's important to recognize the profound contribution made by Eastern thinkers to this tradition. This collection includes the great third-century AD Indian scholar Kauṭilya, whose book on statecraft, *Arthaśāstra*, draws from ancient Hindu wisdom and offers advice for a king on a range of topics, including political theory, public policy, economics, and military strategy. The author advised several emperors of the Maurya Empire, and the text was highly revered in Indian culture, but it disappeared for over a millennium until its rediscovery in the early twentieth century. While little biographical information is known about the author, there is a strong sense of realism in his work that echoes the power politics advised by Chinese legalist Han Fei during the Zhou Dynasty (1046 BC–256 BC), which lasted for nearly eight centuries and produced profound philosophical and technological innovations in agricultural and military life.

It's worth examining Han Fei in greater detail, as his essay "The Difficulties of Persuasion" represents a break from the Roman idealism of Cicero and foreshadows the pragmatism of Machiavelli. He was an aristocrat with a notable stutter that prevented him from speaking in court. He was, however, a talented writer and lamented the poor quality of ministers advising the king of Han. He fiercely opposed corruption in elite classes and implemented systemic reforms to root out mediocrity from the civil service. Later in life, he found himself advising a neighboring king who was considering attacking Han Fei's homeland. Just as he began to make progress and win his affection, a former friend and political rival poisoned him to death, making it look like a suicide.

In this period, Chinese emperors ruled with the "mandate of heaven," and their chief responsibility was maintaining order and harmony on earth, as it is in heaven. Stability—not political freedom—was the first duty for a Zhou ruler. In light of Han Fei's low view of human nature and belief in man's natural propensity for evil, his political advice is rooted in realism. His perspective is largely amoral and interest based, emphasizing power over virtue.

His writing shocks the reader with blunt and pragmatic advice, which is often seasoned with gruesome tales of meting out rewards and punishments to the ruler's ministers. In one particular situation, he describes a confrontation between a ruler and a former court official who was crying after having had a foot amputated as punishment. Bluntly, the king asked the man, "Many people in the world have had their feet amputated—why do you weep so piteously over it?"[8]

On another occasion, Han Fei identifies what he calls the five "vermin of the state," which include analogues to scholars, journalists, defense contractors, lobbyists, and merchants. Han Fei says, quite apocalyptically, "If the rulers do not wipe out such vermin, and in their place encourage men of integrity and public spirit, then they should not be surprised, when they look about the area within the four seas, to see states perish and ruling houses wane and die."[9]

Breaking from the Western tradition, Han Fei advises that rulers keep a low profile and only appear in public when necessary. A ruler should maintain silence and not reveal his motives. His otherworldliness is key to maintaining power, and he should never reveal his inner designs to anyone lest courtiers tailor their suggestions to please the ruler's ears.

In Han Fei's regime, power is centralized, and the individual is entirely subordinate to the interests of the sovereign. Tradition is jettisoned for pragmatism, and subjects are encouraged to abase themselves in service of collective ends. Ministers should be graded on an objective scale and held to the exact standards they set for themselves, no more, no less. Rulers get all the credit for good things, and subordinates take the fall for bad things. Power is never delegated or else the ruler loses his authority as the sole dispenser of justice and mercy, reward and punishment. "The Difficulties of Persuasion," although cruel, offers a penetrating look at human nature and provides useful advice for practicing public speaking, resisting the false counsel of flatterers, and fighting corruption by maintaining the rule of law. While not for the faint of heart, it gives a window into the operating philosophy of today's People's Republic of China.

Before turning our attention to the medieval Christian and Islamic period, it's worth exploring the Jewish traditions of statecraft in ancient Israel. I have included a "Royal Psalm" from the Davidic monarchy, which was recently used in King Charles's coronation ceremony in England, as an example of how Jewish monarchs understood their political and religious duties in a liturgical context. However, because the Jewish people suffered long and hard as a persecuted minority—first at the hands of the Egyptians, Babylonians, Greeks, and Romans, then at the hands of Christians and Muslims in the West—and went without a king for extended periods of time, their leadership handbooks have less to do with princely rule than with how to win the affections of a prince who is hostile to your people's faith and interests.

Three key texts from the Hebrew tradition are the book of Esther, the book of Daniel, and the book of Judith, whose story has been selected for this collection. They provide inspiring tales of heroines and heroes who are as cunning as they are faithful. Esther hides her ethnic and religious identity to marry a Persian king and deliver the Jews from annihilation. Daniel remains faithful to God as a civil servant in Babylon, miraculously avoiding death at the hands of rapacious emperors. And Judith seduces and beheads an Assyrian general, preventing the capture of Jerusalem.

These stories of courage, piety, and duty strike a refreshing balance between the worldly pragmatism of Xenophon and Han Fei and the high-mindedness of Cicero. They demonstrate concretely that it is possible for great men and women to live with principle in a messy and fallen world. When necessary, they prudentially "get their hands dirty" in order to achieve the greater good for their communities. Yet there are limits to their behavior. Namely, they will never forsake their God or betray his covenanted people. At a time when religious believers find themselves in the minority, the Jewish tradition of statecraft in exile provides a blueprint for political engagement.

Medieval

The conversion of the Roman emperor Constantine to Christianity in 312 AD marked a new era of statecraft in the West. What started as a small religious sect grew to become the state religion, informing the political theology of the empire for more than a millennium.

While the Western Roman Empire fell to barbarians in 476, which is considered by many to be the start of the Middle Ages, the Byzantine Empire consciously maintained its Roman identity and survived until 1453, when it fell at the hands of the Ottoman Turks. This period, marked by famine, plague, and invasion, is often caricatured as an era of religious superstition and technological decline. But it was actually defined by the birth and flourishing of Christendom, when the Christian faith fully permeated the political and cultural imaginations of the Western world, transforming its ethics and worldview for centuries to come.

In many important respects, public Christianity tempered the excesses of pagan society and established new moral norms centered on the dignity of the human person, the universality of the human race, and the possibility of grace, mercy, and forgiveness. Largely gone were the days of human sacrifice to the gods, temple prostitution, blood sports where people were fed to animals for public spectacle, and the tyranny of mythical gods who were subject to human-like weaknesses and passions. However, the visible nature of the Church—and the institution's cooperation with the Byzantine Empire—meant that power politics was here to stay.

Nearly every major theologian during this period believed the primary duties of rulers were to restrain lawlessness; protect the people of God from foreign invasion, schism, and heresy; and support the Church in its mission to heal the world and prepare citizens for eternity. Even though the temporal order was lower than the spiritual order in terms of ultimate importance, the medievals had an elevated, even sacramental, view of kingship, inspired by the ancient world. This view diminished in the West after the Great Schism and rise of the universal papal monarchy, despite the best efforts of Germanic western kings who saw themselves as inheritors of the Davidic monarchy from ancient Israel and associated their rule more closely with the person of Christ than did their eastern counterparts.[10]

For the first thousand years of Christianity, the church and empire were part of an organic whole. Separation of powers did not exist, and there were no formal, governmental checks on the emperor's political power. In a very real sense, the emperor was accountable to God, tradition, and his or her conscience alone. On the other hand, institutions like the church, senate, dynastic families, and the military, while subject to the emperor, could restrain imperial behavior if an emperor stepped out of line.

Nevertheless, this lack of earthly accountability raised the stakes for the mirrors-for-princes tradition. A well-timed letter from a theologian or a court minister—or the presentation of a celebrated text upon accession to the throne—could be the best or even the only hope of simultaneously abating vices and educating an emperor or a king in the principles of judicious statecraft.

Six texts from the medieval period—three from the Christian West, two from the Byzantine East, and one from the Islamic Middle East—are particularly notable for their impact during the period and their applicability to present-day concerns: Augustine's *The City of God*, Thomas Aquinas's *On Kingship*, Christine de Pizan's *The Book of the Body Politic*, Eusebius's *Life of Constantine*, Agapetus's *Advice to Emperor Justinian*, and Abu Nasr Muhammad al-Farabi's *Aphorisms of the Statesman*.

Augustine was born in what is today Algeria in 354 AD. African by descent, he was a Roman citizen who was raised speaking Latin. He left the Christianity of his mother when he was a teenager and embraced a gnostic faith called Manichaeism. After moving to Italy, he eventually converted to Christianity under the influence of Saint Ambrose of Milan, entered the priesthood, and became the Bishop of Hippo. His writings on political theology have had a profound impact on Western thought. They were informed by the sacking of Rome in 410 AD, which his pagan neighbors blamed on Christianity for allegedly weakening the empire through its teachings of humility and forgiveness.

Only a portion of his most famous work, *The City of God*, fits into this tradition. Still, it provides an important glimpse into Western Christian thinking on statecraft. Augustine stresses two main points. First, an emperor ought to make political power "the handmaid of His majesty by using it for the greatest possible extension of His worship." Second, earthly happiness is possible only "by hope" in the "eternal felicity" to come in the heavenly kingdom.[11]

While Augustine believed the state should serve as handmaid to the Church, specifically in ratifying moral laws and supporting the Church's evangelical mission, he was less optimistic about baptizing and sanctifying the empire. For him, government exists as a result of the fall of mankind described in the book of Genesis, and its primary concern is to mitigate human vice, not to play a priestly role in ushering in the Kingdom of God on earth, even if cooperation with ecclesial authorities is inevitable. Like Cicero and Xenophon, his self-discipline also comes through in his warnings against taking pleasure in earthly power and delights. The pagans emphasized restraint for the purpose of delayed gratification *in this life*. Augustine takes things a step further by urging restraint for the sake of pleasure in the life to come.

After Saint Augustine, there is no greater Western theologian and philosopher than Saint Thomas Aquinas. He was born into a noble family in Italy in 1225 AD and joined the newly formed Dominican Order in Paris after his studies in Naples. During his life, he served in various posts in Rome, Paris, and Naples. Eventually, he settled in Naples and devoted his days to writing his famous work, the *Summa Theologica*, which synthesized Greek philosophy, particularly the works of Aristotle, with Roman Catholic Christianity.

One of Aquinas's lesser-known works, *On Kingship*, was dedicated to the King of Cyprus and exemplifies the best of the medieval Western mirror-for-princes tradition, elucidating the ends of government and the character traits needed to rule justly. He builds on Augustine's foundations but offers a much more systematic treatise on the nature and function of kingship. His thinking is logical, clear, and thorough, and he provides a robust theoretical framework for the King of Cyprus to better understand his vocation and duties.

In every community, someone must rule or else anarchy reigns. Aquinas believes that monarchy is both natural and superior—although he does recommend the possibility of a mixed regime in the *Summa*—because it is the most efficient way to achieve the end of the political community, which in his view is virtue. To the extent that it's fitting, the ruler should reward virtue and punish vice, while establishing justice, peace, and harmony in the kingdom. More provocatively, he believes that all kings are subject to the Pope of Rome and that temporal power ought to lead man towards his final end in the Kingdom of God.

Perhaps the most striking claim made by Aquinas is that tyrants are sent by God as punishment for wicked behavior. While this echoes much of the Hebrew Scriptures, it's quite a disturbing idea by contemporary standards. We tend to assume that the will of the majority in a democratic society is almost divinely inspired, akin to the College of Cardinals electing a pope. Furthermore, if a democratically elected leader turns to tyranny, we almost always blame the leader, not the people, who are victims of his crimes. Aquinas dissents from this by maintaining that God, in his providence and mercy, uses tyranny as a tool to bring a nation to repentance and renewal.

Finally, Aquinas provides sound moral guidance for aspiring princes who might be tempted by the lure of earthly honors and glories. Quoting the ancient Roman historian Sallust, he laments that many become hypocrites and demagogues in order to win the praise of the people, and he warns about the ephemerality of wealth and pleasure. "For nothing permanent is found in earthly things. . . . Thus, nothing earthly can make men happy, so that it may be a fitting reward for a king."[12]

Christine de Pizan, born in the fourteenth century AD in modern-day Italy, is worth noting as a capstone to the tradition in the medieval West. She is the first known woman to write on the topic and was a learned poet and philosopher in France, providing for her family through writing after her husband's untimely death.[13] Her work *The Book of the Body Politic* begins with the proper education of a young prince with an emphasis on faith, public service, and justice. Moving from domestic matters to the state, she draws from the heroic tales of ancient Romans to extol the virtues of liberality, pity, and clemency for a prince, while not neglecting the need to be feared, which is foundational for any prince who hopes to maintain order and restrain vice.

While the modern relationship between church and state looks nothing like it did during the medieval period, Augustine, Aquinas, and Pizan remind us that good politics should always encourage good living. Moreover, we shouldn't pin our hopes on the fleeting pleasures of this world.

Turning our attention to the Byzantine East, we arrive at Eusebius's *Life of Constantine* and Agapetus's *Advice to Emperor Justinian*. While the differences between Eastern and Western Christendom can be overstated, it's undeniable that the Greeks had a more optimistic view of original sin and human nature, and therefore the possibility of the Roman Empire being baptized and sanctified by the Church. Both Emperors Constantine and Justinian are considered saints in the Orthodox Church, and the former received the honorary title of "Equal to the Apostles" for his conversion of the Empire and for calling and presiding over the Council of Nicaea, which is chronicled in Eusebius's work included in this collection. In the Eastern view, the ideal relationship between church and state is one of symphony or harmony, marked by collaboration between the two powers as part of a single organism, the Roman Empire. After the fall of Constantinople in 1453 AD, this tradition lived on in Imperial Russia, which viewed Moscow as the "Third Rome" and heir to the legacies of Constantine and Justinian.

Agapetus was a tutor to Justinian and served in Constantinople at the church of the Hagia Sophia. Justinian reigned during the sixth century AD and is regarded as the single most powerful and accomplished Byzantine emperor, with the possible exception of Constantine himself. He reconquered many parts of the Western Roman Empire and North Africa that had fallen to invaders; built numerous churches, such as the Hagia Sophia, which stands today in Istanbul; and centralized Roman civil law, creating the *Corpus Juris Civilis* or Code of Justinian, which has served as the template for legal systems in numerous other countries throughout history and today.

Agapetus's letter takes a different course than Augustine and Aquinas in two critical areas. First, while containing both philosophy and theology, it reads more like traditional wisdom literature, providing the emperor with concise adages to inspire or implement in his daily life. "We should, accordingly, see," noted historian Peter N. Bell, "Agapetus as also providing not simply (sensible) general advice and a moral guide, but an (elegant) survival manual for an embattled emperor."[14] Second, unlike the writings of saints and theologians, Agapetus appears more as a civil servant auditioning for a role at court. Therefore, his counsel, while thoroughly Christian in its worldview, is also infused with a sense of political realism absent in the works of the other authors.

There are strong hints of "aristo-populism" (a term I coined in 2018 to describe a love of both what is beautiful and what is common) in Agapetus's view of imperial rule, which is marked by a healthy contempt for elites and a love of the common man.[15] The emperor is nearly divine in his authority and attributes ("given by God to collaborate with him in conferring benefits"). He cultivates hostility towards aristocrats ("Let no one pride himself on the nobility of his ancestors. All men have clay as forefather of their race."). And, importantly, he voices solidarity with the poor and commoners ("inequality must be changed to equality").[16]

Like Cyrus, Agapetus argues that emperors should use rewards to create incentives for good behavior, and should display a moderate degree of anger, without being wrathful, to command respect. Power should be shown to enemies and benevolence to friends. For Agapetus, the union of heaven and earth is more concrete than it is for Augustine, and worldly power is a necessity, not something to shun or from which to hide. If used wisely, he advises, the earthly kingdom can become "a ladder for you to the glory above."[17]

Agapetus concerns himself with how leaders should approach practical challenges, like tensions arising from income inequality or political rivals attempting to destroy the empire from within. His writings are much more pragmatic than those of his Western counterparts, who, following the tradition of Cicero, tend to reduce politics to mere ethics. Being good is very important, but it's not enough. Good rulers must master the art and application of power, and on this point, Agapetus is superior.

Lastly, the Islamic text on statecraft, Abu Nasr Muhammad al-Farabi's *Aphorisms of the Statesman*, contains many similarities to the Greek and Western Christian writings in this tradition. Few details about al-Farabi's life are known; however, he is considered one of the greatest Islamic philosophers of all time and wrote during the eighth and ninth centuries AD in what is now Iraq, Egypt, and Syria. Drawing from Aristotelian and Platonic sources, he focused on the role of the statesman in maintaining the health of the regime. Comparing the king to a doctor, the aim of statecraft is to cure souls by using the power of law to encourage virtue and restrain vice. Taking happiness as his ultimate aim, al-Farabi's statesman is concerned with the highest ends of human life, but does not neglect the practical conditions needed for human flourishing. His work was of great interest to latter-day philosophers like Leo Strauss for his exploration of the tension between philosophy and religion and theory and practice.[18]

While many view the medieval period as notably distinct from the classical era on account of the rise of Christianity and Islam, the continuity between these two periods in the mirrors-for-princes tradition is striking. Citizens or subjects in the medieval world held their rulers to a similar standard as the ancient one. Rulers were viewed as representatives of God on earth called to live virtuously, maintain order and justice, protect the kingdom or city from internal and external threats, promote civic virtue and religiosity, and foster conditions for material prosperity. The modern world, as we will soon see, attempts to separate some of these functions from the domain of politics.

However, the possibility and long-term success of such a revolutionary project have yet to be determined by history.

Renaissance

The Renaissance period began in fourteenth-century AD Italy, with a messy, centuries-long transition from the Middle Ages that climaxed throughout Europe in the fifteenth and sixteenth centuries AD. It was followed by the Protestant Reformation, Enlightenment, and Industrial Revolution, which profoundly altered man's relationship with the material world. The medieval concept of Christendom—a world whose order and sustenance depended on the sacramental vision of the church—came undone, and scholars began to see the state, economy, and physical world as independent entities that were governed by measurable, scientific laws apart from direct providence of the Christian God.

While it's common to credit (or blame) Renaissance thinkers, particularly Machiavelli, for the advent of secularism in Western Europe, its origins go back to the eleventh and twelfth centuries. After the Great Schism between the Roman Catholic and Eastern Orthodox churches, the papacy sought to centralize administrative power in Rome. Through the Gregorian reforms during this period, the Latin church took a firm stand against simony (the selling of church offices) and in favor of clerical celibacy. More importantly, it limited the role of temporal powers in church life and undermined the foundations of sacral kingship, chiefly by denying rulers the authority to appoint local bishops, diminishing and eventually rejecting the sacramental nature of coronation ceremonies, and affirming the nascent idea of "consent of the governed," which had emerged organically through feudal arrangements after the collapse of the Western Roman Empire.[19]

The purpose of these reforms was to root out corruption in the church and to assert the superiority of the spiritual over the temporal orders, even going as far as to assert the pope's prerogative to depose emperors. In attempting to dominate the political sphere, the church intentionally desacralized it, which sowed—often inadvertently—the seeds of secularism, political equality, and representative government that would blossom centuries later. These political and theological innovations would set the Christian West and East on fundamentally different trajectories and give birth to the modern world as we know it.

The Renaissance period marked the pinnacle of the mirrors-for-princes tradition in the West. Scholars first rediscovered classic Roman texts like those of Cicero and Seneca, which were scattered across Europe but not widely studied. Then, with the fall of Constantinople, exiles from the East brought Greek texts by the likes of Homer and Thucydides to Italy, helping popularize them for wider audiences. This spurred the publication of new texts that built upon or, in some cases, openly challenged them.

New authors like Machiavelli, Erasmus, and Saint Thomas More took one of two paths when confronting the historic legacy of the tradition: rupture or synthesis.

Machiavelli was a Florentine diplomat, military leader, and philosopher born in 1469 AD during a chaotic period when the papacy, local city-states, and other European powers were vying for territory throughout Italy. In addition to his diplomatic posts, he formed and led a militia that participated in the successful capture of Pisa in 1509. Eventually, he saw his beloved Republic of Florence fall to the Medici family, his former patrons, who were supported by Pope Julius II. He was banished, imprisoned, and tortured. After his release, he, retook leave to the countryside to work with his hands and write books. Despite his vehement criticism of the Catholic Church, he allegedly made a confession before his death and had a proper Christian burial.

In Machiavelli's writing, we see a rupture between the Christian and pagan traditions in favor of the latter, which placed more emphasis on realism and power than on idealism and charity. By contrast, Erasmus and Thomas More attempt to synthesize Christianity and pagan philosophy, resulting in the birth of Christian humanism, which elevated the role of classical education in the moral and intellectual formation of a Christian leader.

While the notion of universal human rights can trace its origins to the Christian humanism of More and Erasmus, their synthesis of Christian theology and classical philosophy proved to be less enduring than the rupture caused by Machiavelli. The brazen decoupling of politics and religion by Machiavelli ushered in the end of Christendom, hastening a centuries-long process of secularization that began in the eleventh century.

Following the Reformation and Enlightenment, the very idea of a "Christian prince" became a misnomer.

Today, while there are leaders who are Christians, the formal—and now informal—separation of church and state has reduced the significance of traditional religion on public life throughout the Western world. While America had long preserved a rich and decentralized tradition of religious practice and philanthropy, its influence on government, education, and culture has waned. What remains of Christianity in the public square has largely been transformed into a civil religion, which engenders a sense of patriotism and providence around special occasions like presidential inaugurations and Fourth of July parades, but is easily coopted by the ideological currents of the day. That said, the "established churches" that still exist elsewhere in the West—such as the Church of England and the Evangelical Lutheran Church of Finland—have arguably fared even worse in the face of secularism and modernity than the "free churches" throughout the wider Western world.

In order to better understand the revolution in worldviews that took place in Western Europe during this period and continues to impact our world today, it's important to return to Machiavelli and understand the radical nature of his work.

Political theorist Harvey Mansfield, perhaps the greatest living scholar of Machiavelli, boldly wrote that *The Prince* "is the most famous book on politics when politics is thought to be carried on for its own sake, unlimited by anything above it."[20] Machiavelli pioneered the idea of *realpolitik*, which subjected philosophy—and even justice—to experience and the verdict of history and gave teeth to the art of power. Having witnessed first-hand the worldly ambition of the papacy under Julius II, the "warrior pope" who overthrew the Republic of Florence, it's understandable why Machiavelli wanted to separate politics from theology.

For Machiavelli, philosophers—to their detriment—typically deal exclusively with theory and abstractions. Without first establishing practical judgment, their counsels are often of little use to a prince. While it's expedient to lay a foundation in the traditional virtues and to understand one's duty to God, nation, and family, politics is about cunning, and few philosophers really understand how to deal with the day-to-day challenges of ruling. Even fewer understand the application of power, which cannot be avoided in political leadership.

Machiavelli insists there is little to no correlation between being a "good person" and being a "good ruler." Character does not ensure competence any more than religious faith or political ideology. These things are not necessary, although they can be useful. A capable ruler must take stock of the world as it is and master the levers of power that best serve to advance his interests and that of his nation. Machiavelli offers a truly novel contribution that is simultaneously more commanding and disturbing in its presentation than any other work in this tradition since Xenophon.

Erasmus of Rotterdam charts a different course on the issues of character and faith. While he would likely agree that piety without competence is dangerous, he strongly believed that goodness, not cunning, is the foundation for successful political leadership.

Erasmus was born in the late fifteenth century AD. He was a close friend and confidant of Saint Thomas More, and his life's aim was to reform the Catholic Church from within. Humorously, having witnessed Pope Julius II's military conquest of Bologna, he wrote a satirical pamphlet about the pope being denied entry at the gates of heaven by Saint Peter himself, which was widely popular, albeit scandalous, throughout Europe. He maintained cordial relationships with Protestant scholars throughout his life and offered a moderate, liberalizing voice in favor of religious tolerance and the consent of the governed while remaining faithful to Roman Catholicism.

In his famous book *The Education of a Christian Prince*, he embraces Cicero as his mentor, a notable contrast to Machiavelli, who was highly critical of the celebrated Roman. He looks down on pagan histories and urges one to read them with great caution, advising that if "you come across anything in these men's actions which is worthy of a good prince, you will take care to rescue it like a jewel from a dung-heap."[21] He prefers Roman philosophy because of its emphasis on order, discipline, moral cleanliness, and duty, recommending Plutarch, Seneca, and Cicero, and his portrait of an ideal prince is aspirational, and for good reason.

According to Lisa Jardine, Erasmus took the relationship between Pope Adrian VI and Emperor Charles V as a model for emulation in the education of future princes, saying, "Before he became pope, Adrian VI had been tutor to the young Prince Charles. . . . Charles V was a Christian prince, raised according to humanistic principles and values under the guidance of the personal tutor who now reigned as God's representative on earth—an Aristotle to Charles's Alexander, or a Xenophon to Charles's Cyrus."[22]

Perhaps more than anyone since Xenophon, Erasmus believed that "the main hope of getting a good prince hangs on his proper education."[23] Therefore, those charged with educating the prince must be held to the highest of standards. If they succeed, the realm prospers. If they corrupt the mind of the prince, the people perish. He even goes so far as to suggest the death penalty for tutors who fill the prince's mind with wicked ideas. Because few, if any, institutional checks and balances existed to hold a prince accountable, his or her education was of paramount importance, as it was the one thing, beyond God and conscience, that could restrain a prince from lawlessness or incite him to virtuous behavior.

While Erasmus is very idealistic in his understanding of kingship, he does offer practical advice as well: keep taxes low, establish few and straightforward laws, provide for education, fight for the poor, restrain income inequality, punish vice, and reward virtue, among other precepts. There are subtle notes of populism in his prescriptions. Laws should be implemented to protect the poor against being exploited by the powerful. And private property, while important, is not sacrosanct. Erasmus has no problem trying to use state power to achieve a greater balance of prosperity.

If Erasmus possesses the greatest mind of the Christian humanists, his friend Saint Thomas More is the greatest statesman. More was born in London in 1529 AD and served as speaker of the House of Commons and Lord High Chancellor to Henry VIII. He was a beloved family man with a witty sense of humor, who made a conscious decision to provide his wife and daughters with a liberal education. In many respects, More could be considered a Catholic Machiavelli who was able to effectively work the levers of power for the common good, until he was asked to deny his faith, at which point he willfully accepted martyrdom at the command of Henry VIII, dying—with his famous last words—as "the king's good servant, but God's first."

Book I of More's *Utopia* is short, but provides the most profound insight into his approach to statecraft. It contains a dialogue between a fictional civil servant by the name of "Thomas More" and a wayfaring sage named "Raphael." More urges Raphael to offer his learning and experience in service to a prince, but Raphael demurs, calling it "servitude" rather than "service." He lambastes the worldly vanity of court life, bemoans the prospect of having to get his hands dirty in politics and palace intrigue, and asserts that "there is no room for philosophy in the courts of princes."[24]

This display of idealism and philosophical purity repulses More. He views service to king and commonwealth as man's highest earthly duty and blames Raphael's mindset for the troubles plaguing the Western world. "It is no wonder if we are so far from happiness while philosophers will not think it their duty to assist kings with their counsels." More distinguishes between the type of philosophy suited to intellectuals like Raphael and that which is fitting for "political action" in the counsel of princes, the latter being an imaginative exercise in applied ethics based on concrete circumstances and adapted "to the play that is in hand."[25]

In perhaps the most famous passage of *Utopia*, More expounds on his defense of the active life by providing a concise summary of his approach to statesmanship. No matter how bad things are in the regime, "you must not, therefore, abandon the commonwealth, for the same reasons as you should not forsake the ship in a storm because you cannot command the winds."[26] He insists we should use every tool at our disposal, both direct and indirect, to promote what is good and reduce what is harmful.

Playing off the book's title, there is no room for utopian schemes in More's work; in fact, book II of *Utopia* exposes the folly of such logic by sketching the real-world contradictions and consequences of trying to build a regime that ignores human nature. By the grace of God, we are called to enter the political fray on behalf of our fellow citizens and fight to reform the system by whatever means possible and prudent. In light of his service to the crown and eventual martyrdom, there hasn't been an author in the mirror-of-princes tradition since Cicero who more perfectly embodied his principles in the real world than Saint Thomas More.

Modernity

While the popularity of the mirrors-for-princes tradition declined as democracies replaced monarchies throughout the world, it's worth highlighting several texts from the modern era that provide enduring examples of statesmanship today: George Washington's "Farewell Address," Theodore Roosevelt's "Citizenship in a Republic," Winston Churchill's "Consistency in Politics," and Charles de Gaulle's *Edge of the Sword*.

The fundamental principles of political leadership remain constant across the ages, but the understanding of statesmanship changed dramatically in the modern era. While the American order was shaped by English constitutionalism and common law, as well as by Judeo-Christian and Greco-Roman influences, there is something novel in the American experiment as well. For example, the focus of Washington's "Farewell Address," which offers parting advice on the occasion of his retirement from the presidency, is almost entirely institutional. He does not speak of great individuals, but of constitutions, laws, habits, and mores. In doing so, he affirms John Adams's sentiment that one of the chief aims of the American founding was to establish "a government of laws, not of men." More pointedly, the "institutional constitution," operating by the consent of the citizenry, replaced the "institutional individual" (that is, the monarch) as the lead actor on the political stage in America and, eventually, throughout most of the Western world.

Washington was born in colonial Virginia in 1732 AD. While he lacked a formal education by the standard of his social class, his understanding of statesmanship was shaped by studying a sixteenth-century French courtesy manual, which provided advice on manners and morals inspired by classical authors. Washington's knowledge of the world came mostly through mastering the practical challenge of leading other men at a very young age. He became a lieutenant colonel in the Virginia militia at the age of twenty-four and served with distinction in the French and Indian War before being elected to the Virginia House of Burgesses at the age of twenty-six. These formative experiences prepared him well for his future roles as general of the Continental Army and president of the United States and strongly shaped his views on character formation and government. The admonitions contained in his "Farewell Address," which was drafted by James Madison and Alexander Hamilton, largely cohere with the advice offered by other authors in the mirrors-for-princes tradition, even if his focus was more on the institutions that sustain ordered liberty than the statesman himself.

In matters of domestic politics, Washington was a nationalist who believed that the federal constitution was the lynchpin of American unity and the bulwark of "happiness," "safety," and "prosperity." He stood against "domestic factions" and "the fury of party spirit" and maintained that "religion and morality" were "indispensable supports" of "political prosperity." In foreign affairs, he warned against "passionate attachments" to other nations and the threat of "overgrown military establishments" at home. He urged "harmony" and "liberal intercourse with all Nations" in matters of commerce but also asserted in his "First Annual Address to Congress" his belief in economic independence for "essential, particularly military, supplies."[27]

In sum, Washington's statesman was marked by prudence, respect for experience and inherited wisdom, and a love of the common good over individual gain. He shared these sentiments from a place of deep, acknowledged friendship and fatherly concern. When considered in light of history, both Washington's moral character and political accomplishments place him among a handful of statesmen at the pinnacle of political leadership in the West, and his "Farewell Address" deserves to be included in the pantheon of the mirrors-for-princes tradition. Indeed, the U.S. Senate reads the text in full every year on George Washington's birthday as a testimony to the enduring relevance of his admonitions.

By the twentieth century, individuality had eclipsed both the institution of the Constitution, which was the cornerstone of the American Founding, and the institutional individual, who served as the head of state under monarchy. The statesman of modern times was defined less by formal obligations to law or religion and more by charisma, personality, and will. Politics became a popularity contest, and public opinion triumphed over republicanism. Roosevelt, Churchill, and de Gaulle embodied both reform-minded and conservative tendencies. While not monolithic in their views, they both shared a reverence for their nation's distinct customs and institutions, yet were larger-than-life figures who personified America, Great Britain, and France. As such, their writings on statesmanship have a personalized tone and individuality characteristic of their age, even if their observations are rooted in permanent realities.

Theodore Roosevelt, president of the United States between 1901 and 1909, is renowned for establishing America as an empire on the world stage, building the Panama Canal, and fighting concentrated corporate power through vigorous antitrust action. For Roosevelt, the success of a democratic republic depends upon the virtue of ordinary men and women. Without self-government at the local level—in the lives of everyday Americans—the experiment in liberty will fail.

By setting a high bar for the average man and woman, Roosevelt thus raises expectations for leaders. A well-educated, elite class should have "the gifts of sympathy with plain people and of devotion to great ideals." By orienting their vision toward these ends, political leaders can maintain the best qualities of popular and representative government. Finally, echoing the likes of Xenophon and Saint Thomas More, Roosevelt describes his ideal statesman as "the man in the arena" who dares greatly in pursuit of "worthy causes" and "high achievement" while avoiding the fate of critics and cowards "who neither know victory nor defeat."[28]

Winston Churchill served as a member of Parliament for over sixty years and became prime minister on two separate occasions. He was an ardent critic of appeasement and led the Allied powers in the fight against Nazism. In many respects, he was the indispensable man of the twentieth century who preserved freedom against all odds.

In his essay "Consistency in Politics," Churchill takes a more measured tone, reflecting upon the role of prudence in political life and specifically exploring how great statesmen navigate changing political circumstances. For example, he asks how it was possible that someone like Joseph Chamberlain was an ardent defender of free trade in the late nineteenth century but then led the case for protectionism in the twentieth century. Was Chamberlain merely a hypocrite seeking political convenience or a genuine, prudential statesman making decisions based on changing facts and circumstances? It's tough to discern in light of the fact that his arguments were in direct contradiction to each other at different periods of time, both theoretically and practically. However, Churchill offers some sage advice: "A Statesman should always try to do what he believes is best in the long view for his country, and he should not be dissuaded from so acting by having to divorce himself from a great body of doctrine to which he formerly sincerely adhered."[29]

Churchill's treatment of Edmund Burke provides the clearest path for understanding how to be consistent in politics over the course of a lifetime. He contrasts Burke's robust defense of American independence, which was considered a liberal viewpoint at the time, with his vehement condemnation of the French Revolution, which was heralded as a conservative position in his day, and concludes that "the Burke of Liberty" and "the Burke of Authority" only appear to be in tension. Upon closer inspection, Burke was "the same man pursuing the same ends, seeking the same ideals of society and Government, and defending them from assaults, now from one extreme, now from the other."[30]

In assessing the political legacy of any leader, it's important to take the long view. On a month-by-month or year-by-year basis, there are innumerable ups and downs, twists of fate, and perhaps changes in policy. Yet over the course of a lifetime, according to Churchill, the overall trajectory of decision-making will prove consistent for great leaders who have mastered the art of keeping their principles fixed, while adapting their methods to the demands of changing circumstances. On this point, Churchill's vision is quite Aristotelian.

On the subject of Aristotle, a figure who looms large over the entire tradition, Charles de Gaulle's *Edge of the Sword* is the perfect text to conclude the collection. De Gaulle presents a modern-day description of Aristotle's magnanimous man, which has been described as "an anticipatory self-portrait" by André Malraux because it was published in 1932 AD, fore-shadowing the great deeds he would accomplish later in life.[31] De Gaulle, a devout Catholic, led the French resistance to Nazi occupation during World War II and founded the Fifth French Republic in 1958 AD, serving as its president for a decade. He ushered in an era of unprecedented economic growth and national renewal.

For de Gaulle, the archetypical statesman is a figure of heroic proportions. He is self-reliant, takes responsibility for his own actions, and acts independently of higher authorities. The man of character, as de Gaulle describes him, is a born protector, fighter, lover, artist, and risk-taker. He knows when to disobey orders in pursuit of beauty or greatness and, drawing from Cicero, his legacy is judged "in the light of the best examples available," historic or contemporary. He combines both theory and practice, reason and experience, "to launch great undertakings" and sees them through.[32] He is without question the personification of Theodore Roosevelt's man in the arena.

In a moment of crisis, the man or woman of character becomes visible "when the nation is in urgent need of leaders with initiative who can be relied upon." In "serious" times, when people are scared for their lives and lose hope for their children's future, a "ground swell brings the man of character to the surface."[33] In these moments, people rally to the statesman and provide him with the resources he needs to accomplish great deeds on behalf of the community.

With growing economic, political, and cultural unrest at home and the threat of great power conflict abroad, it's paramount that we uphold the examples of de Gaulle, Churchill, Roosevelt, and Washington as inspiration for a new generation of leaders. By teaching the best of the mirrors-for-princes tradition, we raise the probability that one or several heroes will emerge to help us navigate the challenges and opportunities of twenty-first century.

The Present

Throughout history, great mentors have had the opportunity to educate great leaders. In America, perhaps the most notable example was the relationship between George Washington and Alexander Hamilton. At the age of twenty-two, Hamilton was Washington's aide-de-camp. At twenty-six, he was the hero of the Battle of Yorktown. And at thirty-three, he was writing the *Federalist Papers* in defense of the U.S.

Constitution. Later, he served as Washington's Treasury secretary, becoming the architect of American capitalism.

Other significant examples from history include the relationship between Aristotle and Alexander the Great, Pope Adrian VI and Emperor Charles V, as well as that of Thomas More and King Henry VIII. Tragically, with respect to the latter, the pupil not only rejected the advice given to him, but he sent his mentor to the executioner. Without a doubt, counseling princes can be a dangerous enterprise.

In most cases, however, the relationship between a great mentor and great leader spans time, stretching across the centuries through the written word, equipping each new generation of leaders with the education necessary to become great themselves.

The world-altering impact of this cannot be overstated. Imagine setting out to write a book that would be not only read but also thoroughly studied and cherished by someone living a thousand years from today. More pointedly, imagine that the sharpest minds and most accomplished statesmen would carry your book around in their pockets, seeking to implement its precepts in their own lives to found nations, defend peoples, and lead world religions.

It is rumored that Julius Caesar carried scrolls of Xenophon's *The Education of Cyrus* with him on journeys. Thomas Jefferson had two copies of it in his library at Monticello. Cicero's *On Moral Duties* inspired early church fathers, Renaissance philosophers, and American founders. Agapetus's letters to Justinian framed the political theology of the Russian czars, and Han Fei's writings continue to shape the statecraft of Xi Jinping's China.

The mirrors-for-princes texts can be used for good or for ill, depending on the character of the reader and the circumstances of the time. They represent human excellence in all its complexity and provide us with a window into the souls of great leaders and the aspirations of their people. They pose challenging questions about the nature and structure of political rule and offer honest, sometimes brutal advice on the application of power. Moreover, for all the tensions that emerge between the various religious and political traditions represented, there are recurring themes and unifying principles that form a coherent tradition worth rediscovering and reviving today.

These themes can be distilled into twelve laws of leadership that are applicable in all times and places. They are of relevance not only to the statesmen, but also to the CEO, the entrepreneur, the student body president, the captain of a sports team, and anyone striving to become a "prince" in his or her particular domain.

12 Laws of Leadership

1. *Restraint*

   Restraint is the ability to control the base, human passions of lust, greed, anger, gluttony, gossip, sloth, and so forth with the head and the heart. Such discipline is essential for accomplishing any worthy task. Those who forsake restraint and rely merely on raw talent or genius may appear to get away with it for a while, but vice is a cruel master and will eventually corrupt those who indulge its fruits. Restraint is the foundation for commanding respect and accomplishing arduous undertakings.

2. *Piety*

Piety carries negative connotations in contemporary American life. It's often associated with religious hypocrisy, legalism, and sentimentalism. However, true piety is inspirational. It's simply the appropriate display of reverence and respect towards God, country, family, and neighbor. By acknowledging something greater than themselves, leaders demonstrate both humility and a sense of stewardship towards their office and community.

3. *Courage*

Courage is the virtue of pursuing great deeds for the sake of a noble cause in spite of the fear or danger at hand. Most people naturally incline towards cowardice; therefore, those who are courageous often appear to be rash, but their actions are vindicated by their successes—or failures in pursuit of a worthy cause, such as a soldier laying down his life for a friend or a mother sacrificing for her child. Those who are courageous learn to imitate the actions of excellent men and women, either from history or their own day. Without courage, it is impossible for a leader to have self-respect and to inspire others to accomplish important undertakings.

4. *Protection*

Protection is the science of keeping those dependent upon you from both internal and external danger. At the most fundamental level, this means guarding against foreign invasion, suppressing internal rebellion, and preparing for natural disasters. Protection is a bulwark against anarchy and chaos. Those who can protect others without being patronizing fulfill the most elementary of human desires—survival—and will win the affection and trust of those in their care.

5. *Personnel*

Personnel is policy. The most important decision a leader can make is to surround himself with the right people. Even the best of leaders have come undone by choosing poor advisers who undermine their plans. The higher you rise in authority, the more difficult it is to discern who actually has your best interests at heart. Leaders are susceptible to flattery and often surround themselves with people who praise them publicly but blame them privately. It's important to resist flattery, but even more so to use the truth of flattery, that people respond to positive affirmation judiciously given, to build morale and encourage your team to develop their unique talents and abilities.

6. *Prosperity*

Prosperity is establishing the economic conditions needed for broad-based material growth, innovation, entrepreneurial dynamism, and societal flourishing. It ensures that basic human necessities like health, housing, and work are met and provides a foundation for the pursuit of human happiness. If a society isn't growing economically, it is stagnating, decaying, and declining. After protection, it's one of the most basic human needs. The key elements to prosperity include keeping taxes reasonably low, establishing clear and simple laws surrounding commerce that are impartially enforced, rooting out corruption and cronyism, and mitigating destabilizing wealth inequality by strengthening the middle class. Leaders who devote their energy to making those around them better off will never be lacking for resources in a time of need.

7. *Mercy*

Mercy is the practice of showing compassion, care, and concern for those who are suffering, regardless of who or what is to blame. Leaders will be judged not by how they take care of the powerful but by the condition of those in poverty and on the margins of society. Those in authority are uniquely positioned to amplify the voices of the oppressed and to provide dignity, through both material and immaterial means, to those who are forgotten, ignored, or invisible. Leaders who are merciful will receive rewards, not only in the world to come, but also in this present life as there is nothing more attractive and charismatic than humbling oneself before someone in need.

8. *Peace*

Peace is the restful condition of those who are not at war with internal or external enemies. It serves as a prerequisite for safety, prosperity, and happiness. However, the pursuit of peace does not come naturally for those who are inclined to pursue glory and prestige. Proving one's merits on the field of battle and consolidating the support of the military is the quickest and surest path for leaders to rise to power. Peacetime presidents are often forgotten, but wartime presidents become national heroes. The incentives for ambitious leaders to pursue war are in tension with the interests of citizens to maintain peace. Therefore, leaders must soberly and objectively check their own ambitions for military conflict, ensuring that such a course is only pursued for just causes and if the national interest and common good demand it.

9. *Justice*

Justice means giving people their due. It depends upon good laws being faithfully and impartially executed. The law serves as a teacher to inculcate virtue and discourage vicious behavior, particularly actions that inflict harm upon oneself, neighbor, community, or country. Just leaders instill respect, trust, and stability in their regimes and institutions because people have confidence that they will be treated fairly in their personal or professional affairs. When justice is forsaken for favoritism or applied in a haphazard fashion, it threatens the foundations of society, leaving leaders open to criticism, revolt, or worse.

10. *Prudence*

Prudence is the art of identifying the right goals and possessing the talent and ability to achieve them in a given situation. It's not enough for leaders to have mere intellectual knowledge of what ends to pursue, nor is it sufficient to reason quickly from means to ends if leaders have the wrong ends in mind. Prudence demands both thought and action. It's a virtue acquired through personal experience and imitation of those with experience. Like learning a second language, it takes trial and error before one can command his mind and body at a high enough level to see the right things through to their proper ends. Leaders who master prudence are considered wise and possess the queen of the virtues, for they are able to translate beautiful words into great deeds.

11. *Power*

Power is the energy that makes prudent action possible. It is the capacity to marshal political, economic, and relational capital in pursuit of specific goals. Power commands respect from friends and rivals alike, which is essential to the survival of any institution or regime. Power itself is amoral—its value depends on how and why it's used. A leader gains power in three main ways: growing in knowledge and experience, befriending and imitating those with virtue and influence, and gaining access to financial resources. All three components are required for wielding authority and gaining prestige; a leader neglects power at his peril.

12. *Destiny*

Destiny is being in the right place at the right time and seizing the moment. It can go by the name of fortune or providence depending upon one's outlook, and it is often confused with luck. Destiny, however, requires readiness and assertiveness when the great waves of opportunity arise throughout one's life. Often, the timing of these waves is inexplicable, but like the surfer, leaders must be waiting at attention to paddle and ride with all of their strength. When destiny is at one's back, a statesman moves with deliberate speed, knowing that the window of opportunity will close in short order. Success breeds success, and opportunities arise more frequently for those who take advantage of their circumstances. Challenges or obstacles are turned into ladders by which the fortunate climb to greatness. What breaks the coward makes the man of character. Destiny is mysterious, but a prince cannot rise to power without her cooperation.

These laws of leadership from the mirrors-for-princes tradition represent the political wisdom of mankind. In the collection of texts contained in this book, discerning readers will discover that previous generations—among all cultures, creeds, and civilizations—paid serious attention to the qualities they wanted to cultivate in leaders and the education required to do so. What's needed today is a rediscovery and revival of this tradition in order to elevate and inspire a new generation of leaders. This exercise will demand careful reflection on what has been written in the past; the humility to step outside our own circumstances and evaluate our situation in light of historic perspectives; the imagination to understand the complex dynamics shaping political life in distant eras; identification and prudential application of the timeless principles contained in these texts; and the ambition required to widely disseminate these ideas and examples to leaders in positions of influence today.

Most important, it's vital for those with the courage to pursue such an arduous task to understand that this project will only succeed if the teachers, mentors, and pupils involved possess a vision for the flourishing of the whole body politic. The common good—not narrow partisan or class interests—must capture the political imagination and shape the vocabulary of the leaders produced by such an undertaking. Only then, when the totality of the people, laws, culture, and customs are lifted up and transfigured in light of the enduring and ennobling truths from the mirrors-for-princes tradition, can the decline, divisions, and decadence of our present moment begin to heal and happiness spread.

In an age of irony marked by distrust of authority and a fear of failure, it often appears as though the possibility of human excellence is nothing more than a fantasy. The statesmen of old were made of iron and took themselves seriously—today, such qualities garner laughter and scorn more than awe. Is there hope for heroism, greatness, and goodness in our own day?

On this important question, President Theodore Roosevelt offers the only response worthy of those who would take the study of statesmanship seriously:

> It is not the critic who counts; not the man who points out how the strong man stumbles or where the doer of deeds could have done them better. The credit belongs to the man who is actually in the arena, whose face is marred by dust and sweat and blood; who strives valiantly; who errs, who comes short again and again, because there is no effort without error and shortcoming; but who does actually strive to do the deeds; who knows the great enthusiasms, the great devotions; who spends himself in a

worthy cause; who at the best knows in the end the triumph of high achievement, and who at the worst, if he fails, at least fails while daring greatly, so that his place shall never be with those cold and timid souls who neither know victory nor defeat.[34]

John A. Burtka IV
Chester County, Pennsylvania
June 2023

Ancient

Xenophon

The Education of Cyrus
Fourth Century BC, Greece

---

*Ruling human beings does not belong among those
tasks that are impossible, or even among those that
are difficult, if one does it with knowledge.*

Selections from Books I and VIII; Epilogue

Book I

Chapter 1

We have had occasion before now to reflect how often democracies have been overthrown by the desire for some other
type of government, how often monarchies and oligarchies
have been swept away by movements of the people, how often
would-be despots have fallen in their turn, some at the outset
by one stroke, while those who have maintained their rule for

ever so brief a season are looked upon with wonder as marvels of sagacity and success.

The same lesson, we had little doubt, was to be learnt from the family: the household might be great or small—even the master of few could hardly count on the obedience of his little flock. And so, one idea leading to another, we came to shape our reflections thus: drovers may certainly be called the rulers of their cattle and horse-breeders the rulers of their studs—all herdsmen, in short, may reasonably be considered the governors of the animals they guard. If, then, we were to believe the evidence of our senses, was it not obvious that flocks and herds were more ready to obey their keepers than men their rulers? Watch the cattle wending their way wherever their herdsmen guide them, see them grazing in the pastures where they are sent and abstaining from forbidden grounds, the fruit of their own bodies they yield to their master to use as he thinks best; nor have we ever seen one flock among them all combining against their guardian, either to disobey him or to refuse him the absolute control of their produce. On the contrary, they are more apt to show hostility against other animals than against the owner who derives advantage from them. But with man the rule is converse; men unite against none so readily as against those whom they see attempting to rule over them.

As long, therefore, as we followed these reflections, we could not but conclude that man is by nature fitted to govern all creatures, except his fellow man. But when we came to realize the character of Cyrus the Persian, we were led to a change of mind: here is a man, we said, who won for himself obedience from thousands of his fellows, from cities and tribes innumerable: we must ask ourselves whether the government of men is after all an impossible or even a difficult task, provided one set about it in the right way. Cyrus, we know, found the readiest obedience in his subjects, though some of them dwelt at a distance which it would take days and months to traverse, and among them were men who had never set eyes on him, and for the matter of that could never hope to do so, and yet they were willing to obey him. Cyrus did indeed eclipse all other monarchs, before or since, and I include not only those who have inherited their power, but those who have won empire by their own exertions. How far he surpassed them all may be felt if we remember that no Scythian, although the Scythians are reckoned by their myriads, has ever succeeded in dominating a foreign nation; indeed the Scythian would be well content could he but keep his government unbroken over his own tribe and people. The same is true of the Thracians and the Illyrians, and indeed of all other nations within our ken; in Europe, at any rate, their condition is even now one of independence, and of such separation as would seem to be permanent.

Now this was the state in which Cyrus found the tribes and peoples of Asia when, at the head of a small Persian force, he started on his career. The Medes and the Hyrcanians accepted his leadership willingly, but it was through conquest that he won Syria, Assyria, Arabia, Cappadocia, the two Phrygias, Lydia, Caria, Phoenicia, and Babylonia. Then he established his rule over the Bactrians, Indians, and Cilicians, over the Sakians, Paphlagonians, and Magadidians, over a host of other tribes the very names of which defy the memory of the chronicler; and last of all he brought the Hellenes in Asia beneath his sway, and by a descent on the seaboard Cyprus and Egypt also.

It is obvious that among this congeries of nations few, if any, could have spoken the same language as himself, or understood one another, but none the less Cyrus was able so to penetrate that vast extent of country by the sheer terror of his personality that the inhabitants were prostrate before him: not one of them dared lift hand against him. And yet he was able, at the same time, to inspire them all with so deep a desire to please him and win his favor that all they asked was to be guided by his judgment and his alone. Thus he knit to himself a complex of nationalities so vast that it would have taxed a man's endurance merely to traverse his empire in any one direction, east or west or south or north, from the palace which was its center. For ourselves, considering his title to our admiration proved, we set ourselves to inquire what his parentage might have been and his natural parts, and how he was trained and brought up to attain so high a pitch of excellence in the government of men. And all we could learn from others about him or felt we might infer for ourselves we will here endeavor to set forth.

Chapter 2

The father of Cyrus, so runs the story, was Cambyses, a king of the Persians, and one of the Perseidae, who look to Perseus as the founder of their race. His mother, it is agreed, was Mandane, the daughter of Astyages, king of the Medes. Of Cyrus himself, even now in the songs and stories of the East the record lives that nature made him most fair to look upon, and set in his heart the threefold love of man, of knowledge, and of honor. He would endure all labors, he would undergo all dangers, for the sake of glory. Blest by nature with such gifts of soul and body, his memory lives to this day in the mindful heart of ages.

It is true that he was brought up according to the laws and customs of the Persians, and of these laws it must be noted that while they aim, as laws elsewhere, at the common weal, their guiding principle is far other than that which most nations follow. Most states permit their citizens to bring up their own children at their own discretion, and allow the grown men to regulate their own lives at their own will, and then they lay down certain prohibitions, for example, not to pick and steal, not to break into another man's house, not to strike a man unjustly, not to commit adultery, not to disobey the magistrate, and so forth; and on the transgressor they impose a penalty. But the Persian laws try, as it were, to steal a march on time, to make their citizens from the beginning incapable of setting their hearts on any wickedness or shameful conduct whatsoever. And this is how they set about their object.

In their cities they have an open place or square dedicated to Freedom (Free Square they call it), where stand the palace and other public buildings. From this place all goods for sale are rigidly excluded, and all hawkers and hucksters with their yells and cries and vulgarities. They must go elsewhere, so that their clamor may not mingle with and mar the grace and orderliness of the educated classes. This square, where the public buildings stand, is divided into four quarters which are assigned as follows: one for the boys, another for the youths, a third for the grown men, and the last for those who are past the age of military service.

The law requires all the citizens to present themselves at certain times and seasons in their appointed places. The lads and the grown men must be there at daybreak; the elders may, as a rule, choose their own time, except on certain fixed days, when they too are expected to present themselves like the rest. Moreover, the young men are bound to sleep at night round the public buildings, with their arms at their side; only the married men among them are exempt, and need not be on duty at night unless notice has been given, though even in their case frequent absence is thought unseemly.

Over each of these divisions are placed twelve governors, twelve being the number of the Persian tribes. The governors of the boys are chosen from the elders, and those are appointed who are thought best fitted to make the best of their lads: the governors of the youths are selected from the grown men, and on the same principle; and for the grown men themselves and their own governors; the choice falls on those who will, it is hoped, make them most prompt to carry out their appointed duties, and fulfill the commands imposed by the supreme authority. Finally, the elders themselves have presidents of their own, chosen to see that they too perform their duty to the full.

We will now describe the services demanded from the different classes, and thus it will appear how the Persians endeavor to improve their citizens. The boys go to school and give their time to learning justice and righteousness: they will tell you they come for that purpose, and the phrase is as natural with them as it is for us to speak of lads learning their letters. The masters spend the chief part of the day in deciding cases for their pupils: for in this boy-world, as in the grown-up world without, occasions of indictment are never far to seek. There will be charges, we know, of picking and stealing, of violence, of fraud, of calumny, and so forth. The case is heard and the offender, if shown to be guilty, is punished.

Nor does he escape who is found to have accused one of his fellows unfairly. And there is one charge the judges do not hesitate to deal with, a charge which is the source of much hatred among grown men, but which they seldom press in the courts, the charge of ingratitude. The culprit convicted of refusing to repay a debt of kindness when it was fully in his power meets with severe chastisement. They reason that the ungrateful man is the most likely to forget his duty to the gods, to his parents, to his fatherland, and his friends. Shamelessness, they hold, treads close on the heels of ingratitude, and thus ingratitude is the ringleader and chief instigator to every kind of baseness.

Further, the boys are instructed in temperance and self-restraint, and they find the utmost help towards the attainment of this virtue in the self-respecting behavior of their elders, shown them day by day. Then they are taught to obey their rulers, and here again nothing is of greater value than the studied obedience to authority manifested by their elders everywhere. Continence in meat and drink is another branch of instruction, and they have no better aid in this than, first, the example of their elders, who never withdraw to satisfy their carnal cravings until those in authority dismiss them, and next, the rule that the boys must take their food, not with their mother but with their master, and not till the governor gives the sign. They bring from home the staple of their meal, dry bread with [vegetables][1] for a relish, and to slake their thirst they bring a drinking cup, to dip in the running stream. In addition, they are taught to shoot with the bow and to fling the javelin. The lads follow their studies till the age of sixteen or seventeen, and then they take their places as young men.

After that they spend their time as follows. For ten years they are bound to sleep at night round the public buildings, as we said before, and this for two reasons, to guard the community and to practice self-restraint; because that season of life, the Persians conceive, stands most in need of care. During the day they present themselves before the governors for service to the state, and, whenever necessary, they remain in a body round the public buildings. Moreover, when the king goes out to hunt, which he will do several times a month, he takes half the company with him, and each man must carry bow and arrows, a sheathed dagger, or "sagaris," slung beside the quiver, a light shield, and two javelins, one to hurl and the other to use, if need be, at close quarters.

The reason of this public sanction for the chase is not far to seek; the king leads just as he does in war, hunting in person at the head of the field, and making his men follow, because it is

---

1. Brackets on pp. 10–11 were inserted by the editor. All other brackets in this collection were inserted by the author unless otherwise specified.

felt that the exercise itself is the best possible training for the needs of war. It accustoms a man to early rising; it hardens him to endure heat and cold; it teaches him to march and to run at the top of his speed; he must perforce learn to let fly arrow and javelin the moment the quarry is across his path; and, above all, the edge of his spirit must needs be sharpened by encountering any of the mightier beasts: he must deal his stroke when the creature closes, and stand on guard when it makes its rush: indeed, it would be hard to find a case in war that has not its parallel in the chase.

But to proceed: the young men set out with provisions that are ampler, naturally, than the boys' fare, but otherwise the same. During the chase itself they would not think of breaking their fast, but if a halt is called, to beat up the game, or for any hunter's reason, then they will make, as it were, a dinner of their breakfast, and, hunting again on the morrow till dinner-time, they will count the two days as one, because they have only eaten one day's food. This they do in order that, if the like necessity should arise in war, they may be found equal to it. As relish to their bread these young men have whatever they may kill in the chase, or failing that, [vegetables] like the boys. And if one should ask how they can enjoy the meal with [vegetables] for their only condiment and water for their only drink, let him bethink himself how sweet barley bread and wheaten can taste to the hungry man and water to the thirsty.

As for the young men who are left at home, they spend their time in shooting and hurling the javelin, and practicing all they learnt as boys, in one long trial of skill. Besides this, public games are open to them and prizes are offered; and the tribe which can claim the greatest number of lads distinguished for skill and courage and faithfulness is given the meed of praise from all the citizens, who honor, not only their present governor, but the teacher who trained them when they were boys. Moreover, these young men are also employed by the magistrates if garrison work needs to be done or if malefactors are to be tracked or robbers run down, or indeed on any errand which calls for strength of limb and fleetness of foot. Such is the life of the youth. But when the ten years are accomplished they are classed as grown men. And from this time forth for five-and-twenty years they live as follows.

First they present themselves, as in youth, before the magistrates for service to the state wherever there is need for strength and sound sense combined. If an expedition be on foot the men of this grade march out, not armed with the bow or the light shield any longer, but equipped with what are called the close-combat arms, a breastplate up to the throat, a buckler on the left arm (just as the Persian warrior appears in pictures), and for the right hand a dagger or a sword. Lastly, it is from this grade that all the magistrates are appointed except the teachers for the boys. But when the five-and-twenty years are over and the men have reached the age of fifty years or more, then they take rank as elders, and the title is deserved.

These elders no longer go on military service beyond the frontier; they stay at home and decide all cases, public and private both. Even capital charges are left to their decision, and it is they who choose all the magistrates. If a youth or a grown man breaks the law, he is brought into court by the governors of his tribe, who act as suitors in the case, aided by any other citizen who pleases. The cause is heard before the elders and they pronounce judgment; and the man who is condemned is disenfranchised for the rest of his days.

And now, to complete the picture of the whole Persian policy, I will go back a little. With the help of what has been said before, the account may now be brief; the Persians are said to number something like one hundred and twenty thousand men: and of these no one is by law debarred from honor or office. On the contrary, every Persian is entitled to send his children to the public schools of righteousness and justice. As a fact, all who can afford to bring up their children without working do send them there: those who cannot must forego the privilege. A lad who has passed through a public school has a right to go and take his place among the youths, but those who have not gone through the first course may not join them.

In the same way the youths who have fulfilled the duties of their class are entitled eventually to rank with the men, and to share in office and honor: but they must first spend their full time among the youths; if not, they go no further. Finally, those who as grown men have lived without reproach may take their station at last among the elders. Thus these elders form a college, every member of which has passed through the full circle of noble learning; and this is that Persian polity and that Persian training which, in their belief, can win them the flower of excellence.

And even to this day signs are left bearing witness to that ancient temperance of theirs and the ancient discipline that preserved it. To this day it is still considered shameful for a Persian to spit in public, or wipe the nose, or show signs of wind, or be seen going apart for his natural needs. And they could not keep to this standard unless they were accustomed to a temperate diet, and were trained to exercise and toil, so that the humors of the body were drawn off in other ways. Hitherto we have spoken of the Persians as a whole: we will now go back to our starting point and recount the deeds of Cyrus from his childhood.

Chapter 3

Until he was twelve years old or more, Cyrus was brought up in the manner we have described, and showed himself to be above all his fellows in his aptitude for learning and in the noble and manly performance of every duty. . . .

Book VIII

Chapter 7

Thus the years passed on, and Cyrus was now in a ripe old age, and he journeyed to Persia for the seventh time in his reign. His father and mother were long since dead in the course of nature, and Cyrus offered sacrifice according to the law, and led the sacred dance of his Persians after the manner of his forefathers, and gave gifts to every man according to his wont.

But one night, as he lay asleep in the royal palace, he dreamt a dream. It seemed to him that someone met him, greater than a man, and said to him, "Set your house in order, Cyrus: the time has come, and you are going to the gods."

With that Cyrus awoke out of sleep, and he all but seemed to know that the end of his life was at hand. Straightway he took victims and offered sacrifice to Zeus, the god of his fathers, and to the Sun, and all the other gods, on the high places where the Persians sacrifice, and then he made this prayer:

"Zeus, god of my fathers, and thou, O Sun, and all ye gods, accept this sacrifice, my offering for many a noble enterprise, and suffer me to thank you for the grace ye have shown me, telling me all my life, by victims and by signs from heaven, by birds and by the voices of men, what things I ought to do and what I ought to refrain from doing. Deep is my thankfulness that I was able to recognize your care, and never lifted up my heart too high even in my prosperity. I beseech you now to bless my children also, and my wife, and my friends, and my fatherland; and for myself, may my death be as my life has been."

Then Cyrus went home again and lay down on his bed, for he longed to rest. And when the hour was come, his attendants came to him and bade him take his bath. But he said he would rather rest. And others came afterwards, at the usual time, to set the meal before him; but he could not bring himself to take food: he seemed only to thirst, and drank readily. It was the same the second day, and the third, and then he called his sons to his side—it chanced they had followed him to Persia—and he summoned his friends also and the chief magistrates of the land, and when they were all met, he began:

"My sons, and friends of mine, the end of my life is at hand: I know it by many signs. And when I am dead, you must show by word and deed that you think of me as happy. When I was a child, I had all the joys and triumphs of a child, and I reaped the treasures of youth as I grew up, and all the glories of a man when I came to man's estate. And as the years passed, I seemed to find my powers grow with them, so that I never felt my old age weaker than my youth, nor can I think of anything I attempted or desired wherein I failed.

"Moreover, I have seen my friends made happy by my means, and my enemies crushed beneath my hand. This my fatherland, which was once of no account in Asia, I leave at the height of power, and of all that I won I think I have lost nothing. Throughout my whole life I have fared as I prayed to fare, and the dread that was ever with me lest in days to come I might see or hear or suffer evil, this dread would never let me think too highly of myself, or rejoice as a fool rejoices. And if I die now, I leave my sons behind me, the sons the gods have given me; and I leave my fatherland in happiness, and my friends. Surely I may hope that men will count me blessed and cherish my memory.

"And now I must leave instructions about my kingdom, that there may be no dispute among you after my death. Sons of mine, I love you both alike, but I choose the elder-born, the one whose experience of life is the greater, to be the leader in council and the guide in action. Thus was I trained myself, in the fatherland that is yours and mine, to yield to my elders, my brothers or my fellow citizens, in the street, or in the place of meeting, or in the assembly for debate. And thus have I trained both of you, to honor your elders and be honored by those who are younger than yourselves. These are the principles that I leave with you, sanctioned by time, ingrained in our customs, embodied in our laws.

"The sovereignty is yours, Cambyses; the gods have given it to you, and I also, as far as in me lies; and to you, Tanaoxares, I give the satrapy over the Medes and the Armenians and the Cadousians, these three; and though I leave your elder brother a larger empire and the name of king, your inheritance will bring you, I believe, more perfect happiness than his.

"I ask myself what human joy will be lacking to you: all things which gladden the hearts of men will be yours—but the craving for what is out of reach, the load of cares, the restless passion to rival my achievements, the plots and counterplots, they will follow him who wears the crown, and they are things, be well assured, that leave little leisure for happiness.

"And you, Cambyses, you know of yourself, without words from me, that your kingdom is not guarded by this golden scepter, but by faithful friends; their loyalty is your true staff, a scepter which shall not fail. But never think that loyal hearts grow up by nature as the grass grows in the field: if that were so, the same men would be loyal to all alike, even as all natural objects are the same to all mankind. No, every leader must win his own followers for himself, and the way to win them is not by violence but by loving-kindness.

"And if you would seek for friends to stand by you and guard your throne, who so fit to be the first of them as he who is sprung from the self-same loins? Our fellow citizens are nearer to us than foreigners, and our mess-mates dearer than strangers, and what of those who are sprung from the same seed, suckled at the same breast, reared in the same home, loved by the same parents, the same mother, the same father? What the gods have given to be the seal of brotherhood do not make of none effect yourselves. But build upon it: make it the foundation for other loving deeds, and thus the love between you shall never be overcome. The man who takes thought for his brother cares for his own self. For who but a brother can win glory from a brother's greatness? Who can be honored as a brother can through a brother's power? Or who so safe from injury as the brother of the great?

"Let no one, Tanaoxares, be more eager than yourself to obey your brother and support him: to no one can his triumph or his danger come so near. Ask yourself from whom you could win a richer reward for any kindness. Who could give you stouter help in return for your own support? And where is coldness so ugly as between brothers? Or where is reverence so beautiful? And remember, Cambyses, only the brother who holds preeminence in a brother's heart can be safe from the jealousy of the world.

"I implore you both, my sons, by the gods of our fathers, hold each other in honor, if you care at all to do me pleasure: and none of you can say you know that I shall cease to be when I cease to live this life of ours. With your bodily eyes you have never seen my soul, and yet you have discerned its presence through its working. And have you never marked the terrors which the spirits of those who have suffered wrong can send into the hearts of their murderers, and the avenging furies they let loose upon the wicked? Think you the honors of the dead would still abide, if the souls of the departed were altogether powerless?

"Never yet, my sons, could I be persuaded that the soul only lives so long as she dwells within this mortal body, and falls dead so soon as she is quit of that. Nay, I see for myself that it is the soul which lends life to it, while she inhabits there. I cannot believe that she must lose all sense on her separation from the senseless body, but rather that she will reach her highest wisdom when she is set free, pure and untrammeled at last. And when this body crumbles in dissolution, we see the several parts thereof return to their kindred elements, but we do not see the soul, whether she stays or whether she departs. Consider," he went on, "how these two resemble one another, Death and his twin brother Sleep, and it is in sleep that the soul of a man shows her nature most divine, and is able to catch a glimpse of what is about to be, for it is then, perhaps, that she is nearest to her freedom.

"Therefore, if these things are as I believe, and the spirit leaves the body behind and is set free, reverence my soul, O sons of mine, and do as I desire. And even if it be not so, if the spirit must stay with the body and perish, yet the everlasting gods abide, who behold all things, with whom is all power, who uphold the order of this universe, unmarred, unaging, unerring, unfathomable in beauty and in splendor. Fear them, my sons, and never yield to sin or wickedness, in thought or word or deed.

"And after the gods, I would have you reverence the whole race of man, as it renews itself forever; for the gods have not hidden you in the darkness, but your deeds will be manifest in the eyes of all mankind, and if they be righteous deeds and pure from iniquity, they will blazon forth your power: but if you meditate evil against each other, you will forfeit the confidence of every man. For no man can trust you, even though he should desire it, if he sees you wrong him whom above all you are bound to love.

"Therefore, if my words are strong enough to teach you your duty to one another, it is well. But, if not, let history teach you, and there is no better teacher. For the most part, parents have shown kindness to their children and brothers to their brothers, but it has been otherwise with some. Look, then, and see which conduct has brought success, choose to follow that, and your choice will be wise.

"And now maybe I have said enough of this. As for my body, when I am dead, I would not have you lay it up in gold or silver or any coffin whatsoever, but give it back to the earth with all speed. What could be more blessed than to lie in the lap of Earth, the mother of all things beautiful, the nurse of all things good? I have been a lover of men all my life, and methinks I would fain become a part of that which does good to man. And now," he added, "now it seems to me that my life begins to ebb; I feel my spirit slipping away from those parts she leaves the first. If you would take my hand once more, or look into my eyes while life is there, draw near me now; but when I have covered my face, let no man look on me again, not even you, my sons.

"But you shall bid the Persians come, and all our allies, to my sepulcher; and you shall rejoice with me and congratulate me that I am safe at last, free from suffering or sorrow, whether I am with God or whether I have ceased to be. Give all who come the entertainment that is fitting in honor of a man whose life on earth was happy, and so send them away. Remember my last saying: show kindness to your friends, and then shall you have it in your power to chastise your enemies. Goodbye, my dear sons, bid your mother goodbye for me. And all my friends, who are here or far away, goodbye."

And with these words he gave his hand to them, and then he covered his face and died.

Epilogue

Of all the powers in Asia, the kingdom of Cyrus showed itself to be the greatest and most glorious. On the east it was bounded by the Red Sea, on the north by the Euxine, on the west by Cyprus and Egypt, and on the south by Ethiopia. And yet the whole of this enormous empire was governed by the mind and will of a single man, Cyrus: his subjects he cared for and cherished as a father might care for his children, and they who came beneath his rule reverenced him like a father.

But no sooner was he dead than his sons were at strife, cities and nations revolted, and all things began to decay. I can show that what I say is true, and first I will speak of their impiety. In the early days, I am aware, the king and those beneath him never failed to keep the oaths they had sworn and fulfill the promises they had given, even to the worst of criminals.

In fact, if such had not been their character and such their reputation, none of the Hellenic generals who marched up with the younger Cyrus could have felt the confidence they did: they would not have trusted a Persian any more than one trusts them today, now that their perfidy is known. As it was, they relied on their old reputation and put themselves in their power, and many were taken up to the king and there beheaded. And many of the Asiatics who served in the same war perished as they did, deluded by one promise or another.

In other ways also the Persians have degenerated. Noble achievement in the old days was the avenue to fame: the man was honored who risked his life for the king, or brought a city or nation beneath his sway. But now, if some Mithridates has betrayed his father Ariobarzanes, or some Reomithres has left his wife and children and the sons of his friend as hostages at the court of Egypt, and then has broken the most solemn of all pledges—it is they and their like who are loaded with the highest honors, if only they are thought to have gained some advantage for the king.

With such examples before them, all the Asiatics have turned to injustice and impiety. For what the leaders are, that, as a rule, will the men below them be. Thus has lawlessness increased and grown among them. And injustice has grown, and thieving. Not only criminals, but men who are absolutely innocent are arrested and forced to pay fines for no reason whatsoever: to be known to have wealth is more dangerous than guilt, so that the rich do not care to have any dealings with the powerful, and dare not even risk appearing at the muster of the royal troops. Therefore, when any man makes war on Persia, whoever he may be, he can roam up and down the country to his heart's content without striking a blow, because they have forgotten the gods and are unjust to their fellow men. In every way their hearts and minds are lower than in days gone by.

Nor do they care for their bodies as they did of old. It was always their custom neither to spit nor blow the nose, only it is clear this was instituted not from concern for the humors of the body, but in order to strengthen themselves by toil and sweat. But nowadays, though this habit is still in vogue, to harden the body by exercise has quite gone out of fashion. Again, from the first it was their rule only to take a single meal in the day, which left them free to give their time to business and exercise. The single meal is still the rule, but it commences at the earliest hour ever chosen for breakfast, and the eating and drinking goes on till the last moment which the latest reveler would choose for bed.

It was always forbidden to bring chamber pots into the banquet hall, but the reason lay in their belief that the right way to keep body and brain from weakness was to avoid drinking in excess. But today, though as in the old time no such vessels may be carried in, they drink so deep that they themselves are carried out, too weak to stand on their own legs. It was a national custom from the first not to eat and drink on the march nor be seen satisfying the wants of nature, but nowadays, though they still abstain, they make each march so short that no man need wonder at their abstinence.

In the old time they went out to hunt so often that the chase gave enough exercise and training for man and horse alike. But when the day came that Artaxerxes and all his court were the worse for wine, the old custom of the king leading the hunt in person began to pass away. And if any eager spirits hunted with their own followers, it was easy to see the jealousy, and even the hatred, aroused by such superiority.

It is still the habit to bring up the boys at the palace gates, but fine horsemanship has disappeared, for there is no place where the lads can win applause by their skill. The old belief that the children of Persia would learn justice by hearing the judges decide the cases has been turned upside down: the children have only to use their eyes and they see that the verdict goes to the man with the longest purse. Children in former times were taught the properties of plants in order to use the wholesome and avoid the harmful; but now they seem to learn it for the mere sake of doing harm: at any rate, there is no country where deaths from poison are so common.

And the Persian today is far more luxurious than he was in the time of Cyrus. Then they still clung to the Persian style of education and the Persian self-restraint, merely adopting the Median dress and a certain grace of life. But now the old Persian hardihood may perish for all they care, if only they preserve the softness of the Mede. I might give instances of their luxury. They are not content with soft sheets and rugs for their beds, they must have carpets laid under the bedposts to prevent any jarring from the floor. They have given up none of the cooked dishes invented in former days; on the contrary, they are always devising new ones, and condiments to boot: in fact, they keep men for the very purpose. In the winter it is not enough to have the body covered, and the head and the feet, they must have warm sleeves as well and gloves for the hands: and in the summer they are not content with the shade from the trees or the rocks, they must have servants standing beside them with artificial screens.

To have an endless array of cups and goblets is their special pride: and if these are come by unjustly, and all the world knows it, why, there is nothing to blush for in that: injustice has grown too common among them, and ill-gotten gain. Formerly no Persian was ever to be seen on foot, but the sole object of the custom was to make them perfect horsemen. Now they lay more rugs on their horses' backs than on their own beds; it is not a firm seat they care for, but a soft saddle.

As soldiers we may imagine how they have sunk below the ancient standard; in past times it was a national institution that the landowner should furnish troopers from his own estate, and men were bound to go on active service, while the garrison troops in the country received regular pay; but now the Persian grandees have manufactured a new type of cavalry, who earn their pay as butlers and cooks and confectioners and cupbearers and bathmen and flunkeys to serve at table or remove the dishes, and serving-men to put their lords to bed and help them to rise, and perfumers to anoint them and rub them and make them beautiful.

In numbers they make a very splendid show, but they are no use for fighting; as may be seen by what actually takes place: an enemy can move about their country more freely than the inhabitants themselves. It will be remembered that Cyrus put a stop to the old style of fighting at long range, and by arming men and horses with breastplates and giving each trooper a short spear he taught them to fight at close quarters. But nowadays they will fight in neither one style nor the other. The infantry still carry the large shields, the battle-axes, and the swords, as if they meant to do battle as they did in Cyrus' day. But they will never close with the enemy. Nor do they use the scythe-bearing chariots as Cyrus intended. By the honors he gave he raised the dignity and improved the quality of his charioteers till he had a body of men who would charge right into the enemy's ranks; but the generals of today, though they do not even know the charioteers by sight, flatter themselves that untrained men will serve their purpose quite as well as trained.

So the charioteers will dash off, but before they reach the enemy half the men have fallen from their boxes, and the others will jump out of their own accord, and the teams, left without their drivers, will do more harm to their friends than to their foes. And since in their hearts the Persians of today are well aware what their fighting condition really is, they always give up the struggle, and now none of them will take the field at all without Hellenes to help them, whether they are fighting among themselves or whether Hellenes are in arms against them: even then it is a settled thing that they must have the aid of other Hellenes to face them.

I venture to think I have shown the truth of the statement that I made. I asserted that the Persians of today and their allies are less religious than they were of old, less dutiful to their kindred, less just and righteous towards other men, and less valiant in war. And if any man doubts me, let him examine their actions for himself, and he will find full confirmation of all I say.

Aristotle

Nicomachean Ethics
Fourth Century BC, Greece

———————

*A great-souled person . . . is someone who takes
great risks, and when he does take a risk he is without regard for his life, on the ground that it is not
just on any terms that life is worth living.*

Selections from Book IV

The very name of Great-mindedness implies, that great
things are its object-matter; and we will first settle what kind of
things. It makes no difference, of course, whether we regard the
moral state in the abstract or as exemplified in an individual.

Well then, he is thought to be Great-minded who values
himself highly and at the same time justly, because he that does
so without grounds is foolish, and no virtuous character is foolish or senseless. Well, the character I have described is
Great-minded. The man who estimates himself lowly, and at
the same time justly, is modest; but not Great-minded, since
this latter quality implies greatness, just as beauty implies a

large bodily conformation while small people are neat and well made but not beautiful.

Again, he who values himself highly without just grounds is a Vain man: though the name must not be applied to every case of unduly high self-estimation. He that values himself below his real worth is Small-minded, and whether that worth is great, moderate, or small, his own estimate falls below it. And he is the strongest case of this error who is really a man of great worth, for what would he have done had his worth been less?

The Great-minded man is then, as far as greatness is concerned, at the summit, but in respect of propriety he is in the mean, because he estimates himself at his real value (the other characters respectively are in excess and defect). Since then he justly estimates himself at a high, or rather at the highest possible rate, his character will have respect specially to one thing: this term "rate" has reference of course to external goods: and of these we should assume that to be the greatest which we attribute to the gods, and which is the special object of desire to those who are in power, and which is the prize proposed to the most honorable actions: now honor answers to these descriptions, being the greatest of external goods. So the Great-minded man bears himself as he ought in respect of honor and dishonor. In fact, without need of words, the Great-minded plainly have honor for their object-matter: since honor is what the great consider themselves specially worthy of, and according to a certain rate.

The Small-minded man is deficient, both as regards himself, and also as regards the estimation of the Great-minded: while the Vain man is in excess as regards himself, but does not get beyond the Great-minded man. Now the Great-minded man, being by the hypothesis worthy of the greatest things, must be of the highest excellence, since the better a man is the more is he worth, and he who is best is worth the most: it follows then, that to be truly Great-minded a man must be good, and whatever is great in each virtue would seem to belong to the Great-minded. It would no way correspond with the character of the Great-minded to flee spreading his hands all abroad; nor to injure any one; for with what object in view will he do what is base, in whose eyes nothing is great? In short, if one were to go into particulars, the Great-minded man would show quite ludicrously unless he were a good man: he would not be in fact deserving of honor if he were a bad man, honor being the prize of virtue and given to the good.

This virtue, then, of Great-mindedness seems to be a kind of ornament of all the other virtues, in that it makes them better and cannot be without them; and for this reason it is a hard matter to be really and truly Great-minded; for it cannot be without thorough goodness and nobleness of character.

Honor then and dishonor are specially the object-matter of the Great-minded man: and at such as is great, and given by good men, he will be pleased moderately as getting his own, or perhaps somewhat less, for no honor can be quite adequate to perfect virtue: but still he will accept this because they have nothing higher to give him. But such as is given by ordinary people and on trifling grounds he will entirely despise, because these do not come up to his deserts: and dishonor likewise, because in his case there cannot be just ground for it.

Now though, as I have said, honor is specially the object-matter of the Great-minded man, I do not mean but that likewise in respect of wealth and power, and good or bad fortune of every kind, he will bear himself with moderation, fall out how they may, and neither in prosperity will he be overjoyed nor in adversity will he be unduly pained. For not even in respect of honor does he so bear himself; and yet it is the greatest of all such objects, since it is the cause of power and wealth being choice-worthy, for certainly they who have them desire to receive honor through them. So to whom honor even is a small thing to him will all other things also be so; and this is why such men are thought to be [proud].

It seems too that pieces of good fortune contribute to form this character of Great-mindedness: I mean, the nobly born, or men of influence, or the wealthy, are considered to be entitled to honor, for they are in a position of eminence and whatever is eminent by good is more entitled to honor: and this is why such circumstances dispose men rather to Great-mindedness, because they receive honor at the hands of some men.

Now really and truly the good man alone is entitled to honor; only if a man unites in himself goodness with these external advantages he is thought to be more entitled to honor: but they who have them without also having virtue are not justified in their high estimate of themselves, nor are they rightly denominated Great-minded; since perfect virtue is one of the indispensable conditions to such and character.

Further, such men become [proud] and insolent, it not being easy to bear prosperity well without goodness; and not being able to bear it, and possessed with an idea of their own superiority to others, they despise them, and do just whatever their fancy prompts; for they mimic the Great-minded man, though they are not like him, and they do this in such points as they can, so without doing the actions which can only flow from real goodness they despise others. Whereas the Great-minded man despises on good grounds (for he forms his opinions truly), but the mass of men do it at random.

Moreover, he is not a man to incur little risks, nor does he court danger, because there are but few things he has a value for; but he will incur great dangers, and when he does venture he is prodigal of his life as knowing that there are terms on which it is not worth his while to live. He is the sort of man to do kindnesses, but he is ashamed to receive them; the former putting a man in the position of superiority, the latter in that of inferiority; accordingly he will greatly overpay any kindness done to him, because the original actor will thus be laid under obligation and be in the position of the party benefited.

Such men seem likewise to remember those they have done kindnesses to, but not those from whom they have received them: because he who has received is inferior to him who has done the kindness and our friend wishes to be superior; accordingly he is pleased to hear of his own kind acts but not of those done to himself (and this is why, in Homer, Thetis does not mention to Jupiter the kindnesses she had done him, nor did the Lacedaemonians to the Athenians but only the benefits they had received).

Further, it is characteristic of the Great-minded man to ask favors not at all, or very reluctantly, but to do a service very readily; and to bear himself loftily towards the great or fortunate, but towards people of middle station affably; because to be above the former is difficult and so a grand thing, but to be above the latter is easy; and to be high and mighty towards the former is not ignoble, but to do it towards those of humble station would be low and vulgar; it would be like parading strength against the weak.

And again, not to put himself in the way of honor, nor to go where others are the chief men; and to be remiss and dilatory, except in the case of some great honor or work; and to be concerned in few things, and those great and famous. It is a property of him also to be open, both in his dislikes and his likings, because concealment is a consequent of fear. Likewise to be careful for reality rather than appearance, and talk and act openly (for his contempt for others makes him a bold man, for which same reason he is apt to speak the truth, except where the principle of reserve comes in), but to be reserved towards the generality of men.

And to be unable to live with reference to any other but a friend; because doing so is servile, as may be seen in that all flatterers are low and men in low estate are flatterers. Neither is his admiration easily excited, because nothing is great in his eyes; nor does he bear malice, since remembering anything, and specially wrongs, is no part of Great-mindedness, but rather overlooking them; nor does he talk of other men; in fact, he will not speak either of himself or of any other; he neither cares to be praised himself nor to have others blamed; nor again does he praise freely, and for this reason he is not apt to speak ill even of his enemies except to show contempt and insolence.

And he is by no means apt to make laments about things which cannot be helped, or requests about those which are trivial; because to be thus disposed with respect to these things is consequent only upon real anxiety about them. Again, he is the kind of man to acquire what is beautiful and unproductive rather than what is productive and profitable: this being rather the part of an independent man.

Also slow motion, deep-toned voice, and deliberate style of speech, are thought to be characteristic of the Great-minded man: for he who is earnest about few things is not likely to be in a hurry, nor he who esteems nothing great to be very intent: and sharp tones and quickness are the result of these.

Marcus Tullius Cicero

On Moral Duties
First Century BC, Rome

─────────

Nothing is more lovable . . . than the common
possession of . . . moral excellences; for those who
have the same virtuous desires and purposes love
one another as they love themselves.

Selections from Book I

But there are several degrees of relationship among men. To take our departure from the tie of common humanity, of which I have spoken, there is a nearer relation of race, nation, and language, which brings men into very close community of feeling. It is a still more intimate bond to belong to the same city; for the inhabitants of a city have in common among themselves forum, temples, public walks, streets, laws, rights, courts, modes and places of voting, beside companionships and intimacies, engagements and contracts, of many with many.

Closer still is the tie of kindred; for by this from the vast society of the human race one is shut up into a small and narrow circle. Indeed, since the desire of producing offspring is common by nature to all living creatures, the nearest association consists in the union of the sexes; the next, in the relation with children; then, that of a common home and a community of such goods as appertain to the home. Then the home is the germ of the city, and, so to speak, the nursery of the state. The union of brothers comes next in order, then that of cousins less or more remote, who, when one house can no longer hold them all, emigrate to other houses as if to colonies. Then follow marriages and affinities by marriage, thus increasing the number of kindred.

From this propagation and fresh growth of successive generations states have their beginning. But the union of blood, especially, binds men in mutual kindness and affection; for it is a great thing to have the same statues of ancestors, the same rites of domestic worship, the same sepulchers. But of all associations none is more excellent, none more enduring, than when good men, of like character, are united in intimacy. For the moral rectitude of which I have so often spoken, even if we see it in a stranger, yet moves us, and calls out our friendship for him in whom it dwells. Moreover, while every virtue attracts us to itself, and makes us love those in whom it seems to exist, this is emphatically true of justice and generosity. At the same time, nothing is more lovable, and nothing brings men into more intimate relations, than the common possession of these moral excellences; for those who have the same virtuous desires and purposes love one another as they love themselves, and they realize what Pythagoras would have in friendship, the unifying of plurality.

That also is an intimate fellowship which is created by benefits mutually bestowed and received, which, while they give pleasure on both sides, produce a lasting attachment between those who thus live in reciprocal good offices. But when you survey with reason and judgment the entire field of human society, of all associations none is closer, none dearer, than that which unites each of us with our country. Parents are dear, children are dear, so are kindred and friends; but the country alone takes into her embrace all our loves for all, in whose behalf what good man would hesitate to encounter death, if he might thus do her service? The more detestable is the savageness of those who by every form of guilt have inflicted grievous wounds on their country, and are and have been employed in her utter subversion.

Now, if you make an estimate and comparison of the degree of service to be rendered in each relation, the first place must be given to our country and our parents, bound as we are to them by paramount benefits; next come our children, and the entire family which looks to us alone, nor in stress of need can have any other refuge; then, afterward, the kindred with whom we are on pleasant terms, and with whom, for the most part, we are in the same condition of life. For the reasons indicated we owe chiefly to these that I have named the necessary protection of daily life; but companionship, conviviality, counsel, conversation, advice, consolation, sometimes reproof also, have their most fruitful soil in friendship, and that is the most pleasant friendship which is cemented by resemblance in character.

In discharging all these duties, we ought to consider what is most needful for each person, and what each person either can or cannot obtain without our aid. Thus the degrees of relationship will not correspond with those of the occasions for our kind offices; and there are duties which we owe to some rather than to others, on grounds independent of their connection with us. Thus you would help a neighbor rather than a brother or an intimate friend in harvesting his crops; while in a case in court you would appear as an advocate for your kinsman or friend rather than for your neighbor.

These and similar points are to be carefully considered in every department of duty, and we should practice and exercise ourselves so that we may be good calculators of duty, and by adding and subtracting may ascertain the remainder, and thus know how much is due to each person. Indeed, as neither physicians, nor commanders, nor orators, though they understand the rules of their art, can accomplish anything worthy of high commendation without practice and exercise; so, though the precepts for the faithful discharge of duty be delivered, as I am delivering them now, the very greatness of the work which they prescribe demands practice and exercise. I have now shown, with nearly sufficient fullness of detail, how the right, on which duty depends, is derived from the constituent elements of human society.

It is to be observed that of the four sources from which right and duty flow, the greatest admiration attends that consisting in a large and lofty mind which looks down on human fortunes. Thus, when reproach is intended, nothing occurs more readily than utterances like this—

"*Ye, youths, indeed show but a woman's soul;*
    That heroine, a man's;"—

or this—

"*Give, Salmacis, spoils without sweat and blood.*"

On the other hand, in panegyrics, our speech rolls on with a fuller flow when we praise deeds that have been wrought with a large mind, bravely and grandly. Hence the field for eloquent discourse about Marathon, Salamis, Plataea, Thermopylae, Leuctrae; hence the fame of our own fellow countrymen, Cocles, the Decii, Cneius and Publius Scipio; hence the glory of Marcus Marcellus, and of others more than can be numbered; and the Roman people, as a nation, excels other nations chiefly in this very greatness of soul.

In particular, the prevailing love for glory in war is manifested in the almost uniform clothing of statues in military attire. But this loftiness of spirit, manifested in peril and in toil, if devoid of justice, and contending for selfish ends, not for the public good, is to be condemned; for not only does it not appertain to virtue—it belongs rather to a savageness that spurns all human feelings.

Therefore courage is well defined by the Stoics as the virtue that contends for the right. No one, then, who has sought a reputation for courage by treachery and fraud, has won the fame he sought. Nothing that is devoid of justice can be honorable. It was well said by Plato: "Not only is knowledge, when divorced from justice, to be termed subtlety rather than wisdom; but also the soul prompt to encounter danger, if moved thereto by self-interest, and not by the common good, should have the reputation of audacity rather than of courage."

Therefore I would have brave and high-spirited men also good and simple, friends of truth, remote from guile—traits of character which belong to the very heart of justice. But the mischief is, that in this exaltation and largeness of soul obstinacy and an excessive lust of power very easily have birth. For as, according to Plato, the entire character of the Lacedaemonians was set on fire by the desire for victory, so now, in proportion as one surpasses others in grandeur of soul, he is ambitious to hold the foremost place among those in power, or rather, to rule alone.

Now it is hard, when you covet preeminence, to maintain the equity which is the most essential property of justice. Hence it is that such men suffer themselves to be overcome neither in debate nor by any legal or constitutional hindrance, and in the state they, for the most part, employ bribery and intrigue that they may acquire the greatest influence possible, and may rise by force, rather than maintain equality with their fellow citizens by justice. But the greater the difficulty, the greater the glory. Nor is there any occasion that ought to be devoid of justice.

Therefore not those who inflict, but those who repel, wrong ought to be deemed brave and magnanimous. A soul truly and wisely great regards the right to which the nature of man aspires as consisting in deeds, not in fame; it chooses to be chief rather than to seem so. On the other hand, he who depends on the waywardness of the undiscerning multitude does not deserve to be reckoned among great men. But in proportion to a man's towering ambition, he is easily urged by the greed of fame to deeds averse from justice. His is a slippery standing-ground; for we seldom find a man, who, for labors undertaken and dangers encountered, does not demand fame as the price of his exploits.

A brave and great soul is, in fine, chiefly characterized by two things. One of these is the contempt of outward circumstances in the persuasion that a man ought not to admire or wish or seek aught that is not right and becoming, or to yield to human influence, or to passion, or to calamity. The other is that, with this disposition of mind, one should undertake the conduct of affairs great, indeed, and, especially, beneficial, but at the same time arduous in the highest degree, demanding severe toil, and fraught with peril not only of the means of comfortable living, but of life itself. Of these two things, all the luster and renown, and the utility too, belong to the latter: but their cause and the habit of mind that makes men great lie in the former; for in this is inherent that which renders souls truly great, and lifts them above the vicissitudes of human fortune.

Moreover, this first constituent of greatness consists in two things, in accounting the right alone as good, and in freedom from all disturbing passions: for to hold in light esteem, and on fixed and firm principles to despise, objects which to most persons seem excellent and splendid, is the token of a brave and great soul; and to bear those reputedly bitter experiences which are so many and various in human life and fortunes, in such a way as to depart in no wise from the deportment that is natural to you, in no wise from the dignity befitting a wise man, is the index of a strong mind and of great steadfastness of character.

But it is incongruous for one who is not broken down by fear to be broken down by the love of gain, or for him who has shown himself unconquered by labor, to be conquered by sensuality. These failures must be provided against, and the desire for money must especially be shunned. For nothing shows so narrow and small a mind as the love of riches; nothing is more honorable and magnificent than to despise money if you have it not—if you have it, to expend it for purposes of beneficence and generosity.

The greed of fame, also, as I have already said, must be shunned; for it deprives one of liberty, which every high-minded man will strive to the utmost to maintain. Indeed, posts of command ought not to be eagerly sought, nay, they should sometimes rather be refused, sometimes resigned. One should also be free from all disturbing emotions, not only from desire and fear, but equally from solicitude, and sensuality, and anger, that there may be serenity of mind, and that freedom from care which brings with it both evenness of temper and dignity of character.

But there are and have been many who, in quest of the serenity of which I am speaking, have withdrawn from public affairs, and taken refuge in a life of leisure. Among these are the most eminent philosophers, including those of the very first rank, and also some stern and grave men, who could not endure the conduct either of the people or of their rulers. Some, too, have taken up their abode in the country, engrossed in the care of their own property. Their design is the same as that of kings, to lack nothing, to obey no one, to enjoy liberty, the essence of which is to live as one pleases.

While the purpose of living as one pleases is common to those greedy of power and to the men of leisure of whom I have spoken, the former think that they can realize it if they have large resources; the latter, if they are content with what they have, and with little. Nor is either opinion to be despised. But the life of the men of leisure is easier, and safer, and less liable to give trouble or annoyance to others; while that of those who have fitted themselves for the public service and for the management of large affairs, is more fruitful of benefit to mankind, and more conducive to their own eminence and renown.

All things considered, we ought, perhaps, to excuse from bearing part in public affairs those who devote themselves to learning with superior ability, and those who, from impaired health, or for some sufficiently weighty reason, have sought retirement, abandoning to others the power and the praise of civic service.

But as for those who have no such reason, yet say that they despise what most persons admire, places of trust and honor in the military or civil service, this, I think, is to be reckoned to their discredit, not to their praise. They, indeed, deserve approval for despising fame and thinking it of no account. But they seem to dread not only toil and trouble, but a certain imagined shame and disgrace from the disappointments and repulses which they must encounter. For there are those who in opposite circumstances fail to act consistently—who have the utmost contempt for pleasure, yet are unmanned by pain—who scorn fame, yet are broken down by unpopularity; and these are, indeed, manifest incongruities in a man's character.

But those whom nature has endowed with qualities that fit them for the management of public affairs ought, without needless delay, to become candidates for office and to take the interests of the state in charge; for only thus can the state be well governed, and only thus can commanding power of mind be made manifest. At the same time, for those who undertake public trusts, perhaps even more than for philosophers, there is need of elevation of mind, and contempt of the vicissitudes of human fortune, and that serene and unruffled spirit of which I often speak, in order that they may be free from solicitude, and may lead dignified and self-consistent lives.

This is easier for philosophers, inasmuch as their condition in life is less open to the assaults of fortune, their wants are fewer, and in case of adverse events they encounter a less heavy fall. On the other hand, those who hold public trusts are obviously liable to stronger mental excitement, and are more heavily burdened with care than those who live in retirement; and they should therefore bring to their duty a corresponding strength of mind, and independence of the ordinary causes of vexation. But let him who meditates entering on any important undertaking, carefully consider, not only whether the undertaking is right, but also whether he has the ability to carry it through; and here he must beware, on the one hand, lest he too readily despair of success from mere want of spirit, or, on the other hand, lest he be overconfident from excessive eagerness. In fine, in all transactions, before you enter upon them, you should make diligent preparation. . . .

In fine, let those who are to preside over the state obey two precepts of Plato—one, that they so watch for the well-being of their fellow citizens that they have reference to it in whatever they do, forgetting their own private interests; the other, that they care for the whole body politic, and not, while they watch over a portion of it, neglect other portions. For, as the guardian- ship of a minor, so the administration of the state is to be con- ducted for the benefit, not of those to whom it is entrusted, but of those who are entrusted to their care.

But those who take counsel for a part of the citizens, and ne- glect a part, bring into the state an element of the greatest mis- chief, and stir up sedition and discord, some siding with the people, some with the aristocracy, and few being equally the friends of all. From this cause arose great dissensions among the Athenians, and in our republic it has led not only to seditions, but also to destructive civil wars. Partiality of this kind, a citizen who is substantial and brave, and worthy of a chief place in the state, will shun and abhor, and will give himself wholly up to the state, pursuing neither wealth nor power; and he will so watch over the entire state as to consult the well-being of all its citizens. Nor will he expose any one to hatred or envy by false accusation, and he will in every respect so adhere to justice and right as in their behalf to submit to any loss however severe, and to face death itself rather than surrender the principles which I have indicated.

Most pitiful in every aspect is the canvassing and scrambling for preferment, of which it is well said by the same Plato, that those who strive among themselves which shall be foremost in the administration of the state, act like sailors who should quarrel for a place at the helm. The same writer exhorts us to regard as enemies those who bear arms against us, not those who desire to care for the interests of the state in accordance with their own judgment, as in the case of the disagreement without bitterness between Publius Africanus and Quintus Metellus.

Nor are they to be listened to who think that anger is to be cherished toward those who are unfriendly to us on political grounds, and imagine that this betokens a large-minded and brave man; for nothing is more praiseworthy, nothing more befitting a great and eminent man, than placability and clemency. Moreover, in free states and where all have equal rights, there is a demand for courtesy, and for a soul superior to petty causes of vexation, lest if we suffer ourselves to be angry with those who intrude upon us inopportunely, we fall into irritable habits equally harmful and hateful.

Yet an easy and accommodating temper is to be approved only so far as may be consistent with the strictness demanded in public business, without which the state cannot be administered. But all punishment and correction ought to be free from personal insult, and should have reference, not to the pleasure of him who administers punishment or reproof, but to the public good. Care also must be taken lest the punishment be greater than the fault, and lest for the same cause some be made penally responsible, and others not even called to account.

Most of all is anger to be eliminated in punishment; for he who enters on the office of punishment in anger will never preserve that mean between too much and too little, of which the Peripatetics make so great account, and rightly too, if they only would not commend anger, and say that it is implanted by nature for useful ends. On the other hand, it is under all circumstances to be shunned, and it is desirable that those who preside over the state should be like the laws, which are led to inflict punishment, not by anger, but by justice.

Again, in prosperity, and when affairs flow on as we would have them, we should with the utmost care avoid pride, fastidiousness, and arrogance; for it is the token of a frivolous mind to bear either prosperity or adversity otherwise than moderately, and preeminently praiseworthy is an equable temperament in one's whole life, the same countenance and the same [mind] always, as we learn was the case with Socrates, and equally with Caius Laelius.

I regard Philip, king of the Macedonians, though surpassed by his son in achievements and in fame, as having been his superior in affability and kindness. Thus the one was always great, the other often very mean—so as to give good ground for the rule of those who say that the higher our position is, the more meekly we should carry ourselves. Panaetius, indeed, tells us that Africanus, his pupil and friend, used to say, that as it is common to give horses that, from having been often in battle, rear and prance dangerously, into the hands of professional tamers, that they may be ridden more easily, so men, when at loose reins in prosperity, and over self-confident, should be brought, as it were, to the ring of reason and instruction, that they may fully see the frailty of man's estate, and the fickleness of fortune.

Still further, in the extreme of prosperity, especially, resort is to be had to the counsel of friends, and even greater authority to be given to them than under ordinary circumstances. In such a condition we must also take heed lest we open our ears to flatterers, and suffer ourselves to be cajoled. In yielding to [flattery], we are always liable to be deceived, thinking that we deserve the praise bestowed upon us, whence proceed numberless mistakes, men who are inflated by self-conceit becoming the objects of coarse derision, and committing the most egregious eccentricities in conduct. But enough on this point.

From what has been said, it is to be inferred that the most important affairs, and those indicative of the highest tone of spirit, come under the direction of men in public life, their official duty having the widest scope, and extending to the largest number of persons; but that there are and have been many men of great mind in private life, engaged in important investigations or enterprises, yet attending to no affairs but their own; while others, no less great, midway between philosophers and statesmen, are occupied with the care of their property, not, indeed, increasing it by every means in their power, nor yet depriving their friends of the benefit of it, but rather, whenever there is need, giving freely to their friends and to the state.

Property thus held should, in the first place, have been fairly obtained, and not by any mean or offensive calling; then it should show itself of service to as many as possible, if they only be worthy; then, too, it should be increased by industry and frugality, and should not lie open to the demands of sensuality and luxury rather than to those of generosity and beneficence.

He who observes these rules may live in splendor, dignity, and independence, and at the same time with simplicity, with integrity, and in friendly relations with mankind.

Kauṭilya

Arthaśāstra
Fourth–Third Century BC, India

———

Whoever has not his organs of sense under his control, will soon perish, though possessed of the whole earth bounded by the four quarters.

Selections from Books I and VI

Book I—Concerning Discipline

Chapter 6—Restraint of the Organ of Sense: The Shaking Off of the Aggregate of the Six Enemies

Restraint of the organs of sense, on which success in study and discipline depends, can be enforced by abandoning lust, anger, greed, vanity (mána), haughtiness (mada), and overjoy (harsha).

Absence of discrepancy (avipratipatti) in the perception of sound, touch, color, flavor, and scent by means of the ear, the skin, the eyes, the tongue, and the nose, is what is meant by the restraint of the organs of sense. Strict observance of the precepts of sciences also means the same; for the sole aim of all the sciences is nothing but restraint of the organs of sense.

Whosoever is of reverse character, whoever has not his organs of sense under his control, will soon perish, though possessed of the whole earth bounded by the four quarters.

For example: Bhoja, known also by the name Dáṇḍakya, making a lascivious attempt on a Bráhman maiden, perished along with his kingdom and relations.

So also Karála, the Vaideha. Likewise Janamejaya under the influence of anger against Bráhmans, as well as Tálajaṅgha against the family of Bhṛigus.

Aila in his attempt under the influence of greed to make exactions from Bráhmans, as well as Ajabindu, the Sauvīra (in a similar attempt);

Rávaṇa, unwilling under the influence of vanity to restore a stranger's wife, as well as Duryodhana to part with a portion of his kingdom; Dambhodbhava as well as Arjuna of Haihaya dynasty being so haughty as to despise all people.

Vátápi, in his attempt under the influence of overjoy to attack Agastya, as well as the corporation of the Vṛiṣhṇis in their attempt against Dvaipáyana.

Thus these and other several kings, falling a prey to the aggregate of the six enemies, and having failed to restrain their organs of sense, perished together with their kingdom and relations. Having driven out the aggregate of the six enemies, Ambarīṣha of Jámadagnya, famous for his restraint of the organs of sense, as well as Nábhága, long enjoyed the earth.

Chapter 7—Restraint of the Organ of Sense: The Life of a Saintly King

Hence by overthrowing the aggregate of the six enemies, he shall restrain the organs of sense; acquire wisdom by keeping company with the aged; see through his spies; establish safety and security by being ever active; maintain his subjects in the observance of their respective duties by exercising authority; keep up his personal discipline by receiving lessons in the science; and endear himself to the people by bringing them in contact with wealth and doing good to them.

Thus with his organs of sense under his control, he shall keep away from hurting the woman and property of others; avoid not only lustfulness, even in dream, but also falsehood, haughtiness, and evil proclivities; and keep away from unrighteous and uneconomical transactions.

Not violating righteousness and economy, he shall enjoy his desires. He shall never be devoid of happiness. He may enjoy in an equal degree the three pursuits of life, charity, wealth, and desire, which are interdependent upon each other. Any one of these three, when enjoyed to an excess, hurts not only the other two, but also itself.

Kauṭilya holds that wealth, and wealth alone, is important, inasmuch as charity and desire depend upon wealth for their realization.

Those teachers and ministers who keep him from falling a prey to dangers, and who, by striking the hours of the day as determined by measuring shadows (chháyánálikápratodena), warn him of his careless proceedings even in secret, shall invariably be respected.

Sovereignty (rájatva) is possible only with assistance. A single wheel can never move. Hence he shall employ ministers and hear their opinion.

Chapter 8—Creation of Ministers

"The King," says Bháradvája, "shall employ his classmates as his ministers; for they can be trusted by him inasmuch as he has personal knowledge of their honesty and capacity."

"No," says Viśálákṣha, "for, as they have been his playmates as well, they would despise him. But he shall employ as ministers those whose secrets, possessed of in common, are well known to him. Possessed of habits and defects in common with the king, they would never hurt him lest he would betray their secrets."

"Common is this fear," says Paráśara, "for under the fear of betrayal of his own secrets, the king may also follow them in their good and bad acts.

"Under the control of as many persons as are made aware by the king of his own secrets, might he place himself in all humility by that disclosure. Hence he shall employ as ministers those who have proved faithful to him under difficulties fatal to life and are of tried devotion."

"No," says Piśuna, "for this is devotion, but not intelligence (buddhiguṇah). He shall appoint as ministers those who, when employed on financial matters, show as much as, or more than, the fixed revenue, and are thus of tried ability."

"No," says Kauṇapadanta, "for such persons are devoid of other ministerial qualifications; he shall, therefore, employ as ministers those whose fathers and grandfathers had been ministers before; such persons, in virtue of their knowledge of past events and of an established relationship with the king, will, though offended, never desert him; for such faithfulness is seen even among dumb animals; cows, for example, stand aside from strange cows and ever keep company with accustomed herds."

"No," says Vátavyádhi, "for such persons, having acquired complete dominion over the king, begin to play themselves as the king. Hence he shall employ as ministers such new persons as are proficient in the science of polity. It is such new persons who will regard the king as the real scepter-bearer (daṇḍadhara) and dare not offend him."

"No," says the son of Báhudantī (a woman); "for a man possessed of only theoretical knowledge, and having no experience of practical politics, is likely to commit serious blunders when engaged in actual works. Hence he shall employ as ministers such as are born of high family and possessed of wisdom, purity of purpose, bravery and loyal feelings, inasmuch as ministerial appointments shall purely depend on qualifications."

"This," says Kauṭilya, "is satisfactory in all respects; for a man's ability is inferred from his capacity shown in work. And in accordance with the difference in the working capacity.

Having divided the spheres of their powers and having definitely taken into consideration the place and time where and when they have to work, such persons shall be employed not as councilors (mantriṇah), but as ministerial officers (amátyah)."

Chapter 19—The Duties of a King

If a king is energetic, his subjects will be equally energetic. If he is reckless, they will not only be reckless likewise, but also eat into his works. Besides, a reckless king will easily fall into the hands of his enemies. Hence the king shall ever be wakeful.

He shall divide both the day and the night into eight nálikas (1.5 hours), or according to the length of the shadow (cast by a gnomon standing in the sun): the shadow of three puruṣhás (36 aṅgulás or inches), of one puruṣhá (12 inches), of four aṅgulás (4 inches), and absence of shadow denoting midday are the four one-eighth divisions of the forenoon; like divisions (in the reverse order) in the afternoon.

Of these divisions, during the first one-eighth part of the day, he shall post watchmen and attend to the accounts of receipts and expenditure; during the second part, he shall look to the affairs of both citizens and country people; during the third, he shall not only bathe and dine, but also study; during the fourth, he shall not only receive revenue in gold (hiraṇya) but also attend to the appointments of superintendents; during the fifth, he shall correspond in writs (patrasampreṣhaṇena) with the assembly of his ministers, and receive the secret information gathered by his spies; during the sixth, he may engage himself in his favorite amusements or in self-deliberation; during the seventh, he shall superintend elephants, horses, chariots, and infantry; and during the eighth part, he shall consider various plans of military operations with his commander-in-chief.

At the close of the day, he shall observe the evening prayer (sandhya).

During the first one-eighth part of the night, he shall receive secret emissaries; during the second, he shall attend to bathing and supper and study; during the third, he shall enter the bedchamber amid the sound of trumpets and enjoy sleep during the fourth and fifth parts; having been awakened by the sound of trumpets during the sixth part, he shall recall to his mind the injunctions of sciences as well as the day's duties; during the seventh, he shall sit considering administrative measures and send out spies; and during the eighth division of the night, he shall receive benedictions from sacrificial priests, teachers and the high priest, and having seen his physician, chief cook and astrologer, and having saluted both a cow with its calf and a bull by circumambulating round them, he shall get into his court.

Or in conformity to his capacity, he may alter the timetable and attend to his duties.

When in the court, he shall never cause his petitioners to wait at the door, for when a king makes himself inaccessible to his people and entrusts his work to his immediate officers, he may be sure to engender confusion in business, and to cause thereby public disaffection, and himself a prey to his enemies.

He shall, therefore, personally attend to the business of gods, of heretics, of Bráhmans learned in the Vedas, of cattle, of sacred places, of minors, the aged, the afflicted, and the helpless, and of women—all this in order (of enumeration) or according to the urgency or pressure of those works.

All urgent calls he shall hear at once, but never put off; for when postponed, they will prove too hard or impossible to accomplish.

Having seated himself in the room where the sacred fire has been kept, he shall attend to the business of physicians and ascetics practicing austerities; and that in company with his high priest and teacher and after preliminary salutation (to the petitioners).

Accompanied by persons proficient in the three sciences (trividya) but not alone lest the petitioners be offended, he shall look to the business of those who are practicing austerities, as well as of those who are experts in witchcraft and Yóga.

Of a king, the religious vow is his readiness to action; satisfactory discharge of duties is his performance of sacrifice; equal attention to all is the offer of fees and ablution towards consecration.

In the happiness of his subjects lies his happiness; in their welfare his welfare; whatever pleases himself he shall not consider as good, but whatever pleases his subjects he shall consider as good.

Hence the king shall ever be active and discharge his duties; the root of wealth is activity, and of evil its reverse.

In the absence of activity acquisitions present and to come will perish; by activity he can achieve both his desired ends and abundance of wealth.

Book VI—The Source of Sovereign States

Chapter 1—The Elements of Sovereignty

The king, the minister, the country, the fort, the treasury, the army and the friend are the elements of sovereignty.

Of these, the best qualities of the king are:

Born of a high family, godly, possessed of valor, seeing through the medium of aged persons, virtuous, truthful, not of a contradictory nature, grateful, having large aims, highly enthusiastic, not addicted to procrastination, powerful to control his neighboring kings, of resolute mind, having an assembly of ministers of no mean quality, and possessed of a taste for discipline—these are the qualities of an inviting nature.

Inquiry, hearing, perception, retention in memory, reflection, deliberation, inference and steadfast adherence to conclusions are the qualities of the intellect.

Valor, determination of purpose, quickness, and probity are the aspects of enthusiasm.

Possessed of a sharp intellect, strong memory, and keen mind, energetic, powerful, trained in all kinds of arts, free from vice, capable of paying in the same coin by way of awarding punishments or rewards, possessed of dignity, capable of taking remedial measures against dangers, possessed of foresight, ready to avail himself of opportunities when afforded in respect of place, time, and manly efforts, clever enough to discern the causes necessitating the cessation of treaty or war with an enemy, or to lie in wait keeping treaties, obligations and pledges, or to avail himself of his enemy's weak points, making jokes with no loss of dignity or secrecy, never brow-beating and casting haughty and stern looks, free from passion, anger, greed, obstinacy, fickleness, haste and backbiting habits, talking to others with a smiling face, and observing customs as taught by aged persons—such is the nature of self-possession.

The qualifications of a minister have been described in the beginning, middle, and at the close of the work.

Possessed of capital cities both in the center and the extremities of the kingdom, productive of subsistence not only to its own people, but also to outsiders on occasions of calamities, repulsive to enemies, powerful enough to put down neighboring kings, free from miry, rocky, uneven, and desert tracts, as well as from conspirators, tigers, wild beasts, and large tracts of wilderness, beautiful to look at, containing fertile lands, mines, timber and elephant forests, and pasture grounds, artistic, containing hidden passages, full of cattle, not depending upon rain for water, possessed of land and waterways, rich in various kinds of commercial articles, capable of bearing the burden of a vast army and heavy taxation, inhabited by agriculturists of good and active character, full of intelligent masters and servants, and with a population noted for its loyalty and good character;—these are the qualities of a good country.

The excellent qualities of forts have already been described.

Justly obtained either by inheritance or by self-acquisition, rich in gold and silver, filled with an abundance of big gems of various colors and of gold coins, and capable to withstand calamities of long duration, is the best treasury.

Coming down directly from father and grandfather (of the king), ever strong, obedient, happy in keeping their sons and wives well contented, not averse to making a long sojourn, ever and everywhere invincible, endowed with the power of endurance, trained in fighting various kinds of battles, skillful in handling various forms of weapons, ready to share in the weal or woe of the king, and consequently not failing foul with him, and purely composed of soldiers of Kṣhatriya caste, is the best army.

Coming down directly from father and grandfather, long-standing, open to conviction, never falling foul, and capable of making preparations for war quickly and on a large scale, is the best friend.

Not born of a royal family, greedy, possessed of a mean assembly of ministers, with disloyal subjects, ever doing unrighteous acts, of loose character, addicted to mean pleasures, devoid of enthusiasm, trusting to fate, indiscreet in action, powerless, helpless, impotent and ever injurious, is the worst enemy. Such an enemy is easily uprooted.

- Excepting the enemy, these seven elements, possessed of their excellent characteristics are said to be the limb-like elements of sovereignty.
- A wise king can make even the poor and miserable elements of his sovereignty happy and prosperous; but a wicked king will surely destroy the most prosperous and loyal elements of his kingdom.

- Hence a king of unrighteous character and of vicious habits will, though he is an emperor, fall a prey either to the fury of his own subjects or to that of his enemies.
- But a wise king, trained in politics, will, though he possesses a small territory, conquer the whole earth with the help of the best-fitted elements of his sovereignty, and will never be defeated.

Han Fei

The Difficulties of Persuasion
Third Century BC, China

---

*It is not difficult to know a thing; what is difficult is
to know how to use what you know.*

On the whole, the difficult thing about persuading others
is not that one lacks the knowledge needed to state his case nor
the audacity to exercise his abilities to the full. On the whole,
the difficult thing about persuasion is to know the mind of the
person one is trying to persuade and to be able to fit one's words
to it.

If the person you are trying to persuade is out to establish
a reputation for virtue, and you talk to him about making a fat
profit, then he will regard you as low-bred, accord you a shabby
and contemptuous reception, and undoubtedly send you pack-
ing. If the person you are trying to persuade is on the contrary
interested in a fat profit, and you talk to him about a virtuous

reputation, he will regard you as witless and out of touch with reality, and will never heed your arguments. If the person you are trying to persuade is secretly out for big gain but ostensibly claims to be interested in a virtuous name alone, and you talk to him about a reputation for virtue, then he will pretend to welcome and heed you, but in fact will shunt you aside; if you talk to him about making a big gain, he will secretly follow your advice but ostensibly reject you. These are facts that you must not fail to consider carefully.

Undertakings succeed through secrecy but fail through being found out. Though the ruler himself has not yet divulged his plans, if you in your discussions happen to hit upon his hidden motives, then you will be in danger. If the ruler is ostensibly seeking one thing but actually is attempting to accomplish something quite different, and you perceive not only his ostensible objective but the real motives behind his actions as well, then you will likewise be in danger. If you happen to think up some unusual scheme for the ruler which meets with his approval, and some other person of intelligence manages by outside means to guess what it is and divulges the secret to the world, then the ruler will suppose that it was you who gave it away and you will be in danger.

If you have not yet won substantial reward and favor and yet your words are extremely apt and wise, then if the ruler heeds them and the undertaking is successful, he will forget to reward you; and if he does not heed them and the undertaking fails, he will regard you with suspicion and you will be in danger. If some person of eminence takes a brief step in the wrong direction and you immediately launch into a lecture on ritual principles and challenge his misdeed, then you will be in danger. If some eminent person gets hold of a good scheme somewhere and plans to use it to win merit for himself, and you happen to know where he got it, then you will be in danger. If you try forcibly to talk a person into doing what he cannot do, or stopping what he cannot stop, then you will be in danger.

If you talk to the ruler about men of real worth, he will think you are implying that he is no match for them; if you talk to him of petty men, he will think you are attempting to use your influence to get your friends into office; if you talk to him about what he likes, he will suspect you of trying to utilize him; if you talk about what he hates, he will suspect you of trying to test his patience. If you speak too bluntly and to the point, he will consider you unlearned and will shun you; if you speak too eloquently and in too great detail, he will consider you pretentious and will reject you.

If you are too sketchy in outlining your ideas, he will think you a coward who is too fainthearted to say what he really means; if you are too exuberant and long-winded in stating your proposals, he will think you an uncouth bumpkin who is trying to talk down to him. These are the difficulties of persuasion; you cannot afford to be ignorant of them!

The important thing in persuasion is to learn how to play up the aspects that the person you are talking to is proud of, and play down the aspects he is ashamed of. Thus, if the person has some urgent personal desire, you should show him that it is his public duty to carry it out and urge him not to delay. If he has some mean objective in mind and yet cannot restrain himself, you should do your best to point out to him whatever admirable aspects it may have and to minimize the reprehensible ones. If he has some lofty objective in mind and yet does not have the ability needed to realize it, you should do your best to point out to him the faults and bad aspects of such an objective and make it seem a virtue not to pursue it. If he is anxious to make a show of wisdom and ability, mention several proposals which are different from the one you have in mind but of the same general nature in order to supply him with ideas; then let him build on your words, but pretend that you are unaware that he is doing so, and in this way abet his wisdom.

If you wish to urge a policy of peaceful coexistence, then be sure to expound it in terms of lofty ideals, but also hint that it is commensurate with the ruler's personal interests. If you wish to warn the ruler against dangerous and injurious policies, then make a show of the fact that they invite reproach and moral censure, but also hint that they are inimical to his personal interests.

Praise other men whose deeds are like those of the person you are talking to; commend other actions which are based upon the same policies as his. If there is someone else who is guilty of the same vice he is, be sure to gloss it over by showing that it really does no great harm; if there is someone else who has suffered the same failure he has, be sure to defend it by demonstrating that it is not a loss after all. If he prides himself on his physical prowess, do not antagonize him by mentioning the difficulties he has encountered in the past; if he considers himself an expert at making decisions, do not anger him by pointing out his past errors; if he pictures himself a sagacious planner, do not tax him with his failures.

Make sure that there is nothing in your ideas as a whole that will vex your listener, and nothing about your words that will rub him the wrong way, and then you may exercise your powers of rhetoric to the fullest. This is the way to gain the confidence and intimacy of the person you are addressing and to make sure that you are able to say all you have to say without incurring his suspicion.

Yi Yin became a cook and Boli Xi a captive slave, so they could gain the ear of the ruler. These men were sages, and yet they could not avoid shouldering hard tasks for the sake of advancement and demeaning themselves in this way. Therefore you too should become a cook or a slave when necessary; if this enables you to gain the confidence of the ruler and save the state, then it is no disgrace for a man of ability to take such a course.

If you are able to fulfill long years of service with the ruler, enjoy his fullest favor and confidence, lay long-range plans for him without ever arousing suspicion, and when necessary oppose him in argument without incurring blame, then you may achieve merit by making clear to him what is profitable and what is harmful, and bring glory to yourself by your forthright judgments of right and wrong. When ruler and minister aid and sustain each other in this way, persuasion may be said to have reached its fulfillment.

In ancient times Duke Wu of Zheng wanted to attack the state of Hu, and so he first married his daughter to the ruler of

Hu in order to fill his mind with thoughts of pleasure. Then he told his ministers, "I want to launch a military campaign. What would be a likely state to attack?" The high official Guan Qisi replied, "Hu could be attacked," whereupon Duke Wu flew into a rage and had him executed, saying, "Hu is a brother state! What do you mean by advising me to attack it!" The ruler of Hu, hearing of this, assumed that Zheng was friendly towards him and therefore took no precautions to defend himself from Zheng. The men of Zheng then made a surprise attack on Hu and seized it.

Once there was a rich man of Song. When the dirt wall around his house collapsed in a heavy rain, his son said, "If you don't rebuild it, thieves will surely break in," and the old man who lived next door told him the same thing. When night fell, thieves actually broke in and made off with a large share of the rich man's wealth. The rich man's family praised the son for his wisdom, but eyed the old man next door with suspicion.

Both these men—the high official Guan Qisi and the old man next door—spoke the truth, and yet one was actually executed for his words, while the other cast suspicion on himself. It is not difficult to know a thing; what is difficult is to know how to use what you know. Rao Zhao spoke the truth but, though he was regarded as a sage by the men of Jin, he was executed by those of Qin. This is something you cannot afford not to examine.

In ancient times Mi Zixia won favor with the ruler of Wei. According to the laws of the state of Wei, anyone who secretly made use of the ruler's carriage was punished by having his feet amputated. When Mi Zixia's mother fell ill, someone slipped into the palace at night to report this to Mi Zixia. Mi Zixia forged an order from the ruler, got into the ruler's carriage, and went off to see her, but when the ruler heard of it, he only praised him, saying, "How filial! For the sake of his mother he forgot all about the danger of having his feet cut off!"

Another day Mi Zixia was strolling with the ruler in an orchard and, biting into a peach and finding it sweet, he stopped eating and gave the remaining half to the ruler to enjoy. "How sincere is your love for me!" exclaimed the ruler. "You forget your own appetite and think only of giving me good things to eat!" Later, however, when Mi Zixia's looks had faded and the ruler's passion for him had cooled, he was accused of committing some crime against his lord. "After all," said the ruler, "he once stole my carriage, and another time he gave me a half-eaten peach to eat!" Mi Zixia was actually acting no differently from the way he always had; the fact that he was praised in the early days, and accused of a crime later on, was because the ruler's love had turned to hate.

If you gain the ruler's love, your wisdom will be appreciated and you will enjoy his favor as well; but if he hates you, not only will your wisdom be rejected, but you will be regarded as a criminal and thrust aside. Hence men who wish to present their remonstrances and expound their ideas must not fail to ascertain the ruler's loves and hates before launching into their speeches.

The beast called the dragon can be tamed and trained to the point where you may ride on its back. But on the underside of its throat it has scales a foot in diameter that curl back from the body, and anyone who chances to brush against them is sure to die. The ruler of men too has his bristling scales. Only if a speaker can avoid brushing against them will he have any hope for success.

King David

Psalm 72
Tenth Century BC, Israel

Give your judgment, O God, to the king, and your
justice to the king's son, to judge your people with
justice and your poor with judgment.

Psalm 72

Give your judgment, O God, to the king, and your
justice to the king's son, to judge your people with
justice and your poor with judgment.

Let the mountains take up peace for the people, and
the hills, justice.

He will judge the poor of the people, and he will
bring salvation to the sons of the poor. And he will
humble the false accuser.

73

And he will remain, with the sun and before the moon, from generation to generation.

He will descend like rain upon fleece, and like showers showering upon the earth.

In his days, justice will rise like the sun, with abundance of peace, until the moon is taken away.

And he will rule from sea to sea and from the river to the limits of the whole world.

In his sight, the Ethiopians will fall prostrate, and his enemies will lick the ground.

The kings of Tarshish and the islands will offer gifts. The kings of Arabia and of Seba will bring gifts.

And all the kings of the earth shall adore him. All nations will serve him.

For he will free the poor from the powerful, and the poor one who has no helper.

He will spare the poor and the indigent, and he will bring salvation to the souls of the poor.

He will redeem their souls from usuries and from iniquity, and their names shall be honorable in his sight.

And he will live, and to him will be given from the gold of Arabia, and by him they will always adore. They will bless him all day long.

And there will be a firmament on earth, at the summits of mountains: its fruits will be extolled above Lebanon, and those of the city will flourish like the grass of the earth.

May his name be blessed forever; may his name remain before the sun. And all the tribes of the earth will be blessed in him. All nations will magnify him.

Blessed is the Lord, God of Israel, who alone does wondrous things.

And blessed is the name of his majesty in eternity. And all the earth will be filled with his majesty. Amen. Amen.

The praises of David, the son of Jesse, have reached an end.

Book of Judith

Second Century BC, Israel

---

*Behold, the head of Holofernes the leader of the
military of the Assyrians, and behold his canopy,
under which he reclined in his drunkenness, where the
Lord our God struck him by the hand of a woman.*

Chapters 9–13 and 16

Chapter 9

And when they were gone, Judith entered her place of
prayer. And clothing herself with haircloth, she placed ashes
on her head. And prostrating herself to the Lord, she cried out
to the Lord, saying:

"O Lord, God of my father Simeon, you gave him a sword
to defend against foreigners, who stood out as violators by their
defilement, and who uncovered the thigh of the virgin unto
shame. And you gave their wives into plunder, and their daughters into captivity, and all their spoils to be divided to the

servants, who were zealous with your zeal. Bring help, I ask you, O Lord my God, to me, a widow. For you have acted in the past, and you have decided one thing after another. And what you have willed, this too has happened. For all your ways have been prepared, and you have placed your judgments within your providence.

"Look upon the camp of the Assyrians now, just as you deigned to look upon the camp of the Egyptians, when their weapons rushed after your servants, trusting in their four-horse chariots, and in their horsemen, and in a multitude of warriors. But you gazed upon their camp, and darkness wearied them.

"The abyss took hold of their feet, and the waters covered them. So may it be with these also, O Lord, who trust in their multitude, and in their swift chariots, and in their pikes, and in their shields, and in their arrows, and the glory in their lances. And they do not know that you are our God, who crushes wars from the beginning, and the Lord is your name.

"Raise up your arm, just as from the beginning, and throw down their power by your power. Let their power fall, in their anger, for they promise themselves to violate your sanctuary, and to pollute the tabernacle of your name, and to cut down by their sword the horn of your altar. Act, O Lord, so that his arrogance may be cut off with his own sword. Let him be seized by the snare of his own eyes in my regard, and may you strike him by the attraction of my lips. Give me constancy in my soul, so that I may hold him in contempt, and give me virtue, so that I may overthrow him. For this will be a memorial to your name, when he will be overthrown by the hand of a woman.

"For your power, O Lord, is not in numbers, nor is your will with the strength of horses, nor from the beginning have the arrogant been pleasing to you. But the pleas of the humble and the meek have always pleased you. O God of the heavens, Creator of the waters, and Lord of all creation, heed me, a miserable thing, pleading you and depending on your mercy. Remember, O Lord, your covenant, and put your words in my mouth, and reinforce the plan in my heart, so that your house may continue with your sanctification, and so that all the nations may acknowledge that you are God, and there is no other beside you."

Chapter 10

And it happened that, when she had ceased to cry out to the Lord, she arose from the place where she lay prostrate before the Lord. And she called her handmaid, and descending into her house, she took away from herself the haircloth, and she put away from herself the garments of her widowhood, and she washed her body, and she anointed herself with the best ointment, and she plaited the hair of her head, and she put a headdress on her head, and she clothed herself with the garments of her elegance, and she put sandals on her feet, and she put on her little bracelets, and lilies, and earrings, and rings, and she adorned herself with all her ornaments.

And also, the Lord conferred upon her a splendor. For all this dressing up did not proceed from sensuality, but from virtue. And therefore, the Lord increased this, her beauty, so that she appeared with incomparable honor before the eyes of all.

And so, she appointed to her handmaid a wineskin, and a vessel of oil, and parched grain, and dried figs, and bread, and cheese, and they departed.

And when they came to the gate of the city, they found Uzziah and the elders of the city waiting. And when they saw her, being astounded, they wondered at her surpassing beauty. So, not questioning her at all, they dismissed her to go forth, saying: "May the God of our fathers give you grace, and may he strengthen all the advice of your heart with his virtue, so that Jerusalem may glory over you, and your name may be counted among the holy and the just." And those who were there, all with one voice, said: "Amen. Amen." In truth, Judith was praying to the Lord as she crossed through the gates, she and her handmaid.

But it happened that, when she descended the mountain at about the break of day, the scouts of the Assyrians met her, and they stopped her, saying, "Where are you coming from? And where are you going?" And she answered: "I am a daughter of the Hebrews. This is why I have fled from their face: because I realized that in the future they would be given over to you with pillaging, for they hold you in contempt, and they would never be willing to surrender themselves, so that they might find mercy in your sight. For this reason, I thought to myself, saying: I will go to the face of the leader Holofernes, so that I may reveal to him their secrets, and show him by what means he may be able to prevail over them, without one man of his army being slain."

And when the men had heard her words, they beheld her face, and their eyes were astounded, because they wondered exceedingly at her beauty. And they said to her: "You have preserved your life by following such an excellent plan, to descend to our lord. But know this, that when you will stand in his sight, he will treat you well, and you will be very pleasing to his heart." And they led her to the tabernacle of Holofernes, announcing her. And when she had entered before his face, immediately Holofernes was captivated by his eyes.

And his attendants said to him, "Who can hold the people of the Hebrews in contempt, who have such beautiful women? So, we ought to think it not worthwhile, for their sakes, to fight against them." And so, Judith looked upon Holofernes, sitting under a canopy, which was woven from purple and gold, with emeralds and precious stones. And, after she had gazed into his face, she showed reverence for him, prostrating herself to the ground. And the servants of Holofernes lifted her up, at the command of their lord.

Chapter 11

Then Holofernes said to her: "Be steadfast in soul, and do not be terrified in your heart. For I have never harmed a man who was willing to serve king Nebuchadnezzar. But if your people had not despised me, I would not have lifted up my lance over them. But now, tell me, for what reason have you withdrawn from them, and why has it pleased you to come to us?" And Judith said to him: "Receive the words of your maidservant. For, if you will follow the words of your maidservant, the Lord will accomplish an excellent thing by you.

"For, as Nebuchadnezzar the king of the earth lives, and as his power lives, which is with you for the chastising of all straying souls: not only men serve him through you, but also the beasts of the field are submissive to him. For the diligence of your mind is being reported to all nations, and it has been revealed to all of this age that you alone are good and powerful in all his kingdom, and your discipline is being announced beforehand in all the provinces. This is not hidden, what Achior has said, nor are we ignorant of what you have ordered to befall him. For it is agreed that our God is so offended with sins that he has commanded, through his prophets to the people, that he will deliver them up for their sins. And since the sons of Israel know that they have offended their God, your trembling is upon them. Moreover, now also a famine has assailed them, and, by drought of water, they are already counted among the dead.

"And finally, they have a plan to put to death their herds, and to drink their blood. And the sacred things of the Lord their God, which God instructed them not to touch, among the grain, wine, and oil, these they have decided to expend, and they are willing to consume the things that they ought not to touch with their hands. Therefore, because they do these things, it is certain that they will be given over to perdition. And I, your maidservant, knowing this, have fled from them, and the Lord has sent me to report to you these same things. For I, your maidservant, worship God even now that I am with you, and your maidservant will go out, and I will pray to God. And he will tell me when he will repay them for their sins, and I will return and announce it to you, so that I may bring you through the midst of Jerusalem, and you will hold all the people of Israel, like sheep that have no shepherd, and there will not be so much as one dog that barks against you.

"For these things have been told to me through the providence of God. And because God has been angry with them, I have been sent to report these same things to you." And so, all these words were pleasing before Holofernes, and before his servants, and they wondered at her wisdom, and they said to one another: "There is not another woman so great upon the earth: in appearance, in beauty, and in charming words." And Holofernes said to her: "God has done well, who sent you ahead of the people, so that you may give them into our hands. And if your promise is good, if your God will do this for me, he will also be my God, and you will be great in the house of Nebuchadnezzar, and your name will be renowned through all the earth."

Chapter 12

Then he ordered her to enter where his valuables were stored, and he ordered her to wait there, and he appointed what should be given to her from his own feast. And Judith responded to him, and she said: "Now, I am not able to eat from these things which you instructed to be allotted to me, lest an offense come upon me. But I will eat from that which I have brought." And Holofernes said to her, "If these things that you have brought with you should fail you, what shall we do for you?" And Judith said, "As your soul lives, my lord, your maidservant will not expend all these things, until God accomplishes by my hand what I have in mind." And his servants led her into the tabernacle, as he instructed.

And, as she was entering, she requested that it be permitted to her to go outside at night, before daylight, in order to pray and to petition the Lord. And he instructed his chamberlains that she may exit and enter, just as it may please her, to adore her God, for three days. And she went out in the nights into the valley of Bethulia, and she washed herself in a fountain of water. And, as she climbed up, she prayed to the Lord God of Israel that he would direct her way, to the liberation of his people.

And entering, she remained pure in the tabernacle, until she received her own food in the evening.

And it happened on the fourth day that Holofernes made a supper for his servants, and he said to Vagao his eunuch: "Go, and persuade that Hebrew woman to willingly consent to live with me. For it is disgraceful among the Assyrians, if a woman mocks a man, acting so as to pass through with immunity from him." Then Vagao entered toward Judith, and he said, "May she not dread, my good young woman, to enter to my lord, so that she may be honored before his face, so that she may eat with him and drink wine with cheerfulness."

Judith answered him: "Who am I, that I should contradict my lord? All that will be good and best before his eyes, I will do. Moreover, whatever will please him, to me, that will be what is best, all the days of my life." And she arose and dressed herself with her garments, and entering, she stood before his face. But the heart of Holofernes was struck. For he was burning with desire for her. And Holofernes said to her, "Drink now, and recline with cheerfulness, for you have found favor before me." And Judith said, "I will drink, my lord, because my soul has been magnified this day, beyond all my days." And she accepted and ate and drank in his sight what her handmaid had prepared for her. And Holofernes became pleased with her, and he drank very much wine, more than he had ever drunk in his life.

Chapter 13

So then, when it had become late, his servants hurried to their lodgings, and Vagao closed the chamber doors, and he went away. But they were all drowsy from the wine. And Judith was alone in the chamber.

Moreover, Holofernes, being very inebriated, was fast asleep, reclining on his bed. And Judith told her handmaid to stand outside before the chamber, and to watch. And Judith stood in front of the bed, praying with tears, and her lips moved in silence, saying: "Confirm me, O Lord God of Israel, and in this hour look kindly upon the works of my hands, so that, just as you promised, you may raise up Jerusalem, your city, and so that, believing through you that this plan is able to be accomplished, I may succeed." And when she had said this, she approached the pillar, which was at the head of the bed, and she released his blade, which was hanging tied to it.

And when she had unsheathed it, she grabbed him by the hair of his head, and she said, "Confirm me, O Lord God, in this hour." And she struck him twice on his neck, and she cut off his head, and she took off his canopy from the pillars, and she rolled away the trunk of his body. And after a little while, she went out, and she delivered the head of Holofernes to her handmaid, and she ordered her to put it in her bag. And the two went out, according to their custom, as if to prayer, and they passed through the camp, and having circled around the valley, they came to the gate of the city. And Judith, from a distance, spoke to the watchmen on the walls, "Open the gates, for God is with us, and he has acted with his power in Israel."

And it happened that, when the men had heard her voice, they called the elders of the city. And all rushed toward her, from the least to the greatest. For, until then, they held no hope that she would return. And, enflaming the lights, they gathered all around her. But she climbed up to a higher place, and she ordered them to be made silent. And when all had quieted down, Judith said: "Praise the Lord our God, who has not abandoned those who hope in him. And by me, his handmaid, he has fulfilled his mercy, which he promised to the house of Israel. And he has killed the enemy of his people, by my hand this night."

Then, taking the head of Holofernes from the bag, she displayed it to them, saying: "Behold, the head of Holofernes the leader of the military of the Assyrians, and behold his canopy, under which he reclined in his drunkenness, where the Lord our God struck him by the hand of a woman. But, as the Lord himself lives, his angel has been my guardian both from my departure, and while staying there, and when returning from there. And the Lord has not permitted me, his handmaid, to be defiled, but he has called me back to you without the pollution of sin, rejoicing in his victory, in my escape, and in your liberation. Confess everything to him, for he is good, for his mercy is with every generation." Then everyone adored the Lord, and they said to her, "The Lord has blessed you by his power, because, through you, he has reduced our enemies to nothing."

Furthermore, Uzziah, the leader of the people of Israel, said to her: "O daughter, you have been blessed by the Lord, the most high God, above all the women on earth. Blessed is the Lord, who made heaven and earth, who has guided you in harming the head of the leader of our enemies. For he has so magnified your name this day, that your praise will not retire from the mouth of men, who will be mindful of the power of the Lord forever, because you have risked your life for the sake of the distress and tribulation of your people, and you have prevented our ruin before the sight of our God." And all the people said: "Amen. Amen."

And so, Achior was called, and he drew near, and Judith said to him: "The God of Israel, to whom you gave testimony, has avenged himself on his enemies. He has cut down the head of all unbelievers, by my hand this night. And, so that you may determine that this is so, behold, the head of Holofernes, who, in the contempt of his pride, despised the God of Israel and threatened Israel with ruin, saying, 'When the people of Israel have been captured, I will instruct your sides to be pierced through with a sword.'" Then Achior, seeing the head of Holofernes, and being distressed by fear, fell upon his face on the ground, and his soul became agitated. In truth, after this, when he had recovered his breath, he fell down before her feet, and he showed reverence for her, and he said: "Blessed are you by your God, in every tabernacle of Jacob, for in every nation that will hear of your name, the God of Israel will be magnified over you."

Chapter 16 (selections)

And after those days, each one returned to his own house, and Judith became great in Bethulia, and she had great splendor in all the land of Israel. For chastity was one with her virtue, so that she did not know man all the days of her life, after the passing away of her husband, Manasseh. And then, on feast days, she came forth with great glory. But she remained in her husband's house for one hundred and five years, and she set her handmaid free. And she passed away and was buried with her husband in Bethulia. And all the people mourned her, for seven days.

And, during all the time of her life, there was no one who disturbed Israel, nor for many years after her death. Moreover, the day of the festivity of this victory was accepted by the Hebrews in the numbering of holy days, and it was religiously observed by the Jews, from that time, even to the present day.

Medieval

Eusebius

Life of Constantine
Fourth Century AD, Caesarea

---

*My own desire is, for the general advantage of the
world and all mankind, that Thy people should enjoy
a life of peace and undisturbed concord.*

Selections from Books I, II, and IV

Book I

*Chapter 3—How God Honors Pious Princes, but Destroys
Tyrants*

And whereas He has given assurance that those who glorify
and honor Him will meet with an ample recompense at His hands,
while those who set themselves against Him as enemies and adversaries will compass the ruin of their own souls; already has He
established the truth of these His own declarations. He has shown
that the lives of those tyrants who denied and opposed Him have
had a fearful end, and at the same time has made it manifest that

even the death of His servant, as well as his life, is worthy of admiration and praise, and justly claims the memorial, not merely of perishable, but of immortal records. Mankind have indeed devised some consolation for the frail and precarious duration of human life, and have thought by the erection of monuments to secure immortal honors to the memory of their ancestors. Some have employed the vivid delineations and colors of painting; some have carved statues from lifeless blocks of wood; while others, by engraving their inscriptions deep on tablets and monuments of wood and stone, have sought to keep the virtues of those whom they honored in perpetual remembrance.

All these indeed are perishable, and consumed by the lapse of time, being representations of the corruptible body, and incapable of expressing the image of the immortal soul. And yet these seemed sufficient to those who had no well-grounded hope of happiness after the termination of this mortal life. But God, that God, I say, who is the Preserver of the universe, has treasured up with Himself, for those who love godliness, greater blessings than human thought has conceived; and, by giving the earnest and firstfruits of future rewards even here, assures, in some sort, immortal hopes to mortal eyes. The ancient oracles of the prophets, delivered to us in the Scripture, declare this; the lives of pious men, who shone in old time with every virtue, attest the same; and our own days prove it to be true, wherein CONSTANTINE, who alone of all that ever wielded the Roman power was the friend of God the Sovereign of all, has appeared to all mankind so bright an example of a godly life.

Chapter 43—Constantine's Liberality to the Poor

He likewise distributed money largely to those who were in need. And not only so, but his kindness and beneficence extended even to the heathen who had no claim on him; and he provided not money only, or necessary food, but also decent clothing for the poor outcasts who begged alms in the forum. But in the case of those who had once been prosperous, and had experienced a reverse of circumstances, his aid was still more lavishly bestowed. On such persons, in a truly royal spirit, he conferred magnificent benefactions; giving grants of land to some, and honoring others with various offices of trust. To unfortunate orphans he sustained the relation of a careful father, while he relieved the forlorn condition of widows, and cherished them with special care. Nay, he even gave virgins, left unprotected by their parents' death, in marriage to wealthy men with whom he was personally acquainted. But this he did after first bestowing on the brides such portions as it was fitting they should bring to their future husbands. In short, as the sun, when he rises upon the earth, liberally imparts his rays of light to all, so did Constantine, proceeding at early dawn from the imperial palace, and rising as it were with the heavenly luminary, impart the rays of his own beneficence to all who approached his person. It was scarcely possible to be near him without receiving some benefit, nor did it ever happen that any who had expected to obtain his assistance were disappointed in their hope.

Chapter 44—How He Was Present at the Synods of Bishops

Such, then, was his general conduct towards all. But he exercised a peculiar care over the Church of God: and whereas, in the several provinces there were some who differed from each other in judgment, he assumed as it were the functions of a general bishop constituted by God, and convened synods of His ministers. Nor did he disdain to be present and sit with them in their assembly, but bore a share in their deliberations, endeavoring to minister to them all what pertained to the peace of God. He took his seat too in the midst of them, as an individual amongst many, dismissing his guards and soldiers, and all whose duty it was to defend his person; feeling himself sufficiently protected by the fear of God, and secure in the affection of his most faithful Christian friends. Those whom he saw inclined to a sound judgment, and exhibiting a calm and conciliatory temper, received his high approbation, for he evidently delighted in a general harmony of sentiment; while he regarded the refractory and obstinate with aversion.

Chapter 45—How He Bore with Irrational Opponents

Moreover he endured with patience some who were exasperated against himself, directing them in mild and gentle terms to conduct themselves with temper, and not excite seditious tumults. And some of these respected his admonitions, and desisted; but as to those who proved incapable of sound judgment, he left them entirely at the disposal of God, and never himself resolved on severe measures against any one. Hence it naturally happened that the disaffected in Africa advanced so far in a course of licentiousness as even to venture on overt acts of audacity; some evil spirit, as it seems probable, being jealous of the present great prosperity, and impelling these men to atrocious deeds, that he might excite the emperor's anger against them. He gained nothing, however, by this malicious conduct; for the emperor treated these proceedings with contempt, and declared that he recognized their origin to be from the evil one; inasmuch as these were not the actions of sober persons, but of those who were either utterly devoid of reason, or else possessed by some evil spirit; and that such should be pitied rather than punished; since, though justice might check the fury of madmen, refined humanity had rather sympathize with their condition.

Book II

Chapter 24—Law of Constantine Respecting Piety towards God, and the Christian Religion

"Victor Constantinus, Maximus Augustus, to the inhabitants of the province of Palestine.

"To all who entertain just and wise sentiments respecting the character of the Supreme Being, it has long been most clearly evident, and beyond the possibility of doubt, how vast a difference there has ever been between those who maintain a careful observance of the hallowed duties of the Christian religion, and those who treat this religion with hostility or contempt. But at this present time, we may see by still more manifest proofs, and still more decisive instances, both how unreasonable it were to question this truth, and how mighty is the power of the Supreme

God: since it appears that they who faithfully observe His holy laws, and shrink from the transgression of His commandments, are rewarded with abundant blessings, and are endued with well-grounded hope as well as ample power for the accomplishment of their undertakings. On the other hand, they who have cherished impious sentiments have experienced results corresponding to their evil choice. For how is it to be expected that any blessing would be obtained by one who neither desired to acknowledge nor duly to worship that God who is the source of all blessing? Indeed, facts themselves are a confirmation of what I say. . . ."

Chapter 45—Statutes Which Forbade Sacrifice, and Enjoined the Building of Churches

Soon after this, two laws were promulgated about the same time; one of which was intended to restrain the idolatrous abominations which in time past had been practiced in every city and country; and it provided that no one should erect images, or practice divination and other false and foolish arts, or offer sacrifice in any way. The other statute commanded the erection of oratories on a loftier scale, and the enlargement of the churches of God; as though the hope were entertained that, now the madness of polytheism was wholly removed, almost all mankind would henceforth attach themselves to the service of God. His own personal piety induced the emperor to devise and address these instructions to the governors of the several provinces: and the law further admonished them not to spare the expenditure of money, but to draw supplies from the imperial treasury itself. Similar instructions were written also to the bishops of the several churches; and the emperor was pleased to transmit the same to myself, being the first letter which he personally addressed to me.

Chapter 56—He Prays That All May Be Christians, but Compels None

"My own desire is, for the general advantage of the world and all mankind, that Thy people should enjoy a life of peace and undisturbed concord. Let those, therefore, who are still blinded by error, be made welcome to the same degree of peace and tranquility which they have who believe. For it may be that this restoration of equal privileges to all will have a powerful effect in leading them into the path of truth. Let no one molest another in this matter, but let every one be free to follow the bias of his own mind. Only let men of sound judgment be assured of this, that those only can live a life of holiness and purity, whom Thou callest to an acquiescence in Thy holy laws. With regard to those who will hold themselves aloof from us, let them have, if they please, their temples of lies: *we* have the glorious edifice of Thy truth, which Thou hast given us as our native home. We pray, however, that they too may receive the same blessing, and thus experience that heartfelt joy which unity of sentiment inspires. . . ."

Book IV

Chapter 18—He Enjoins the General Observance of the Lord's Day, and the Day before the Sabbath

He ordained, too, that one day should be regarded as a special occasion for prayer: I mean that which is truly the first and chief of all, the day of our Lord and Savior. The entire care of his household was entrusted to deacons and other ministers consecrated to the service of God, and distinguished by gravity of life and every other virtue: while his trusty bodyguard, strong in affection and fidelity to his person, found in their emperor an instructor in the practice of piety, and like him held the Lord's salutary day in honor, and performed on that day the devotions which he loved. The same observance was recommended by this blessed prince to all classes of his subjects; his earnest desire being gradually to lead all mankind to the worship of God. Accordingly he enjoined on all the subjects of the Roman empire to observe the Lord's day, as a day of rest, and also to honor the day which precedes the sabbath; in memory, I suppose, of what the Savior of mankind is recorded to have achieved on that day. And since his desire was to teach his whole army zealously to honor the Savior's day (which derives its name from light, and from the sun), he freely granted to those among them who were partakers of the divine faith, leisure for attendance on the services of the Church of God, in order that they might be able, without impediment, to perform their religious worship.

Chapter 31—He Is Derided Because of His Excessive Clemency
Meantime, since there was no fear of capital punishment to deter from the commission of crime, for the emperor himself was uniformly inclined to clemency, and none of the provincial governors visited offenses with their proper penalties, this state of things drew with it no small degree of blame on the general administration of the empire; whether justly or not, let every

one form his own judgment: for myself, I only ask permission to record the fact.

Chapter 75—He Surpassed All Preceding Emperors in Devotion to God

Standing, as he did, alone and preeminent among the Roman emperors as a worshipper of God; alone as the bold proclaimer to all men of the doctrine of Christ; having alone rendered honor, as none before him had ever done, to His Church; having alone abolished utterly the superstitious worship of a plurality of gods, and discountenanced idolatry in every form: so, both during life and after death, was he accounted worthy of such honors as none can say have been attained to by any other; so that no one, whether Greek or Barbarian, nay, of the ancient Romans themselves, has ever been presented to us as worthy of comparison with him.

Saint Augustine

The City of God
Fifth Century AD, Rome

*But we say that [Christian Emperors] are happy if
they rule justly; if they are not lifted up amid the
praises of those who pay them sublime honors, and
the obsequiousness of those who salute them with an
excessive humility, but remember that they are men.*

Selections from Book V

Chapter 24—What Was the Happiness of the Christian Emperors, and How Far It Was True Happiness

For neither do we say that certain Christian emperors were therefore happy because they ruled a long time, or, dying a peaceful death, left their sons to succeed them in the empire, or subdued the enemies of the republic, or were able both to guard against and to suppress the attempt of hostile citizens rising against them. These and other gifts or comforts of this sorrowful life even certain worshippers of demons have merited to receive, who do not belong to the kingdom of God to which these belong; and this is to be traced to the mercy of God, who would not have those who believe in Him desire such things as the highest good.

But we say that they are happy if they rule justly; if they are not lifted up amid the praises of those who pay them sublime honors, and the obsequiousness of those who salute them with an excessive humility, but remember that they are men; if they make their power the handmaid of His majesty by using it for the greatest possible extension of His worship; if they fear, love, worship God; if more than their own they love that kingdom in which they are not afraid to have partners; if they are slow to punish, ready to pardon; if they apply that punishment as necessary to government and defense of the republic, and not in order to gratify their own enmity; if they grant pardon, not that iniquity may go unpunished, but with the hope that the transgressor may amend his ways; if they compensate with the lenity of mercy and the liberality of benevolence for whatever severity they may be compelled to decree; if their luxury is as much restrained as it might have been unrestrained; if they prefer to govern depraved desires rather than any nation whatever; and if they do all these things, not through ardent desire of empty glory, but through love of eternal felicity, not neglecting to offer to the true God, who is their God, for their sins, the sacrifices of humility, contrition, and prayer. Such Christian emperors, we say, are happy in the present time by hope, and are destined to be so in the enjoyment of the reality itself, when that which we wait for shall have arrived.

Chapter 25—Concerning the Prosperity Which God Granted to the Christian Emperor Constantine

For the good God, lest men, who believe that He is to be worshipped with a view to eternal life, should think that no one could attain to all this high estate, and to this terrestrial dominion, unless he should be a worshipper of the demons—supposing that these spirits have great power with respect to such things—for this reason He gave to the Emperor Constantine, who was not a worshipper of demons, but of the true God Himself, such fullness of earthly gifts as no one would even dare wish for. To him also He granted the honor of founding a city, a companion to the Roman empire, the daughter, as it were, of Rome itself, but without any temple or image of the demons. He reigned for a long period as sole emperor, and unaided held and defended the whole Roman world. In conducting and carrying on wars he was most victorious; in overthrowing tyrants he was most successful.

He died at a great age, of sickness and old age, and left his sons to succeed him in the empire. But again, lest any emperor should become a Christian in order to merit the happiness of Constantine, when everyone should be a Christian for the sake of eternal life, God took away Jovian far sooner than Julian, and permitted that Gratian should be slain by the sword of a tyrant. But in his case there was far more mitigation of the calamity than in the case of the great Pompey, for he could not be avenged by Cato, whom he had left, as it were, heir to the civil war. But Gratian, though pious minds require not such consolations, was avenged by Theodosius, whom he had associated with himself in the empire, though he had a little brother of his own, being more desirous of a faithful alliance than of extensive power.

Agapetus the Deacon

Advice to the Emperor Justinian
Sixth Century AD, Constantinople

Like a helmsman, the many-eyed intellect of the
emperor remains ever vigilant, holding secure the
rudder of good government and firmly pushing back
the torrents of lawlessness.

Selections

1. Since you have a dignity beyond all other honor, Emperor,
    honor—beyond all others—God, who dignified you. For it
    was in the likeness of the Heavenly Kingdom that he gave
    you the scepter of earthly rule that you might teach men
    the protection of justice and drive away the howling of
    those who rave against it, just as you are ruled by the laws
    of justice and rule lawfully those subject to you.

2. Like a helmsman, the many-eyed intellect of the emperor remains ever vigilant, holding secure the rudder of good government and firmly pushing back the torrents of lawlessness, so that the vessel of the universal state may not founder in the waves of injustice.

3. The divine and first lesson we men are taught is: "Know thyself." Who knows himself, will know God; who knows God, will become like God; who will become like God has become worthy of God. He who does nothing unworthy of God becomes worthy of God, but thinks the things of God, says what he thinks and does what he says.

4. Let no one pride himself on the nobility of his ancestors. All men have clay as forefather of their race: those who flaunt themselves in purple and fine linen; those worn out by poverty and disease; those invested with the diadem, [and those lying exposed, seeking alms]. Let us not therefore flaunt our descent from clay, but let us pride ourselves on the goodness of our ways.

7. Among earthly things, the instability of wealth imitates the course of rivers' currents: for a short time, it flows towards men who think they possess it; but after a short time, it flows away, and departs to others. Only the treasure of good deeds remains fixed for those who possess it, since the blessing of good deeds reverts to their doers.

8. You are unapproachable to men because of the height of your kingship here below; yet you are approachable to those in need because of the might of the power above. You open your ears to those besieged by poverty, so that you may find the ear of God open. For as we treat our fellow slaves, so shall we find our Master treating us.

10. As on a voyage, when a sailor makes a mistake, he brings little harm to those sailing with him. But when the helmsman does so, he brings about the destruction of the whole ship. So too with cities: if a subject errs, he does not so much harm society as himself. But if the ruler does wrong, then he damages the whole state. Since he will be held severely to account if he should neglect to do anything that is necessary, let him say and do everything with great precision.

11. A wheel of human affairs goes round, now taking them in one direction, now in another, and turning them around. And their inequality lies in the fact that none of the things present remains the same. In the face of this rapid change, mightiest of Emperors, you must, therefore, maintain your pious way of thinking unchanged.

15. More than all the glories of empire, it is the chaplet of piety that adorns the emperor. Wealth passes; glory vanishes. But the renown of a life inspired by God stretches to immortal ages, and places beyond oblivion those who possess it.

16. It seems to me very strange indeed that rich and poor suffer the same harm from different things. The former burst with surfeiting; the latter perish from hunger. The one possesses the ends of the earth; the other has nowhere to place the sole of his foot. So that both may achieve health, they must be treated by the method of addition and subtraction: inequality must be changed to equality.

19. If you wish to reap honor from all men, become the common benefactor of all. For nothing so attracts goodwill as the favor of good deeds given to those in need. But reverence which arises from fear is dressed-up flattery, which under the fictitious name of honor deceives those who rely on it.

20. Your rule over us is justly venerated because to enemies it shows its power, but to subjects it dispenses benevolence. Having subdued the former by the power of arms, it is overcome by the unarmed love of your own people. In the distance between a wild animal and a sheep can be reckoned the difference between both.

21. In his bodily essence, the emperor is the equal of every man, but in the power of his rank he is like God over all men. He has no one on earth who is higher than he. Like a man, therefore, he must not be puffed up; like God, he must not be angry. For if he is honored for his divine image, he is nevertheless bound to his earthly image through which he is taught his equality with other men.

27. Impose on yourself the necessity of keeping the laws, since you have on earth no one able to compel you. You will thus display the majesty of the laws by revering them yourself above all others, and it will be clear to your subjects that acting unlawfully is not without danger.

35. Consider yourself to reign safely when you rule willing subjects. For the unwilling subject rebels when he has the opportunity. But he who is ruled by the bonds of goodwill is firm in his obedience to his ruler.

41. Do not distinguish between your friends and foes when giving judgment. Neither favor those who wish you well on account of their well-wishing, nor resist those who are enemies because of their hatred. It is equally absurd to give a favorable verdict to the unjust man, even though he is a friend, and an unfavorable one to the just man, even though he is an enemy. The evil is the same in both cases, even if it is found in opposite circumstances.

46. As the eye is implanted in the body, so is the emperor fitted into the world—given by God to collaborate with Him in conferring benefits. He must, therefore, take thought for all men, as for his own limbs, so that they make progress in things good, and do not stumble in things evil.

55. The ruler must be sharp in all things, especially in reaching judgment on difficult issues, but exceedingly slow to wrath.

Since the complete absence of anger does not earn respect, let him both be moderately angry and not angry: the first, so that he may check the impulse of the wicked; the second, so that he may [track down the motives for murders].

59. Use fittingly your kingdom here below so that it may become a ladder for you to the glory above. Those who rule well the one are, together with this one, judged worthy of the other. Those who rule well here display paternal love for those they rule, and receive in return from them the fear due to a ruler. Thus they bring their faults under control by threats; and not by inflicting on them the test of punishment.

66. For a private individual, I say, wickedness is to do mean things worthy of punishment; for a ruler it is *not* to do what is good and assists salvation. Abstaining from evil does not justify a ruler, but the provision of good crowns him. Let him, therefore, not only consider abstaining from wickedness, but strive also to hold fast to justice.

67. Death is not abashed by the splendors of rank: he sinks his all-devouring fangs into everyone. Before his inexorable arrival, therefore, let us transfer our abundance of treasure to heaven. For no one takes away there, once he has departed, what he collects in the world: but having left behind everything on earth, he is called naked to account for his life.

70. The transitory state of our present life resembles the passage of a seafaring ship which escapes the notice of us, its sailors. Little by little it sweeps off course, and escorts us each to our end. If this is how things are, therefore, let us run past the changing affairs of the world, and hasten to those that remain to the ages of ages.

72. Strive forever, unconquerable emperor. And, as those who have begun to climb a ladder do not cease their upward progress until they have reached the highest rung, so you also hold firm to the ascent in goodness that you may enjoy the kingdom above. May Christ, the King of those who rule and are ruled, grant this to you and your consort, for ever and ever. Amen.

Abu Nasr Muhammad al-Farabi

Aphorisms of the Statesman
Eighth or Ninth Century AD, Syria

*The one who cures bodies is the physician; and the
one who cures souls is the statesman.*

Aphorisms 1–5, 30–32, 58–59, 95–96

*Analogies between the Soul and the Body Politic (Aphorisms
1–5)*

1. Aphorism. The soul has health and sickness just as the
body has health and sickness. The health of the soul is for its
traits and the traits of its parts to be traits by which it can always
do good things, fine things, and noble actions. Its sickness is
for its traits and the traits of its parts to be traits by which it
always does evil things, wicked things, and base actions. The
health of the body is for its traits and the traits of its parts to be
traits by which the soul does its actions in the most complete
and perfect way, whether those actions that come about by
means of the body or its parts are good ones or evil ones. Its
sickness is for its traits and the traits of its parts to be traits by

which the soul does not do its actions that come about by means of the body or its parts, or does them in a more diminished manner than it ought or not as was its wont to do them.

2. Aphorism. The traits of the soul by which a human being does good things and noble actions are virtues. Those by which he does evil things and base actions are vices, defects, and villainies.

3. Aphorism. Just as the health of the body is an equilibrium of its temperament and its sickness is a deviation from equilibrium, so, too, are the health of the city and its uprightness an equilibrium of the moral habits of its inhabitants and its sickness a disparity found in their moral habits. When the body deviates from equilibrium in its temperament, the one who brings it back to equilibrium and preserves it there is the physician. So, too, when the city deviates from equilibrium with respect to the moral habits of its inhabitants, the one who brings it back to uprightness and preserves it there is the statesman. So the statesman and physician have their two actions in common and differ with respect to the two subjects of their two arts. For the subject of the former is souls and the subject of the latter, bodies. And just as the soul is more eminent than the body, so, too, is the statesman more eminent than the physician.

4. Aphorism. The one who cures bodies is the physician; and the one who cures souls is the statesman, and he is also called the king. However, the intention of the physician in curing bodies is not to make its traits such that the soul does good things or wicked ones by means of them. Rather, he intends

only to make its traits such that by means of them the actions of the soul coming about by means of the body and its parts are more perfect, whether those actions are wicked things or fine ones.

The physician who cures the body does so only to improve a human being's strength, regardless of whether he uses that improved strength in fine things or wicked ones. The one who cures the eye intends thereby only to improve sight, regardless of whether he uses that in what he ought and becomes fine or in what he ought not and becomes base. Therefore, to look into the health of the body and its sickness from this perspective is not up to the physician insofar as he is a physician, but up to the statesman and the king. Indeed, the statesman by means of the political art and the king by means of the art of kingship determine where it ought to be done, with respect to whom it ought to be done and with respect to whom not done, and what sort of health bodies ought to be provided with and what sort they ought not to be provided with.

Therefore, the case of the kingly and the political art with respect to the rest of the arts in cities is that of the master builder with respect to the builders. For the rest of the arts in cities are carried out and practiced only so as to complete by means of them the purpose of the political art and the kingly art, just as the ruling art among the arts of the builders uses the rest of them in order to complete its intention by means of them.

5. Aphorism. The physician who cures bodies needs to be cognizant of the body in its entirety and of the parts of the body, of what sicknesses occur to the whole of the body and to each

one of its parts, from what they occur, from how much of a thing, of the way to make them cease, and of the traits that when attained by the body and its parts make the actions coming about in the body perfect and complete. Likewise, the statesman and the king who cure souls need to be cognizant of the soul in its entirety and of its parts, of what defects and vices occur to it and to each one of its parts, from what they occur, from how much of a thing, of the traits of the soul by which a human does good things and how many they are, of the way to make the vices of the inhabitants of cities cease, of the devices to establish these traits in the souls of the citizens, and of the way of governing so as to preserve these traits among them so that they do not cease. And yet he ought to be cognizant of only as much about the soul as is needed in his art just as the physician needs to be cognizant of only as much about the body as is needed in his art, and the carpenter with respect to wood or the smith with respect to iron only as much as is needed in his art.

On the King in Truth (Aphorisms 30–32)

30. Aphorism. The king in truth is the one whose purpose and intention concerning the art by which he governs cities are to provide himself and the rest of the inhabitants of the city true happiness. This is the goal and the purpose of the kingly craft. It necessarily follows that the king of the virtuous city be the most perfect among the inhabitants of the city in happiness since he is the reason for their being happy.

31. Aphorism. One group is of the opinion that the goal intended in kingship and the governance of cities is majesty;

honor; domination; executing command and prohibition; and being obeyed, made great, and magnified. They prefer honor for its own sake, not for any other thing they might gain by means of it. They set down the actions by which cities are governed as actions by which they arrive at this purpose, and they set down the traditional laws of the city as traditional laws by which they arrive at this purpose through the inhabitants of the city. Some arrive at that by practicing virtue with the inhabitants of the city, acting well toward them, bringing them to the good things that are good things according to the inhabitants of the city, preserving these for them, and giving them preference in these things over themselves. They gain great honor thereby, and these are the most virtuous among the rulers of honor.

Others are of the opinion that they will become deserving of honor by means of wealth, and they endeavor to be the wealthiest inhabitants of the city and to be themselves unique in wealth so as to achieve honor. Some are of the opinion that they will be honored for descent alone. Others do that by conquering the inhabitants of the city, dominating them, humiliating them, and terrorizing them.

Others among the governors of cities are of the opinion that the purpose of governing cities is wealth. They set down as the actions by which they govern cities actions by which they arrive at wealth. And they set down traditional laws for the inhabitants of the city by means of which they arrive at wealth through the inhabitants of the city. If they prefer a certain good or do anything, they prefer it and do it only so that they attain wealth.

It is known that there is a major difference between one who prefers wealth so as to be honored for it and one who prefers honor and to be obeyed so that he will become affluent and arrive at wealth. The latter are called the inhabitants of the vile rulership.

Others among the governors of cities are of the opinion that the goal of governing cities is the enjoyment of pleasures.

A group of others is of the opinion that it is all three of these brought together—namely, honor, wealth, and pleasures. They rule despotically and set the inhabitants of the city down as things similar to tools for them to gain pleasures and wealth.

Not one of these is called king by the Ancients.

32. Aphorism. The king is king by means of the kingly craft, the art of governing cities, and the ability to use the kingly craft at any moment whatsoever as a rulership over a city—whether he is reputed for his art or not, finds the tools to use or not, finds a group who accepts him or not, is obeyed or not.

So, too, the physician is a physician by means of the medical craft—whether he is recognized by people for it or not, is furnished with the tools of his art or not, finds a group who serves him by executing his actions or not, comes upon sick persons who accept his statement or not. Nor is his medicine diminished by his not having any of these. Similarly, the king is king by means of the craft and the ability to use the art—whether he has dominion over a group or not, is honored or not, is wealthy or poor.

A group of others is of the opinion that they not apply the name king to anyone who has the kingly craft without being obeyed and honored in a city. Others add wealth to that. And others are of the opinion to add to that dominion by conquest, humiliation, terror, and provoking fear.

None of these is among the stipulations of kingship. Yet they are results that sometimes follow the kingly craft, and it is therefore presumed that they are kingship.

The Virtuous City (Aphorisms 58–59)

58. Aphorism. The rulers and governors of this city are of four sorts.

One is the king in truth; he is the supreme ruler and the one in whom six stipulations come together: wisdom, complete prudence, excellent persuasion, excellent imaginative evocation, bodily capability for struggle, and having nothing in his body that prevents him from carrying out the things pertaining to struggle. One in whom all of these qualities come together is the model, someone to be copied in his ways of life and his actions, someone whose declarations and counsels are to be accepted, and one who may govern as he thinks and wishes.

The second is for no human being to exist in whom all of these have come together. But they do exist dispersed among a group so that one of them gives the goal, the second gives what leads to the goal, the third has excellent persuasion and excellent imaginative evocation, and another the capability for struggle. So this group all together takes the place of the king, and they are called superior rulers and the possessors of virtues. Their rulership is called the rulership of the virtuous.

The third is for these not to exist either, so the ruler of the city is then the one in whom [the following] exist together: [a] that he is knowledgeable of the preceding divine and traditional laws the first leaders brought forth to govern cities; [b] then, that he is excellent at distinguishing the places and conditions in which one ought to apply those traditional laws in accordance with the intention of the first [leaders]; [c] then, that he has the capability to infer what was not explicitly declared in the previous traditional laws that were preserved and written down, following in the traces of the prior traditional laws in what he infers; [d] then, that he has excellent opinion and prudence with respect to the events that occur one by one and, not being such as to have come about in the previous ways of life, are such as to preserve the prosperity of the city; [e] that he is excellent in persuasion and imaginative evocation; [f] and that he has, in addition, the capability for struggle. This one is called the traditional king and his rulership is called traditional kingship.

The fourth is for no single human being to exist in whom all of these come together; yet they are dispersed among a group. So altogether they take the place of the traditional king, and these as a group are called traditional rulers.

59. Aphorism. In each of the parts of the city there is a ruler who has none of the inhabitants of that section over him as a ruler, a person ruled who has no rulership over any human being at all, and someone who is a ruler over those beneath him while being ruled by those above him.

The Virtue of Calculation and Degrees of Health (Aphorisms 95–96)

95. Aphorism. The virtue of calculation is what enables a human being to make an excellent inference about what is more useful with respect to a virtuous goal shared by nations, a nation, or a city when there is a shared occurrence. Some of it is inference for what changes over short periods, and this is called the faculty for the sorts of temporary, particular governorships for the occurrence of things that occur gradually to nations, a nation, or a city. The faculty of calculation that infers what is useful for a goal that is evil is not a virtue of calculation.

96. Aphorism. With respect to our bodies, it is not possible for us to acquire all the sorts of health with its temperaments, or its constitutional elements, its customs, the kind of dwelling particular to it, the art by which to make a living, or what is similar to that. This is the condition of most bodies. And in some places, it is possible for the inhabitants to acquire only a slight amount of the sorts of health. The case is the same with [our] souls, in that they cannot acquire the virtues, or most of them, or can acquire only a slight amount of them.

It is not up to the virtuous leader and the supreme ruler to establish virtues in someone the nature and substance of whose soul do not accept the virtues. For souls like this, it is up to him to obtain as much of the virtues as is possible for them and for their existence in accordance with what is useful for the inhabitants of the city.

Likewise, for bodies in the condition that has been described, it is not up to the virtuous physician to obtain the most perfect levels nor the highest degrees of health. It is up to him to obtain as much health as is possible for their nature and substance in accordance with the actions of the soul. Now the body is for the sake of the soul, and the soul is for the sake of final perfection—namely, happiness. And with respect to virtue, the soul is for the sake of wisdom and virtue.

Saint Thomas Aquinas

On Kingship
Thirteenth Century AD, Italy

For nothing permanent is found in earthly things.
Consequently there is nothing earthly which can
calm desire. Thus, nothing earthly can make man
happy, so that it may be a fitting reward for a king.

Selections from Book I

To the King of Cyprus

As I was turning over in my mind what I might present to Your Majesty as a gift at once worthy of Your Royal Highness and befitting my profession and office, it seemed to me a highly appropriate offering that, for a king, I should write a book on kingship, in which, so far as my ability permits, I should carefully expound, according to the authority of Holy Writ and the teachings of the philosophers as well as the practice of worthy princes, both the origin of kingly government and the things which pertain to the office of a king, relying for the beginning, progress and accomplishment of this work, on the help of Him,

Who is King of Kings, Lord of Lords, through Whom kings rule, God the Mighty Lord, King great above all gods.

Book I

Chapter 1 (selections)

From this it is clearly shown that the idea of king implies that he be one man who is chief and that he be a shepherd, seeking the common good of the multitude and not his own.

Chapter 2 (selections)

This question may be considered first from the viewpoint of the purpose of government. The aim of any ruler should be directed towards securing the welfare of that which he undertakes to rule. The duty of the pilot, for instance, is to preserve his ship amidst the perils of the sea. and to bring it unharmed to the port of safety. Now the welfare and safety of a multitude formed into a society lies in the preservation of its unity, which is called peace. If this is removed, the benefit of social life is lost and, moreover, the multitude in its disagreement becomes a burden to itself.

The chief concern of the ruler of a multitude, therefore, is to procure the unity of peace. It is not even legitimate for him to deliberate whether he shall establish peace in the multitude subject to him, just as a physician does not deliberate whether he shall heal the sick man encharged to him, for no one should deliberate about an end which he is obliged to seek, but only about the means to attain that end. Wherefore the Apostle, having commended the unity of the faithful people, says: "Be ye careful to keep the unity of the spirit in the bond of peace." Thus, the more efficacious a government is in keeping the unity of peace, the more useful it will be. For we call that more useful which leads more directly to the end. Now it is manifest that what is itself one can more efficaciously bring about unity than several—just as the most efficacious cause of heat is that which is by its nature hot. Therefore the rule of one man is more useful than the rule of many.

Chapter 7

Since, according to what has been said thus far, it is the king's duty to seek the good of the multitude, the task of a king may seem too burdensome unless some advantage to himself should result from it. It is fitting therefore to consider wherein a suitable reward for a good king is to be found.

By some men this reward was considered to be nothing other than honor and glory. Whence Tullius says in the book *On the Republic* [*De Republica* V, 7, 9]: "The prince of the city should be nourished by glory," and Aristotle seems to assign the reason for this in his Book on *Ethics* [V, 10: 1134b 7]: "because the prince for whom honor and glory is not sufficient consequently turns into a tyrant." For it is in the hearts of all men to seek their proper good. Therefore, if the prince is not content with glory and honor, he will seek pleasures and riches and so will resort to plundering and injuring his subjects.

However, if we accept this opinion a great many incongruous results follow. In the first place, it would be costly to kings if so many labors and anxieties were to be endured for a reward so perishable, for nothing, it seems, is more perishable among human things than the glory and honor of men's favor since it depends upon the report of men and their opinions, than which nothing in human life is more fickle. And this is why the Prophet Isaiah calls such glory "the flower of grass."

Moreover, the desire for human glory takes away greatness of soul. For he who seeks the favor of men must serve their will in all he says and does, and thus, while striving to please all, he becomes a slave to each one. Wherefore the same Tullius says in his book *On Duties* [*De officiis*, I, 20, 68] that "the inordinate desire for glory is to be guarded against; it takes away freedom of soul, for the sake of which high-minded men should put forth all their efforts." Indeed there is nothing more becoming to a prince who has been set up for the doing of good works than greatness of soul. Thus, the reward of human glory is not enough for the services of a king.

At the same time it also hurts the multitude if such a reward be set up for princes, for it is the duty of a good man to take no account of glory, just as he should take no account of other temporal goods. It is the mark of a virtuous and brave soul to despise glory as he despises life, for justice's sake: whence the strange thing results that glory ensues from virtuous acts, and out of virtue glory itself is despised: and therefore, through his very contempt for glory, a man is made glorious—according to the sentence of Fabius: "He who scorns glory shall have true glory," and as Sallust [*Bellum Catilinae* 54, 6] says of Cato: "The less he sought glory the more he achieved it." Even the disciples of Christ

"exhibited themselves as the ministers of God in honor and dishonor, in evil report and good report" (2 Cor. 6:8). Glory is,
therefore, not a fitting reward for a good man; good men spurn
it. And, if it alone be set up as the reward for princes, it will follow
that good men will not take upon themselves the chief office of
the city, or if they take it, they will go unrewarded. . . .

Moreover, the desire for glory has another vice akin to it,
namely, hypocrisy. Since it is difficult to acquire true virtues, to
which alone honor and glory are due, and it is therefore the lot
of but a few to attain them, many who desire glory become
simulators of virtue. On this account, as Sallust says [*Bellum
Catilinae* 10, 5]: "Ambition drives many mortals to become false.
They keep one thing shut up in their heart, another ready on
the tongue, and they have more countenance than character."

But our Savior also calls those persons hypocrites, or simulators, who do good works that they may be seen by men.
Therefore, just as there is danger for the multitude, if the prince
seek pleasures and riches as his reward, that he become a plun-
derer and abusive, so there is danger, if glory be assigned to him
as reward, that he become presumptuous and a hypocrite.

Looking at what the above-mentioned wise men intended
to say, they do not seem to have decided upon honor and glory
as the reward of a prince because they judged that the king's
intention should be principally directed to that object, but because it is more tolerable for him to seek glory than to desire
money or pursue pleasure. For this vice is akin to virtue inasmuch as the glory which men desire, as Augustine says [*De civ.
Dei* V, 12], is nothing else than the judgment of men who think

well of men. So the desire for glory has some trace of virtue in it, at least so long as it seeks the approval of good men and is reluctant to displease them.

Therefore, since few men reach true virtue, it seems more tolerable if one be set up to rule who, fearing the judgment of men, is restrained from manifest evils. For the man who desires glory either endeavors to win the approval of men in the true way, by deeds of virtue, or at least strives for this by fraud and deceit. But if the one who desires to domineer lacks the desire for glory, he will have no fear of offending men of good judgment and will commonly strive to obtain what he chooses by the most open crimes. Thus he will surpass the beasts in the vices of cruelty and lust, as is evidenced in the case of the Emperor Nero, who was so effete, as Augustine says [*loc. cit.*], "that he despised everything virile, and yet so cruel that nobody would have thought him to be effeminate." Indeed all this is quite clearly contained in what Aristotle says in his *Ethics* [IV, 7:1124a 16] regarding the magnanimous man: true, he does seek honor and glory, but not as something great which could be a sufficient reward of virtue. And beyond this he demands nothing more of men, for among all earthly goods the chief good, it seems, is this, that men bear testimony to the virtue of a man.

Chapter 8

Therefore, since worldly honor and human glory are not a sufficient reward for royal cares, it remains to inquire what sort of reward is sufficient.

It is proper that a king look to God for his reward, for a servant looks to his master for the reward of his service. The king is indeed the minister of God in governing the people, as the Apostle says: "All power is from the Lord God" (Rom. 13:1) and God's minister is "an avenger to execute wrath upon him who does evil" (Rom. 13:4). And in the Book of Wisdom (6:5), kings are described as being ministers of God. Consequently, kings ought to look to God for the reward of their ruling. Now God sometimes rewards kings for their service by temporal goods, but such rewards are common to both the good and the wicked.

Wherefore the Lord says to Ezekiel (29:18): "Nebuchadnezzar, king of Babylon, has made his army to undergo hard service against Tyre, and there has been no reward given him nor his army for Tyre, for the service he rendered Me against it," for that service namely, by which, according to the Apostle, power is "the minister of God and the avenger to execute wrath upon him who does evil." Afterwards He adds, regarding the reward: "Therefore, thus says the Lord God, 'I will set Nebuchadnezzar the king of Babylon in the land of Egypt, and he shall rifle the spoils thereof, and it shall be wages for his army.'"

Therefore, if God recompenses wicked kings who fight against the enemies of God, though not with the intention of serving Him but to execute their own hatred and cupidity, by giving them such great rewards as to yield them victory over their foes, subject kingdoms to their sway and grant them spoils to rifle, what will He do for kings who rule the people of God and assail His enemies from a holy motive? He promises them not an earthly reward indeed but an everlasting one and in none other than in Himself. As Peter says to the shepherds of the people (1 Pet. 5:2, 4): "Feed the flock of God that is among you and when the prince of pastors shall appear (i.e. the King of kings, Christ) you shall receive a never-fading crown of glory," concerning which Isaiah says (28:5): "The Lord shall be a crown of glory and a garland of joy to His people."

This is also clearly shown by reason. It is implanted in the minds of all who have the use of reason that the reward of virtue is happiness. The virtue of anything whatsoever is explained to be that which makes its possessor good and renders his deed good. Moreover, everyone strives by working well to attain that which is most deeply implanted in desire, namely, to be happy. This, no one is able not to wish. It is therefore fitting to expect as a reward for virtue that which makes man happy. Now, if to work well is a virtuous deed, and the king's work is to rule his people well, then that which makes him happy will be the king's reward.

What this is has now to be considered. Happiness, we say, is the ultimate end of our desires. Now the movement of desire does not go on to infinity else natural desire would be vain, for infinity cannot be traversed. Since, then, the desire of an intellectual nature is for universal good, that good alone can make it truly happy which, when attained, leaves no further good to be desired. Whence happiness is called the perfect good inasmuch as it comprises in itself all things desirable. But no earthly good is such a good.

They who have riches desire to have more, they who enjoy pleasure desire to enjoy more, and the like is clear for the rest:

and if they do not seek more, they at least desire that those they have should abide or that others should follow in their stead. For nothing permanent is found in earthly things. Consequently there is nothing earthly which can calm desire. Thus, nothing earthly can make man happy, so that it may be a fitting reward for a king.

Again, the last perfection and perfect good of anything one chooses depends upon something higher, for even bodily things are made better by the addition of better things and worse by being mixed with baser things. If gold is mingled with silver, the silver is made better, while by an admixture of lead it is rendered impure. Now it is manifest that all earthly things are beneath the human mind. But happiness is the last perfection and the perfect good of man, which all men desire to reach. Therefore there is no earthly thing which could make man happy, nor is any earthly thing a sufficient reward for a king. For, as Augustine says, "we do not call Christian princes happy merely because they have reigned a long time, or because after a peaceful death they have left their sons to rule, or because they subdued the enemies of the state, or because they were able to guard against or to suppress citizens who rose up against them.

"Rather do we call them happy if they rule justly, if they prefer to rule their passions rather than nations, and if they do all things not for the love of vainglory but for the love of eternal happiness. Such Christian emperors we say are happy, now in hope, afterwards in very fact when that which we await shall come to pass." But neither is there any other created thing which would make a man happy and which could be set up as the reward for a king. For the desire of each thing tends towards its source, whence is the cause of its being. But the cause of the human soul is none other than God Who made it to His own image. Therefore it is God alone Who can still the desires of man and make him happy and be the fitting reward for a king.

Furthermore, the human mind knows the universal good through the intellect, and desires it through the will: but the universal good is not found except in God. Therefore there is nothing which could make man happy, fulfilling his every desire, but God, of Whom it is said in the Psalm (102:5): "Who satisfies your desire with good things." In this, therefore, should the king place his reward. Wherefore, King David, with this in mind, said (Ps. 72:25, 28): "What have I in heaven? And besides You what do I desire upon earth?" and he afterwards adds in answer to this question: "It is good for me to adhere to my God and to put my hope in the Lord God." For it is He Who gives salvation to kings, not merely temporal salvation by which He saves both men and beasts together, but also that salvation of which He says by the mouth of Isaiah (51:6): "But my salvation shall be forever," that salvation by which He saves man and makes them equal to the angels.

It can thus also be verified that the reward of the king is honor and glory. What worldly and frail honor can indeed be likened to this honor that a man be made a "citizen with the Saints and a kinsman of God" (Eph. 2:19), numbered among the sons of God, and that he obtain the inheritance of the heavenly kingdom with Christ? This is the honor of which King David, in desire and wonder, says (Ps. 138:17): "Your friends, O

God, are made exceedingly honorable." And further, what glory of human praise can be compared to this, not uttered by the false tongue of flatterers nor the fallacious opinion of men, but issuing from the witness of our inmost conscience and confirmed by the testimony of God, Who promises to those who confess Him that He will confess them before the Angels of God in the glory of the Father? They who seek this glory will find it and they will win the glory of men which they do not seek: witness Solomon, who not only received from the Lord wisdom which he sought, but was made glorious above other kings.

Chapter 9 (selections)

For if happiness is the reward of virtue, it follows that a higher degree of happiness is due to greater virtue. Now, that indeed is signal virtue by which a man can guide not only himself but others, and the more persons he rules the greater his virtue. Similarly, in regard to bodily strength, a man is reputed to be more powerful the more adversaries he can beat or the more weights he can lift. Thus, greater virtue is required to rule a household than to rule one's self, and much greater to rule a city and a kingdom. To discharge well the office of a king is therefore a work of extraordinary virtue. To it, therefore, is due an extraordinary reward of happiness. . . .

Likewise, if I may use the words of Gregory [*Regula Pastoralis* I, 9]: "What else is it (for a king) to be at the pinnacle of power if not to find himself in a mental storm? When the sea is calm even an inexperienced man can steer a ship straight; when the sea is troubled by stormy waves, even an experienced sailor is bewildered. Whence it frequently happens that in the business of government the practice of good works is lost which in tranquil times was maintained." For, as Augustine says [*De civ. Dei* V, 24], it is very difficult for rulers "not to be puffed up amid flattering and honoring tongues and the obsequiousness of those who bow too humbly, but to remember that they are men." It is said also in Sirach (31:8, 10): "Blessed is the rich man who has not gone after gold nor put his trust in money nor in treasures, who could have transgressed with impunity and did not transgress, who could do evil and did not do it."

Wherefore, having been tried in the work of virtue, he is found faithful and so, according to the proverb of Bias [Aristotle, *Eth. Nic.* V, 3:1130a 1]: "Authority shows the man." For many who seemed virtuous while they were in lowly state fall from virtue when they reach the pinnacle of power. The very difficulty, then, of acting well, which besets kings, makes them more worthy of greater reward; and if through weakness they sometimes do amiss, they are rendered more excusable before men and more easily obtain forgiveness from God provided, as Augustine says (*De civ. Dei*, V, 24), they do not neglect to offer up to their true God the sacrifice of humility, mercy, and prayer for their sins. As an example of this, the Lord said to Elijah concerning Ahab, king of Israel, who had sinned a great deal: "Because he has humbled himself for My sake, I will not bring the evil in his days."

Chapter 10 (selections)

This is very clear, too, if we consider the means by which a tyrannical government is upheld. It is not upheld by love, since there is little or no bond of friendship between the subject multitude and the tyrant, as is evident from what we have said. On the other hand, tyrants cannot rely on the loyalty of their subjects, for such a degree of virtue is not found among the generality of men, that they should be restrained by the virtue of fidelity from throwing off the yoke of unmerited servitude, if they are able to do so. Nor would it perhaps be a violation of fidelity at all, according to the opinion of many, to frustrate the wickedness of tyrants by any means whatsoever.

It remains, then, that the government of a tyrant is maintained by fear alone and consequently they strive with all their might to be feared by their subjects. Fear, however, is a weak support. Those who are kept down by fear will rise against their rulers if the opportunity ever occurs when they can hope to do it with impunity, and they will rebel against their rulers all the more furiously the more they have been kept in subjection against their will by fear alone, just as water confined under pressure flows with greater impetus when it finds an outlet. That very fear itself is not without danger, because many become desperate from excessive fear, and despair of safety impels a man boldly to dare anything. Therefore the government of a tyrant cannot be of long duration. . . .

All this becomes still more evident if we consider the divine judgment, for, as we read in Job (34:30), "He makes a man who is a hypocrite to reign for the sins of the people." No one, indeed, can be more truly called a hypocrite than the man who assumes the office of king and acts like a tyrant, for a hypocrite is one who mimics the person of another, as is done on the stage. Hence God permits tyrants to get into power to punish the sins of the subjects. In Holy Scripture it is customary to call such punishment the anger of God.

Thus in Hosea (13:11) the Lord says: "I will give you a king in my wrath." Unhappy is a king who is given to the people in God's wrath, for his power cannot be stable, because "God does not forget to show mercy nor does He shut up His mercies in His anger" (Ps. 76:10). On the contrary, as we read in Joel (2:13): "He is patient and rich in mercy and ready to repent of the evil." So God does not permit tyrants to reign a long time, but after the storm brought on the people through these tyrants, He restores tranquility by casting them down. Therefore the Wise Man says (Sirach 10:17): "God has overturned the thrones of proud princes and hath set up the meek in their stead."

Chapter 12 (selections)

Therefore let the king recognize that such is the office which he undertakes, namely, that he is to be in the kingdom what the soul is in the body, and what God is in the world. If he reflect seriously upon this, a zeal for justice will be enkindled in him when he contemplates that he has been appointed to this position in place of God, to exercise judgment in his kingdom; further, he will acquire the gentleness of clemency and mildness when he considers as his own members those individuals who are subject to his rule.

Chapter 14 (selections)

Now the same judgment is to be formed about the end of society as a whole as about the end of one man. If, therefore, the ultimate end of man were some good that existed in himself, then the ultimate end of the multitude to be governed would likewise be for the multitude to acquire such good, and persevere in its possession. If such an ultimate end either of an individual man or a multitude were a corporeal one, namely, life and health of body, to govern would then be a physician's charge. If that ultimate end were an abundance of wealth, then knowledge of economics would have the last word in the community's government.

If the good of the knowledge of truth were of such a kind that the multitude might attain to it, the king would have to be a teacher. It is, however, clear that the end of a multitude gathered together is to live virtuously. For men form a group for the purpose of *living well....*

Yet through virtuous living man is further ordained to a higher end, which consists in the enjoyment of God, as we have said above. Consequently, since society must have the same end as the individual man, it is not the ultimate end of an assembled multitude to live virtuously, but through virtuous living to attain to the possession of God.

If this end could be attained by the power of human nature, then the duty of a king would have to include the direction of men to it. We are supposing, of course, that he is called king to whom the supreme power of governing in human affairs is entrusted. Now the higher the end to which a government is ordained, the loftier that government is. Indeed, we always find that the one to whom it pertains to achieve the final end commands those who execute the things that are ordained to that end.

For example, the captain, whose business it is to regulate navigation, tells the shipbuilder what kind of ship he must construct to be suitable for navigation; and the ruler of a city, who makes use of arms, tells the blacksmith what kind of arms to make. But because a man does not attain his end, which is the possession of God, by human power but by divine according to the words of the Apostle (Rom. 6:23): "By the grace of God life everlasting"— therefore the task of leading him to that last end does not pertain to human but to divine government. . . .

Thus, in order that spiritual things might be distinguished from earthly things, the ministry of this kingdom has been entrusted not to earthly kings but to priests, and most of all to the chief priest, the successor of St. Peter, the Vicar of Christ, the Roman Pontiff. To him all the kings of the Christian People are to be subject as to our Lord Jesus Christ Himself. For those to whom pertains the care of intermediate ends should be subject to him to whom pertains the care of the ultimate end, and be directed by his rule.

Chapter 15

As the life by which men live well here on earth is ordained, as to its end, to that blessed life which we hope for in heaven, so too whatever particular goods are procured by man's agency—whether wealth, profits, health, eloquence, or learning—are ordained to the good life of the multitude. If, then, as we have said, the person who is charged with the care of our ultimate end ought to be over those who have charge of things ordained to that end, and to direct them by his rule, it clearly follows that, just as the king ought to be subject to the divine government administered by the office of priesthood, so he ought to preside over all human offices, and regulate them by the rule of his government.

Now anyone on whom it devolves to do something which is ordained to another thing as to its end is bound to see that his work is suitable to that end; thus, for example, the armorer so fashions the sword that it is suitable for fighting, and the builder should so lay out the house that it is suitable for habitation. Therefore, since the beatitude of heaven is the end of that virtuous life which we live at present, it pertains to the king's office to promote the good life of the multitude in such a way as to make it suitable for the attainment of heavenly happiness, that is to say, he should command those things which lead to the happiness of Heaven and, as far as possible, forbid the contrary. . . .

When virtuous living is set up in the multitude by the efforts of the king, it then remains for him to look to its conservation. Now there are three things which prevent the permanence of the public good. One of these arises from nature. The good of the multitude should not be established for one time only; it should be in a sense perpetual. Men, on the other hand, cannot abide forever, because they are mortal. Even while they are alive they do not always preserve the same vigor, for the life of man is subject to many changes, and thus a man is not equally suited to the performance of the same duties throughout the whole span of his life.

A second impediment to the preservation of the public good, which comes from within, consists in the perversity of the wills of men, inasmuch as they are either too lazy to perform what the commonweal demands, or, still further, they are harmful to the peace of the multitude because, by transgressing justice, they disturb the peace of others. The third hindrance to the preservation of the commonweal comes from without, namely, when peace is destroyed through the attacks of enemies and, as it sometimes happens, the kingdom or city is completely blotted out.

In regard to these three dangers, a triple charge is laid upon the king. First of all, he must take care of the appointment of men to succeed or replace others in charge of the various offices. Just as in regard to corruptible things (which cannot remain the same forever) the government of God made provision that through generation one would take the place of another in order that, in this way, the integrity of the universe might be maintained, so too the good of the multitude subject to the king will be preserved through his care when he sets himself to attend to the appointment of new men to fill the place of those who drop out.

In the second place, by his laws and orders, punishments and rewards, he should restrain the men subject to him from wickedness and induce them to virtuous deeds, following the example of God, Who gave His law to man and requites those who observe it with rewards, and those who transgress it with punishments. The king's third charge is to keep the multitude entrusted to him safe from the enemy, for it would be useless to prevent internal dangers if the multitude could not be defended against external dangers.

Finally, for the proper direction of the multitude there remains the third duty of the kingly office, namely, that he be solicitous for its improvement. He performs this duty when, in each of the things we have mentioned, he corrects what is out of order and supplies what is lacking, and if any of them can be done better he tries to do so. This is why the Apostle exhorts the faithful to be "zealous for the better gifts" (1 Cor. 12:31).

These then are the duties of the kingly office, each of which must now be treated in greater detail.

Christine de Pizan

The Book of the Body Politic
Fourteenth–Fifteenth Century AD, France

Rule must include kindness and mercy as well as justice and power.

Selections from Chapters 6, 14–16, and 21

Chapter 6 (selections): Here It Tells What the Young Prince Should Do When He Begins to Govern

When the time comes that the son of the prince has grown, and come of age to rule, and comes into his heritage by succession, whether it is a kingdom or another lordship, just as the fruit appears after the tree blossoms, so in him ought to appear the perfection of virtue, following the example of the wise king of France, Charles V. Because from the moment of his coronation, even though it was in the flower of his youth, no one could find anything dishonest in him and he occupied his time in suitable and virtuous things. I have plainly spoken elsewhere of him in my book on his deeds and good manners.

The virtues of a prince are seen in three things, without which he will not achieve this crown of reputation, good name, and consequently, honor. The first and most important, is to love, fear, and serve God without dishonesty, but with good deeds rather than spending time withdrawn in long prayers.

Another is this: he ought solely to love the good and benefit of his country and his people. All his ability, power, and the study of his free time ought to be for this, rather than his own benefit. The third is that he must love justice above all, guarding it and keeping it without restraint, and must do equity to all people. By keeping these three points well, the prince will be crowned with glory in heaven and on earth.

Chapter 14: On Liberality in Princes and Examples of the Romans

We will continue our subject of the second of the three things that are necessary to the good prince, which is that he love the public good.

The good prince, who loves the universal good more than his own should be liberal, a very necessary quality from which he will profit triply; first it is for the good of his soul (if he is discreet), secondly, for the praise and honor of his reputation; thirdly, he will attract the hearts of his own subjects to himself as well as those of strangers. There is no doubt that nothing profits a prince as much as discreet generosity. Oh, how much the Romans profited from it! Once when the ambassadors of Carthage came to Rome to ransom the prisoners who had been taken in battle during the wars between them, the Romans returned freely, without ransom, 1,747 noble young men, who were rich and of high rank. Valerius exalts and praises this three-fold generosity in three ways. "O what marvelous generosity, to free such a great force of the enemy, to deprive themselves of such a ransom, to pardon such injuries. I believe," he said, "that the ambassadors marveled at such generosity." Then he added, "Oh Roman magnificence, equal to the kindness of gods, for this gesture was more generous than your enemies could dare ask." There is no doubt that because of their liberality, the Romans acquired sovereignty and dominion more than by force because foreign countries seeing their nobles and free customs, yielded to them, not in hopes of being servants, but in order to be free. And Valerius said the same, that the empire of Rome, that is, its superiority, did not increase so much from the strength of their bodies as from the vigor of their courage. Valerius tells us (which I have quoted from his book word-for-word because of its beauty and substance) that he could give generosity no better company than humanity and mercy, for they deserve all kinds of praise. And he says that generosity shows itself to those who are poor and suffering, who need one to be generous and liberal to them. Humanity is shown to those who are ill or in prison or insecure in their bodies or their goods. He who has power and right to punish and to pardon, pardons and alleviates their miseries by the power of the prince. He is responsible for healing them his poor subjects compassionately, by the above virtues, maintaining the order of justice and not too rigorously, and especially in those things that are not contrary to nature. And even though, said Valerius, you do not know which of those virtues to praise most, nonetheless, it seems that the one that is highest is that which takes its name from God, and this means liberality which is so like divine virtue, extending itself to all and by which one acquires the most friends. And as it is more in the power of princes than in other persons to be liberal and also they are most in need of friends and well wishers, I say that it is most necessary and appropriate and even enhances their glory. It is written in the third book, thirteenth chapter of the *Policraticus*, that Titus the Emperor by his liberality atoned for the vice of avarice which had been his father's, in such a manner that he was called by all the darling and delight of the human race. And Tully, in book 2 of *On Duties*, said that there is no worse vice in a prince or in those who govern the republic than avarice.

But since we say so often that the good prince ought to be generous, it is important to say in what manner on and what things he should extend his liberality. So Seneca declares in the second book of *On Benefices*, that the prince or the giver must understand his own power and authority, and also the power and rank of him to whom he would give, so as not to give a lesser gift than is appropriate, nor to give more than appropriate. The prince or the donor ought to consider to whom and why he gives the gift, because there is a difference between giving for merit, as a reward for something well done, and giving out of the frank generosity of pure courtesy.

Because, if merited, the prince ought to look closely that the gift be such that it cannot be blamed as shabby or cheap. It ought always to be as generous as is merited. But when the gift is given without great desert or merit, although it is the role of a prince or powerful person to give as great a gift as appropriate, nonetheless they can also give small ones to poor and indigent persons. This liberality must also be moderate and tempered by discretion as Tully says in the book quoted above. For let us suppose that the prince or another gives willingly and generously from his wealth, he ought to consider how he will continue in that virtue and not be like those who give foolishly and distribute without any order. This generosity ought to be from his own wealth and not that of some other person. As St. Ambrose said in the first book of *On Duties*, it is not "liberality" when one gives to one and takes from others, nothing is generous if it is not just. This is why generosity is the divine virtue in the good prince. And it is always appropriate for the prince to reward the friendship which others give him, and not in this case to apportion the gift to the weakness of the persons who did him service, but to the grandeur of the recipient, who can reward well. As is written of King Darius [I] of Persia. . . . This Darius was not yet wealthy. A man named Philomites out of his goodness and without being asked, gave him a cloak which pleased Darius greatly. When Darius came to be king, he did not forget this courtesy and gave him the city and the whole island of Samos, which is a good island, where Pythagoras the philosopher was born. Thus Darius did not consider the price of the gift, but rather the generosity of the giver, and the power of the person giving the reward.

Also, Mithridates, the wealthy king who ruled twenty-two countries, showed his great generosity by rewarding one of his knights, who was named Leonicus by getting him out of the prison of his enemies, for he had been captured in battle. He turned over a very large number of prisoners [in exchange], because he preferred to increase the number of his enemies than leave unrewarded someone who well deserved it.

Chapter 15: On the Humane Pity of the Prince

We have spoken enough of the liberality of the good prince, now we ought to speak of the other two virtues which accompany the first in merit and praise; that is humanity and clemency. These are necessary to have in a good prince, and to prove this we will use examples.

There was the humanity that the worthy Roman prince Lucius Emilius Paulus showed to King Perses who was defeated in a battle so completely that Perses was taken prisoner. But when he knew who stood before him, the noble man would not allow Perses to kneel before him. He took him kindly by the hand and brought him with him, comforted him and honored him, made him sit at table and in council with him, despite Perses' hesitation, and thus treated him as gently as a brother. Ah, what a noble virtue in a prince and in all captains and soldiers, to have pity and be humane to those they have conquered.

There is the example of Hector of Troy of whom one reads that no lion was more fierce or cruel than he was in battle. But when his enemies came before him humiliated and crying, then no lamb could be more gentle nor more good-natured than he was, and so he treated them most gently, as his brothers, by which he profited as much, for his great good nature brought many to surrender to him.

So every noble brave prince and good man ought to act thus, not do as many lords and soldiers do today. When they conquer lands, fortresses, cities, or other places, they act like famished dogs when they enter the city, without pity for the horrible massacres they inflict on Christians—dishonoring women and leaving everything in ruin. Alas, what hearts these men have, when such cruelty can be done to others in their likeness, which is against nature and against divine law! Are they not afraid that the fierce devils of Hell will snatch them for the city of Hell? For there is no doubt that they will come to that at the end. And certainly such people ought rather to have the face and flesh of a horrible serpent, rather than human ones, for under the human form, they wear the cruelty of the treasonable detestable beast!

Marcus Marcellus, who was one of the princes of Rome with great authority, did not do this. When by his great valor, he captured the strong and noble city of Syracuse, he went up to the highest castle to survey the fortune of the city, and considered the power which was maintained, by such noble kings, and the power it had on land and sea. It was then filled with sorrow and so brought down that he had pity on his enemy, and he started to weep.

Yet there are those who are so cruel and inhumane towards their prisoners that because of greed they force them to pay a larger ransom than they can. It is horrible to hear and see the varied tortures that many do to their prisoners, so cruel and

horrible that the Saracens could do no worse! And if such tor-
turers die a good death it seems to me that God and nature do
them a great wrong, but I do not doubt that they are punished,
for God is just.

Ah, the very excellent Prince Pompey never did such, he
who was so superior in excellence of arms that he conquered
every part of the Orient with his sword. But when he had sub-
jugated King Tigranes of Armenia, among others, and killed
40,000 of his men, and had him brought before him, Tigranes
took his crown off and placed it at the feet of Pompey, and
weeping thought to kneel down before him. But Pompey would
not allow him to. Then he very gently raised him up, put his
crown back on his head, comforted him, and reestablished him
in his rank under obedience to the Romans. It seemed to him
that it was as great an honor to make a king as to defeat one.

Chapter 16: On the Clemency and Good Nature Which the Prince Must Have

We have spoken of the humanity of the good prince. Now
we will speak of the virtue of clemency which he ought especially
to have towards his subjects in order to tie their hearts to him
and confirm them in greatest affection. For without doubt there
is nothing more sweet nor more favorable to a subject than to
see his lord and prince gentle and kind to him, and nothing can
satisfy the hearts of his men and his familiars more than mercy,
gentleness and kindness do when wisely and discretely done. Not
that he abases himself among them so that they respect him less,
but while keeping the honor which a sovereign deserves to

receive from his subjects, he is gentle and kind with their requests and petitions, and of gentle speech. He should not show great annoyance or disdain towards any of them for some small thing or misdeed, because the higher and stronger foundation a tower has, the less it will take the shock of a little stone.

Philocrates, the king or duke of Athens, had great good nature. He had a friend named Transippus. At supper together, in the heat of anger he said many injurious and hateful things to Philocrates. But he did not lose his temper nor say anything to injure him, but he begged him not to be angry nor to go away angry from supper. Transippus, compelled by his anger, then spat in his face, but despite this he did not become angry. Then he sent his sons out, because they wanted passionately to kill him and avenge the majesty of their father. The next day Philocrates knew that Transippius was overcome with shame and anger with himself for what he had done and said, and he wanted to kill himself, and Philocrates was moved to great pity. He went immediately to him, embraced him and comforted him, and pardoned him gently, and he gave his word that he was and would be in his grace as before.

Yet more on the good nature of this prince Philocrates. He had a most beautiful young daughter. A young man loved her so much that he thought he would die. Once, he saw her walking with her mother down the street. The young man was so struck by love that he could not control himself and kissed her in front of everyone when he passed her. The mother of the girl, Philocrates' wife, wanted the young man to be executed for this and strongly insisted on this to her lord. But Philocrates answered, compassionately, "if

we kill those that love us, what could we do to those that hate us?"
This response was most humane.

Also Pompey, the brave man spoken of before, is described
as having such great courage that he was not lightly moved. He
endured many injuries from the envious, for he was very careful
to preserve and increase the public good. But despite them, he
never let up, from which it appears to be true, as Valerius said
in the first chapter of the third book of *On Patience*; patience is
so like strength that it is born of it and with it.

Should we not give another little example of good nature
of the very chivalrous prince and king, Pyrrhus of whom we
have spoken already many times? He had very great courage
and many virtues. He honored the good and valiant as he often
showed the Romans during the wars between them. Once in
battle he defeated the Romans, but however, he was not arrogant to them like nowadays, when some are proud of a lucky
victory (which is a great folly, because one ought to remember
that fortune is distributed as she wills, and often gives such
victories and then the next time, the wheel turns and luck
changes). But this Pyrrhus, who knew how brave the Romans
were, despite his victory, when their ambassadors came, he
knew they came to reclaim their prisoners, and he received and
honored them greatly and sent his knights there to honor them.

*Chapter 21 (selections): How a Good Prince, despite Being
Good-Natured and Kind, Ought to Be Feared*

The nature of justice and what it serves and to what extent
is well known and understood; it is appropriate for the good

prince to punish (or have punished) evildoers. And so I will pass by this for a time and proceed to that which also befits the good prince: The virtue of justice, which renders to each that which is his due, according to his power. If he keeps this rule, which is just, he will not fail to do equity in everything, and thus, he will render to himself his due. For it is rational that he has the same right he gives to everyone, which means that he would be obeyed and feared by right and by reason, as is appropriate to the majesty of a prince.

For in whatever land or place where a prince is not feared, there is no true justice. How it is appropriate for the prince to be feared is shown by the worthy man Clearcus who was Duke of Lacedaemonia (which is a large part of Greece where there once was a marvelously valiant people). This duke was so chivalrous and great a warrior that his people were more afraid to flee than to die. He told them that soldiers should be more afraid of their prince than death and their enemies. Because of his words and also the punishment that he gave malefactors and cowards, they gave themselves without sparing, by which they achieved marvelous things. There is no doubt that the good prince ought to be feared despite being gentle and benign. His kindness ought to be considered a thing of grace which one ought to particularly heed rather than scorn. It is for this reason the ancients painted the goddess of lordship as a seated lady of very high rank on a royal throne, holding in one hand an olive branch and in the other a naked sword, showing that rule must include kindness and mercy as well as justice and power.

Renaissance

Machiavelli

The Prince
1532 AD, Italy

Princes become great when they overcome difficulties made for them and opposition made to them. So fortune, specially when she wants to make a new prince great . . . makes enemies arise for him and makes them undertake enterprises against him, so that he has cause to overcome them and to climb higher on the ladder that his enemies have brought for him.

Chapters 14–15 and 17–18

Chapter 14—That Which Concerns a Prince on the Subject of the Art of War

A prince ought to have no other aim or thought, nor select anything else for his study, than war and its rules and discipline; for this is the sole art that belongs to him who rules, and it is of such force that it not only upholds those who are born princes, but it often enables men to rise from a private station to that rank. And, on the contrary, it is seen that when princes have thought more of ease than of arms they have lost their states. And the first cause of your losing it is to neglect this art; and what enables you to acquire a state is to be master of the art.

Francesco Sforza, through being martial, from a private person became Duke of Milan; and the sons, through avoiding the hardships and troubles of arms, from dukes became private persons. For among other evils which being unarmed brings you, it causes you to be despised, and this is one of those ignominies against which a prince ought to guard himself, as is shown later on. Because there is nothing proportionate between the armed and the unarmed; and it is not reasonable that he who is armed should yield obedience willingly to him who is unarmed, or that the unarmed man should be secure among armed servants. Because, there being in the one disdain and in the other suspicion, it is not possible for them to work well together.

And therefore a prince who does not understand the art of war, over and above the other misfortunes already mentioned, cannot be respected by his soldiers, nor can he rely on them. He ought never, therefore, to have out of his thoughts this subject of war, and in peace he should addict himself more to its exercise than in war; this he can do in two ways, the one by action, the other by study.

As regards action, he ought above all things to keep his men well organized and drilled, to follow incessantly the chase, by which he accustoms his body to hardships, and learns something of the nature of localities, and gets to find out how the mountains rise, how the valleys open out, how the plains lie, and to understand the nature of rivers and marshes, and in all this to take the greatest care.

Which knowledge is useful in two ways. Firstly, he learns to know his country, and is better able to undertake its defense; afterwards, by means of the knowledge and observation of that locality, he understands with ease any other which it may be necessary for him to study hereafter; because the hills, valleys, and plains, and rivers and marshes that are, for instance, in Tuscany, have a certain resemblance to those of other countries, so that with a knowledge of the aspect of one country one can easily arrive at a knowledge of others. And the prince that lacks this skill lacks the essential which it is desirable that a captain should possess, for it teaches him to surprise his enemy, to select quarters, to lead armies, to array the battle, to besiege towns to advantage.

Philopoemen, Prince of the Achaeans, among other praises which writers have bestowed on him, is commended because in time of peace he never had anything in his mind but the rules of war; and when he was in the country with friends, he often stopped and reasoned with them: "If the enemy should be upon that hill, and we should find ourselves here with our army, with whom would be the advantage? How should one best advance to meet him, keeping the ranks? If we should wish to retreat, how ought we to pursue?" And he would set forth to them, as he went, all the chances that could befall an army; he would listen to their opinion and state his, confirming it with reasons, so that by these continual discussions there could never arise, in time of war, any unexpected circumstances that he could not deal with.

But to exercise the intellect the prince should read histories, and study there the actions of illustrious men, to see how they have borne themselves in war, to examine the causes of their victories and defeat, so as to avoid the latter and imitate the former; and above all do as an illustrious man did, who took as an exemplar one who had been praised and famous before him, and whose achievements and deeds he always kept in his mind, as it is said Alexander the Great imitated Achilles, Caesar Alexander, Scipio Cyrus.

And whoever reads the life of Cyrus, written by Xenophon, will recognize afterwards in the life of Scipio how that imitation was his glory, and how in chastity, affability, humanity, and liberality Scipio conformed to those things which have been written of Cyrus by Xenophon. A wise prince ought to observe some such rules, and never in peaceful times stand idle, but increase his resources with industry in such a way that they may be available to him in adversity, so that if fortune chances it may find him prepared to resist her blows.

Chapter 15—Concerning Things for Which Men, and Especially Princes, Are Praised or Blamed

It remains now to see what ought to be the rules of conduct for a prince towards subject and friends. And as I know that many have written on this point, I expect I shall be considered presumptuous in mentioning it again, especially as in discussing it I shall depart from the methods of other people. But, it being my intention to write a thing which shall be useful to him who apprehends it, it appears to me more appropriate to follow up the real truth of the matter than the imagination of it; for many have pictured republics and principalities which in fact have never been known or seen, because how one lives is so far distant from how one ought to live, that he who neglects what is done for what ought to be done, sooner effects his ruin than his preservation; for a man who wishes to act entirely up to his professions of virtue soon meets with what destroys him among so much that is evil.

Hence it is necessary for a prince wishing to hold his own to know how to do wrong, and to make use of it or not according to necessity. Therefore, putting on one side imaginary things concerning a prince, and discussing those which are real, I say that all men when they are spoken of, and chiefly princes for being more highly placed, are remarkable for some of those qualities which bring them either blame or praise; and thus it is that one is reputed liberal, another miserly, using a Tuscan term (because an avaricious person in our language is still he who desires to possess by robbery, whilst we call one miserly who deprives himself too much of the use of his own); one is reputed generous, one rapacious; one cruel, one compassionate; one faithless, another faithful; one effeminate and cowardly, another bold and brave; one affable, another haughty; one lascivious, another chaste; one sincere, another cunning; one hard, another easy; one grave, another frivolous; one religious, another unbelieving, and the like.

And I know that every one will confess that it would be most praiseworthy in a prince to exhibit all the above qualities that are considered good; but because they can neither be entirely possessed nor observed, for human conditions do not permit it, it is necessary for him to be sufficiently prudent that he may know how to avoid the reproach of those vices which would lose him his state; and also to keep himself, if it be possible, from those which would not lose him it; but this not being possible, he may with less hesitation abandon himself to them. And again, he need not make himself uneasy at incurring a reproach for those vices without which the state can only be saved with difficulty, for if everything is considered carefully, it will be found that something which looks like virtue, if followed, would be his ruin; whilst something else, which looks like vice, yet followed brings him security and prosperity.

Chapter 17—Concerning Cruelty and Clemency, and Whether It Is Better to Be Loved Than Feared

Coming now to the other qualities mentioned above, I say that every prince ought to desire to be considered clement and not cruel. Nevertheless he ought to take care not to misuse this clemency. Cesare Borgia was considered cruel; notwithstanding, his cruelty reconciled the Romagna, unified it, and restored it to peace and loyalty. And if this be rightly considered, he will be seen to have been much more merciful than the Florentine people, who, to avoid a reputation for cruelty, permitted Pistoia to be destroyed. Therefore a prince, so long as he keeps his subjects united and loyal, ought not to mind the reproach of cruelty; because with a few examples he will be more merciful than those who, through too much mercy, allow disorders to arise, from which follow murders or robberies; for these are wont to injure the whole people, whilst those executions which originate with a prince offend the individual only.

And of all princes, it is impossible for the new prince to avoid the imputation of cruelty, owing to new states being full of dangers. Hence Virgil, through the mouth of Dido, excuses the inhumanity of her reign owing to its being new, saying:

> "Res dura, et regni novitas me talia cogunt
>   Moliri, et late fines custode tueri."

Nevertheless he ought to be slow to believe and to act, nor should he himself show fear, but proceed in a temperate manner with prudence and humanity, so that too much confidence may not make him incautious and too much distrust render him intolerable.

Upon this a question arises: whether it be better to be loved than feared or feared than loved? It may be answered that one should wish to be both, but, because it is difficult to unite them in one person, it is much safer to be feared than loved, when, of the two, either must be dispensed with. Because this is to be asserted in general of men, that they are ungrateful, fickle, false, cowardly, covetous, and as long as you succeed they are yours entirely; they will offer you their blood, property, life, and children, as is said above, when the need is far distant; but when it approaches they turn against you.

And that prince who, relying entirely on their promises, has neglected other precautions, is ruined; because friendships that are obtained by payments, and not by greatness or nobility of mind, may indeed be earned, but they are not secured, and in time of need cannot be relied upon; and men have less scruple in offending one who is beloved than one who is feared, for love is preserved by the link of obligation which, owing to the baseness of men, is broken at every opportunity for their advantage; but fear preserves you by a dread of punishment which never fails.

Nevertheless a prince ought to inspire fear in such a way that, if he does not win love, he avoids hatred; because he can endure very well being feared whilst he is not hated, which will always be as long as he abstains from the property of his citizens and subjects and from their women. But when it is necessary for him to proceed against the life of someone, he must do it on proper justification and for manifest cause, but above all things he must keep his hands off the property of others, because men more quickly forget the death of their father than the loss of their patrimony.

Besides, pretexts for taking away the property are never wanting; for he who has once begun to live by robbery will always find pretexts for seizing what belongs to others; but reasons for taking life, on the contrary, are more difficult to find and sooner lapse. But when a prince is with his army, and has under control a multitude of soldiers, then it is quite necessary for him to disregard the reputation of cruelty, for without it he would never hold his army united or disposed to its duties.

Among the wonderful deeds of Hannibal this one is enumerated: that having led an enormous army, composed of many various races of men, to fight in foreign lands, no dissensions arose either among them or against the prince, whether in his bad or in his good fortune. This arose from nothing else than his inhuman cruelty, which, with his boundless valor, made him revered and terrible in the sight of his soldiers, but without that cruelty, his other virtues were not sufficient to produce this effect. And short-sighted writers admire his deeds from one point of view and from another condemn the principal cause of them.

That it is true his other virtues would not have been sufficient for him may be proved by the case of Scipio, that most excellent man, not only of his own times but within the memory of man, against whom, nevertheless, his army rebelled in Spain; this arose from nothing but his too great forbearance, which gave his soldiers more license than is consistent with military discipline. For this he was upbraided in the Senate by Fabius Maximus, and called the corrupter of the Roman soldiery.

The Locrians were laid waste by a legate of Scipio, yet they were not avenged by him, nor was the insolence of the legate punished, owing entirely to his easy nature. Insomuch that someone in the Senate, wishing to excuse him, said there were many men who knew much better how not to err than to correct the errors of others. This disposition, if he had been continued in the command, would have destroyed in time the fame and glory of Scipio; but, he being under the control of the

Senate, this injurious characteristic not only concealed itself, but contributed to his glory.

Returning to the question of being feared or loved, I come to the conclusion that, men loving according to their own will and fearing according to that of the prince, a wise prince should establish himself on that which is in his own control and not in that of others; he must endeavor only to avoid hatred, as is noted.

Chapter 18—Concerning the Way in Which Princes Should Keep Faith

Every one admits how praiseworthy it is in a prince to keep faith, and to live with integrity and not with craft. Nevertheless our experience has been that those princes who have done great things have held good faith of little account, and have known how to circumvent the intellect of men by craft, and in the end have overcome those who have relied on their word.

You must know there are two ways of contesting, the one by the law, the other by force; the first method is proper to men, the second to beasts; but because the first is frequently not sufficient, it is necessary to have recourse to the second. Therefore it is necessary for a prince to understand how to avail himself of the beast and the man. This has been figuratively taught to princes by ancient writers, who describe how Achilles and many other princes of old were given to the Centaur Chiron to nurse, who brought them up in his discipline; which means solely that, as they had for a teacher one who was half beast and half man, so it is necessary for a prince to know how to make use of both natures, and that one without the other is not durable. A prince, therefore, being compelled knowingly to adopt the beast, ought to choose the fox and the lion; because the lion cannot defend himself against snares and the fox cannot defend himself against wolves. Therefore, it is necessary to be a fox to discover the snares and a lion to terrify the wolves. Those who rely simply on the lion do not understand what they are about. Therefore a wise lord cannot, nor ought he to, keep faith when such observance may be turned against him, and when the reasons that caused him to pledge it exist no longer.

If men were entirely good this precept would not hold, but because they are bad, and will not keep faith with you, you too are not bound to observe it with them. Nor will there ever be wanting to a prince legitimate reasons to excuse this non-observance. Of this endless modern examples could be given, showing how many treaties and engagements have been made void and of no effect through the faithlessness of princes; and he who has known best how to employ the fox has succeeded best.

But it is necessary to know well how to disguise this characteristic, and to be a great pretender and dissembler; and men are so simple, and so subject to present necessities, that he who seeks to deceive will always find someone who will allow himself to be deceived. One recent example I cannot pass over in silence. Alexander the Sixth did nothing else but deceive men, nor ever thought of doing otherwise, and he always found victims; for there never was a man who had greater power in asserting, or who with greater oaths would affirm a thing, yet would observe it less; nevertheless his deceits always succeeded according to his wishes, because he well understood this side of mankind.

Therefore it is unnecessary for a prince to have all the good qualities I have enumerated, but it is very necessary to appear to have them. And I shall dare to say this also, that to have them and always to observe them is injurious, and that to appear to have them is useful; to appear merciful, faithful, humane, religious, upright, and to be so, but with a mind so framed that should you require not to be so, you may be able and know how to change to the opposite.

And you have to understand this, that a prince, especially a new one, cannot observe all those things for which men are esteemed, being often forced, in order to maintain the state, to act contrary to fidelity, friendship, humanity, and religion. Therefore it is necessary for him to have a mind ready to turn itself accordingly as the winds and variations of fortune force it, yet, as I have said above, not to diverge from the good if he can avoid doing so, but, if compelled, then to know how to set about it.

For this reason a prince ought to take care that he never lets anything slip from his lips that is not replete with the above-named five qualities, that he may appear to him who sees and hears him altogether merciful, faithful, humane, upright, and religious. There is nothing more necessary to appear to have than this last quality, inasmuch as men judge generally more by the eye than by the hand, because it belongs to everybody to see you, to few to come in touch with you.

Every one sees what you appear to be, few really know what you are, and those few dare not oppose themselves to the opinion of the many, who have the majesty of the state to defend them; and in the actions of all men, and especially of princes, which it is not prudent to challenge, one judges by the result.

For that reason, let a prince have the credit of conquering and holding his state, the means will always be considered honest, and he will be praised by everybody; because the vulgar are always taken by what a thing seems to be and by what comes of it; and in the world there are only the vulgar, for the few find a place there only when the many have no ground to rest on.

One prince of the present time, whom it is not well to name, never preaches anything else but peace and good faith, and to both he is most hostile, and either, if he had kept it, would have deprived him of reputation and kingdom many a time.

Erasmus

The Education of a Christian Prince
1516 AD, Netherlands

A prince who is about to assume [office] . . . must be advised at once that the main hope of a state lies in the proper education of its youth.

The Arts of Peace

Although the writers of antiquity divided the whole theory of state government into two sections, war and peace, the first and most important objective is the instruction of the prince in the matter of ruling wisely during times of peace, in which he should strive his utmost to preclude any future need for the science of war. In this matter it seems best that the prince should first know his own kingdom. This knowledge is best gained from [a study of] geography and history and from frequent visits through his provinces and cities.

Let him first be eager to learn the location of his districts and cities, with their beginnings, their nature, institutions, customs, laws, annals, and privileges. No one can heal the body until he is thoroughly conversant with it. No one can properly till a field which he does not understand. To be sure, the tyrant takes great care in such matters, but it is the spirit, not the act, which singles out the good prince. The physician studies the functions of the body so as to be more adept in healing it; the poisoning assassin, to more surely end it!

Next, the prince should love the land over which he rules just as a farmer loves the fields of his ancestors or as a good man feels affection toward his household. He should make it his especial interest to hand it over to his successor, whosoever he may be, better than he received it. If he has any children, devotion toward them should urge him on; if he has no family, he should be guided by devotion to his country; and he should always keep kindled the flame of love for his subjects. He should consider his kingdom as a great body of which he is the most outstanding member and remember that they who have entrusted all their fortunes and their very safety to the good faith of one man are deserving of consideration.

He should keep constantly in mind the example of those rulers to whom the welfare of their people was dearer than their own lives; for it is obviously impossible for a prince to do violence to the state without injuring himself. In the second place the prince will see to it that he is loved by his subjects in return, but in such a way that his authority is no less strong among them. There are some who are so stupid as to strive to win goodwill for themselves by incantations and magic rings, when there is no charm more efficacious than good character itself;

nothing can be more lovable than that, for, as this is a real and immortal good, so it brings a man true and undying goodwill. The best formula is this: let him love, who would be loved, so that he may attach his subjects to him as God has won the peoples of the world to Himself by His goodness.

They are also wrong who win the hearts of the masses by largesses, feasts, and gross indulgence. It is true that some popular favor, instead of affection, is gained by these means, but it is neither genuine nor permanent. In the meanwhile the greed of the populace is developed, which, as happens, after it has reached large proportions thinks nothing is enough. Then there is an uprising, unless complete satisfaction is made to their demands. By this means your people are not won, but corrupted.

And so by this means the [average] prince is accustomed to win his way into the hearts of the people after the fashion of those foolish husbands who beguile their wives with blandishments, gifts, and complaisance, instead of winning their love by their character and good actions. So at length it comes about that they are not loved; instead of a thrifty and well mannered wife they have a haughty and intractable one. . . .

The wife should first learn the ways and means of loving her husband and then let him show himself worthy of her love. And so with the people—let them become accustomed to the best, and let the prince be the source of the best things. Those who begin to love through reason, love long. In the first place, then, he who would be loved by his people should show himself a prince worthy of love; after that it will do some good to consider how best he may win his way into their hearts.

The prince should do this first so that the best men may have the highest regard for him and that he may be accepted by those who are lauded by all. They are the men he should have for his close friends; they are the ones for his counselors; they are the ones on whom he should bestow his honors and whom he should allow to have the greatest influence with him. By this means everyone will come to have an excellent opinion of the prince, who is the source of all goodwill. I have known some princes who were not really evil themselves who incurred the hatred of the people for no other reason than that they granted too much liberty to those whom universal public sentiment condemned. The people judged the character of the prince by these other men.

For my part, I should like to see the prince born and raised among those people whom he is destined to rule, because friendship is created and confirmed most when the source of goodwill is in nature itself. The common people shun and hate even good qualities when they are unknown to them, while evils which are familiar are sometimes loved. This matter at hand has a twofold advantage to offer, for the prince will be more kindly disposed toward his subjects and certainly more ready to regard them as his own. The people on their part will feel more kindness in their hearts and be more willing to recognize his position as prince. For this reason I am especially opposed to the accepted [idea of] alliances of the princes with foreign, particularly with distant, nations. . . .

There are two factors, as Aristotle tells us in his *Politics*, which have played the greatest roles in the overthrow of empires. They are hatred and contempt. Goodwill is the opposite of hatred; respected authority, of contempt. Therefore it will be the duty of the prince to study the best way to win the former and avoid the latter. Hatred is kindled by an ugly temper, by violence, insulting language, sourness of character, meanness, and greediness; it is more easily aroused than allayed. A good prince must therefore use every caution to prevent any possibility of losing the affections of his subjects. You may take my word that whoever loses the favor of his people is thereby stripped of a great safeguard.

On the other hand, the affections of the populace are won by those characteristics which, in general, are farthest removed from tyranny. They are clemency, affability, fairness, courtesy, and kindliness. This last is a spur to duty, especially if they who have been of good service to the state, see that they will be rewarded at the hands of the prince. Clemency inspires to better efforts those who are aware of their faults, while forgiveness extends hope to those who are now eager to make recompense by virtuous conduct for the shortcomings of their earlier life and provides the steadfast with a happy reflection on human nature. Courtesy everywhere engenders love—or at least assuages hatred. This quality in a great prince is by far the most pleasing to the masses.

Contempt is most likely to spring from a penchant for the worldly pleasures of lust, for excessive drinking and eating, and for fools and clowns—in other words, for folly and idleness. Authority is gained by the following varied characteristics: in the first place wisdom, then integrity, self-restraint, seriousness, and alertness. These are the things by which a prince should commend himself, if he would be respected in his authority over his subjects. Some have the absurd idea that if they make the greatest confusion possible by their appearance, and dress with pompous display, they must be held in high esteem among their subjects. Who thinks a prince great just because he is adorned with gold and precious stones?

Everyone knows he has as many as he wants. But in the meanwhile what else does the prince expose except the misfortunes of his people, who are supporting his extravagance to their great cost? And now lastly, what else does such a prince sow among his people, if not the seeds of all crime? Let the good prince be reared in such a manner and [continue to] live in such a manner that from the example of his life all the others (nobles and commoners alike) may take the model of frugality and temperance. Let him so conduct himself in the privacy of his home as not to be caught unawares by the sudden entrance of anyone.

And in public it is unseemly for a prince to be seen anywhere, unless always in connection with something that will benefit the people as a whole. The real character of the prince is revealed by his speech rather than by his dress. Every word that is dropped from the lips of the prince is scattered wide among the masses. He should exercise the greatest care to see that whatever he says bears the stamp of [genuine] worth and evidences a mind becoming a good prince.

Aristotle's advice on this subject should not be overlooked. He says that a prince who would escape incurring the hatred of his people and would foster their affection for him should delegate to others the odious duties and keep for himself the tasks which will be sure to win favor. Thereby a great portion of any unpopularity will be diverted upon those who carry out the administration, and especially will it be so if these men are unpopular with the people on other grounds as well. In the matter of benefits, however, the genuine thanks redound to be prince alone. I should like to add also that gratitude for a favor will be returned twofold if it is given quickly, with no hesitation, spontaneously, and with a few words of friendly commendation. If anything must be refused, refusal should be affable and without offense. If it is necessary to impose a punishment, some slight diminution of the penalty prescribed by law should be made, and the sentence should be carried out as if the prince were being forced [to act] against his own desires.

It is not enough for the prince to keep his own character pure and uncorrupted for his state. He must give no less serious attention, in so far as he can, to see that every member of his household—his nobles, his friends, his ministers, and his magistrates—follows his example. They are one with the prince, and any hatred that is aroused by their vicious acts rebounds upon the prince himself.

But, someone will say, this supervision is extremely difficult to accomplish. It will be easy enough if the prince is careful to admit only the best men into his household, and if he makes them understand that the prince is most pleased by that which is best for the people. Otherwise it too often turns out that, due to the disregard of the prince in these matters or even his connivance in them, the most criminal men (hiding under cover of the prince) force a tyranny upon the people, and while they appear to be carrying out the affairs of the prince, they are doing the greatest harm to his good name.

What is more, the condition of the state is more bearable when the prince himself is wicked than when he has evil friends; we manage to bear up under a single tyrant. Somehow or other the people can sate the greed of one man without difficulty: it is not a matter of great effort to satisfy the wild desires of just one man or to appease the vicious fierceness of a single individual, but to content so many tyrants is a heavy burden. The prince should avoid every novel idea in so far as he is capable of doing so; for even if conditions are bettered thereby, the very innovation is a stumbling block. The establishment of a state, the unwritten laws of a city, or the old legal code are never changed without great confusion. Therefore, if there is anything, of this sort that can be endured, it should not be changed but should either be tolerated or happily diverted to a better function. As a last resort, if there is some absolutely unbearable condition, the change should be made, but [only] gradually and by a practiced hand.

The end which the prince sets for himself is of the greatest consequence, for if he shows little wisdom in its selection he must of necessity be wrong in all his plans. The cardinal principle of a good prince should be not only to preserve the present prosperity of the state but to pass it on more prosperous than when he received it.

To use the jargon of the Peripatetics, there are three kinds of "good"—that of the mind, that of the body, and the external good. The prince must be careful not to evaluate them in reverse order and judge the good fortune of his state mainly by the external good, for these latter conditions should only be judged good in so far as they relate to the good of the mind and of the body; that is, in a word, the prince should consider his subjects to be most fortunate not if they are very wealthy or in excellent bodily health but if they are most honorable and self-controlled, if they have as little taste for greed and quarreling as could be hoped for, and if they are not at all factious but live in complete accord with one another.

He must also beware of being deceived by the false names of the fairest things, for in this deception lies the fountainhead from which spring practically all the evils that abound in the world. It is no true state of happiness in which the people are given over to idleness and wasteful extravagance, any more than it is true liberty for everyone to be allowed to do as he pleases. Neither is it a state of servitude to live according to the letter of just laws. Nor is that a peaceful state in which the populace bows to every whim of the prince; but rather [is it peaceful] when it obeys good laws and a prince who has a keen regard for the authority of the laws. Equity does not lie in giving everyone the same reward, the same rights, the same honor; as a matter of fact, that is sometimes a mark of the greatest unfairness.

A prince who is about to assume control of the state must be advised at once that the main hope of a state lies in the proper education of its youth. This Xenophon wisely taught in his *Cyropaedia*. Pliable youth is amenable to any system of training. Therefore the greatest care should be exercised over public and private schools and over the education of the girls, so that the children may be placed under the best and most trustworthy instructors and may learn the teachings of Christ and that good literature which is beneficial to the state. As a result of this scheme of things, there will be no need for many laws or punishments, for the people will of their own free will follow the course of right.

Education exerts such a powerful influence, as Plato says, that a man who has been trained in the right develops into a sort of divine creature, while on the other hand, a person who has received a perverted training degenerates into a monstrous sort of savage beast. Nothing is of more importance to a prince than to have the best possible subjects.

The first effort, then, is to get them accustomed to the best influences, because any music has a soothing effect to the accustomed ear, and there is nothing harder than to rid people of those traits which have become second nature to them through habit. None of those tasks will be too difficult if the prince himself adheres to the best manners. It is the essence of tyranny, or rather trickery, to treat the common citizen as animal trainers are accustomed to treat a savage beast: first they carefully study the way in which these creatures are quieted or aroused, and then they anger them or quiet them at their pleasure. This Plato has painstakingly pointed out. Such a course is an abuse of the emotions of the masses and is no help to them. However, if the people prove intractable and rebel against what is good for them, then you must bide your time and gradually lead them over to your end, either by some subterfuge or by some helpful pretense. This works just as wine does, for when that is first taken it has no effect, but when it has gradually flowed through every vein it captivates the whole man and holds him in its power.

If sometimes the whirling course of events and public opinion beat the prince from his course, and he is forced to obey the [exigencies of the] time, yet he must not cease his efforts as long as he is able to renew his fight, and what he has not accomplished by one method he should try to effect by another.

On Tributes and Taxes

If anyone will merely glance through the annals of the ancients he will discover that a great many seditions have arisen from immoderate taxation. The good prince must be careful that the feelings of the commoners be not aroused by such actions. He should rule without expense if he possibly can. The position of the prince is too high to be a mercenary one; and besides, a good prince has all that his loving subjects possess.

There were many pagans who took home with them only glory as a result of their public activities which they had honorably discharged. . . . How much more should a Christian prince be content with a clear conscience, especially since he is in the service of Him who amply rewards every good deed! There are certain ones in the circles of princes who do nothing else except extort as much as possible from the people on every new pretext they can find and then believe that they have properly served the interests of their princes, as if they were the open enemies of their subjects. But whoever is willing to hearken to such men, should know that he by no means comes under the title of "prince"!

A prince should studiously endeavor to minimize his demands on the people. The most desirable way of increasing the revenue is to cut off the worse than useless extravagances, to abolish the idle ministries, to avoid wars and long travels, which are very like wars [in their bad effects], to suppress graft among the office holders, and to be interested in the proper administration of the kingdom rather than in the extension of its boundaries. But if the prince is going to measure the amount of taxes by his greed or ambitions, what bounds or limits will there be to his demands? Greed knows no end and continually presses and extends what it has started until, as the old proverb goes, too great a strain breaks the rope, and finally the patience of the people is exhausted and they break into an uprising, which is the very thing that has been the undoing of kingdoms that once were most prosperous.

If, however, circumstances force the levying of taxes on the people, then it is the part of a good prince to raise them according to such a system that as little as possible of the hardships will fall upon the poor. It is perhaps desirable to bring the wealthy to a simple life, but to reduce the poor to starvation and chains is most inhuman, as well as extremely dangerous. The conscientious king, at the time when he wants to increase his court, to obtain an excellent alliance for his granddaughter or his sister, to raise all his children to rank with him, to fill the coffers of the nobility, to flaunt his wealth in the face of other nations by extended travels, should ponder again and again in his own mind how inhuman it is for so many thousands of men with their wives and children to starve to death, to be plunged into debt and driven to the last degrees of desperation, so that he can accomplish these ends.

I should not even consider such persons under the class of human beings—much less princes—when they extort from the lowest paupers what they sinfully squander on lewd women and on gambling. And yet we hear of some men who think that even such actions come under their rights.

The prince should also give a good deal of thought to this fact, that whatever is once introduced as a temporary expedient and appears to be connected with the purse strings of prince or nobles, can never be set aside. When the occasion for the taxation is removed, not only should the burden be removed from the people, but recompense made by replacing, as far as possible, the former expenditures. He who has his people's interests at heart will avoid introducing a calamitous precedent; but if he takes pleasure in the disasters of his subjects, or even disregards them, he is in no way a prince, regardless of his title whatever it may be.

The prince should try to prevent too great an inequality of wealth. I should not want to see anyone deprived of his goods, but the prince should employ certain measures to prevent the wealth of the multitude being hoarded by a few. Plato did not want his citizens to be too rich, neither did he want them extremely poor, for the pauper is of no use and the rich man will not use his ability for public service.

It happens that princes like those [which I have just de-scribed] are sometimes not even enriched by these levies. Whoever would like to find out for himself has only to recall how much less our ancestors received from their peoples and how much more beneficent they were and how much more they possessed in every way, because a great part of this money slips through the fingers of the collecting and receiving agents and a very small portion gets to the prince himself.

A good prince will tax as lightly as possible those commodi-ties which are used even by the poorest members of society; e.g., grain, bread, beer, wine, clothing, and all the other staples without which human life could not exist. But it so happens that these very things bear the heaviest tax in several ways; in the first place, by the oppressive extortion of the tax farmers, commonly called *assisiae*, then by import duties which call for their own set of extortionists, and finally by the monopolies by which the poor are sadly drained of their funds in order that the prince may gain a mere trifling interest. As I have brought out, the best way of increasing the prince's treasury is to follow the old proverb, "Parsimony is a great revenue," and carefully check expenditures. However, if some taxation is absolutely necessary and the affairs of the people render it essential, bar-barous and foreign goods should be heavily taxed because they are not the essentials of livelihood but the extravagant luxuries and delicacies which only the wealthy enjoy; for example, linen, silks, dyes, pepper, spices, unguents, precious stones, and all the rest of that same category. But by this system only those who can well afford it feel the pinch. They will not be reduced

to straitened circumstances as a result of this outlay but per-
chance may be made more moderate in their desires so that the
loss of money may be replaced by a change for the better in
their habits.

In the minting of his money the good prince should observe that faith which he owes to God and his own people and
not allow himself a liberty by which he inflicts the direst penalties on others. In this matter there are four ways of robbing the
people, a fact which was only too clearly brought before us at
the death of Charles, when a long period of anarchy more
blighting than any tyranny you could name afflicted your kingdom. The first way is to debase the coinage with alloys, the
second is to make them short weight, the third is to clip them,
and the fourth is to bring about intentional fluctuation of value
to suit the needs of the prince's treasury.

On Enacting or Amending Laws

The best laws under the best princes make a city or a kingdom most fortunate. The most felicitous condition exists when
the prince is obeyed by everyone, the prince himself obeys the
laws, and the laws go back to the fundamental principles of
equity and honesty, with no other aim than the advancement
of the commonwealth.

A good, wise, and upright prince is nothing else than a sort
of living law. He will make it his effort to pass not many laws
but the best possible ones that will prove most beneficial to the
state. A very few laws suffice for a well organized state under a

good prince and honorable officials. Under any other conditions no number, however great, will be enough. A sick person does not get along best with an unskilled physician prescribing one medicine after another.

In the promulgation of laws, the first concern is to see that they do not savor of royal financial plans nor of private gain for the nobility but that they are drawn up on an honest plan and that everything looks to the welfare of the people. This welfare is to be judged not by the popular opinion but according to the dictates of wisdom, which should always be present in the councils of the prince. Even the pagans admitted that a law is really no law at all if it is not just, fair, and intended for public benefit. That is not a law which merely pleases the prince, but rather that which pleases a good and wise prince who has no interest in anything which is not honorable and for the good of his state. But if those standards by which evils are to be corrected are themselves distorted, there can be only one result from laws of this kind, namely, that even good things are perverted to evil.

Plato desired that the laws should be as few as possible, especially on the less important matters, such as agreements, commercial business, and taxes; for no more benefit accrues to the state from a mass of laws than would come [to a person] from a multitude of medicines. When the prince is a man of unquestioned character and the officials fulfill their responsibilities, there is no need of many laws. Under other conditions, however, the abuse of the laws is turned into the destruction of the state, for even the good laws are perverted into other meanings, due to the dishonesty of these men. . . .

The laws should then not only provide punishments for the transgressors but also by means of rewards stimulate good conduct in the service of the state. We find many examples of this type among the ancients: whoever fought bravely in war, hoped for a reward; if he fell fighting, his children were reared by the state. Whoever saved a fellow citizen, whoever drove one of the enemy from the walls, whoever assisted the state by wise counsel, had his reward.

Although a good citizen should follow the path of honor even when no reward is offered, still inducements of that sort are desirable to spur on to an eagerness for good living the minds of those citizens who are still but little developed. Those who have more character are more interested in the honor; those who are on a lower level are influenced by the money also.

A law should have its effect, then, in all these ways—honor and disgrace, profit and loss. Of course those who really are of a servile, or rather, bestial, character must be controlled by chains and floggings. Let your subjects grow up from childhood with this sense of honor and ignominy so that they will realize that rewards are not won through wealth or birth, but by good deeds. In a word, the watchful prince should use every means not only to see that offenses are punished but to look and reach much further back than that. He should see in the first place that no deed is committed which calls for punishment.

The better physician is the one who prevents and wards off disease, not the one that cures the disease with drugs once it is contracted. Just so, it is not a little the more worthwhile achievement to prevent the inception of crime than to inflict punishment once crime is committed. The former will be accomplished if the prince will discover the causes from which most crimes spring and then cut them out if he can, or at any rate, suppress them and deprive them of their force. . . .

It is advisable, then, that the laws be as few as possible, and secondly, that they be as just as possible, and [prepared] with a view to the welfare of the state; in addition they should be very thoroughly familiar to the people. On this very account the ancients used to exhibit the laws publicly written in the records and on tablets so that they might be plainly discernible by all. Some follow the abominable theory of using the law in place of nets with the one purpose of catching as many as they can, with no regard for the state, but just as if they were capturing spoils.

Finally, let the laws be set forth in clear language with as few complexities as possible, so that there will be no urgent need for that most grasping type of man who calls himself "jurisconsult" and "advocate." This profession was once open only to men of the highest standing and carried with it a very high position and very little money. But now the lust for gold which has sapped everything has corrupted this field. Plato says that there can be no enemy more blighting to the state than the person who subjects the laws to the human will. But the laws are at the peak under a good prince.

Saint Thomas More

Utopia
1516 AD, England

Therefore go through with the play that is acting the best you can, and do not confound it because another that is pleasanter comes into your thoughts. . . . If ill opinions cannot be quite rooted out, and you cannot cure some received vice according to your wishes, you must not, therefore, abandon the commonwealth, for the same reasons as you should not forsake the ship in a storm because you cannot command the winds.

Selections

Henry VIII, the unconquered King of England, a prince adorned with all the virtues that become a great monarch, having some differences of no small consequence with Charles the most serene Prince of Castile, sent me into Flanders, as his ambassador, for treating and composing matters between them. I was colleague and companion to that incomparable man Cuthbert Tonstal, whom the King, with such universal applause, lately made Master of the Rolls; but of whom I will say nothing; not because I fear that the testimony of a friend will be suspected, but rather because his learning and virtues are too great for me to do them justice, and so well known, that they need not my commendations, unless I would, according to the proverb, "Show the sun with a lantern."

Those that were appointed by the Prince to treat with us, met us at Bruges, according to agreement; they were all worthy men. The Margrave of Bruges was their head, and the chief man among them; but he that was esteemed the wisest, and that spoke for the rest, was George Temse, the Provost of Casselsee: both art and nature had concurred to make him eloquent: he was very learned in the law; and, as he had a great capacity, so, by a long practice in affairs, he was very dexterous at unraveling them. After we had several times met, without coming to an agreement, they went to Brussels for some days, to know the Prince's pleasure; and, since our business would admit it, I went to Antwerp.

While I was there, among many that visited me, there was one that was more acceptable to me than any other, Peter Giles, born at Antwerp, who is a man of great honor, and of a good rank in his town, though less than he deserves; for I do not know if there be anywhere to be found a more learned and a better bred young man; for as he is both a very worthy and a very knowing person, so he is so civil to all men, so particularly kind to his friends, and so full of candor and affection, that there is not, perhaps, above one or two anywhere to be found, that is in all respects so perfect a friend: he is extraordinarily modest, there is no artifice in him, and yet no man has more of a prudent simplicity. His conversation was so pleasant and so innocently cheerful, that his company in a great measure lessened any longings to go back to my country, and to my wife and children, which an absence of four months had quickened very much.

One day, as I was returning home from mass at St. Mary's, which is the chief church, and the most frequented of any in Antwerp, I saw him, by accident, talking with a stranger, who seemed past the flower of his age; his face was tanned, he had a long beard, and his cloak was hanging carelessly about him, so that, by his looks and habit, I concluded he was a seaman.

As soon as Peter saw me, he came and saluted me, and as I was returning his civility, he took me aside, and pointing to him with whom he had been discoursing, he said, "Do you see that man? I was just thinking to bring him to you." I answered, "He should have been very welcome on your account." "And on his own too," replied he, "if you knew the man, for there is none alive that can give so copious an account of unknown nations and countries as he can do, which I know you very much desire." "Then," said I, "I did not guess amiss, for at first sight I took him for a seaman." "But you are much mistaken," said he, "for he has not sailed as a seaman, but as a traveler, or rather a philosopher.

"This Raphael, who from his family carries the name of Hythloday, is not ignorant of the Latin tongue, but is eminently learned in the Greek, having applied himself more particularly to that than to the former, because he had given himself much to philosophy, in which he knew that the Romans have left us nothing that is valuable, except what is to be found in Seneca and Cicero.

"He is a Portuguese by birth, and was so desirous of seeing the world, that he divided his estate among his brothers, ran the same hazard as Americus Vesputius, and bore a share in three of his four voyages that are now published; only he did not return with him in his last, but obtained leave of him, almost by force, that he might be one of those twenty-four who were left at the farthest place at which they touched in their last voyage to New Castile. The leaving him thus did not a little gratify one that was more fond of traveling than of returning home to be buried in his own country; for he used often to say, that the way to heaven was the same from all places, and he that had no grave had the heavens still over him. Yet this disposition of mind had cost him dear, if God had not been very gracious to him; for after he, with five Castalians, had traveled over many countries, at last, by strange good fortune, he got to Ceylon, and from thence to Calicut, where he, very happily, found some Portuguese ships; and, beyond all men's expectations, returned to his native country."

When Peter had said this to me, I thanked him for his kindness in intending to give me the acquaintance of a man whose conversation he knew would be so acceptable; and upon that Raphael and I embraced each other. After those civilities were past which are usual with strangers upon their first meeting, we all went to my house, and entering into the garden, sat down on a green bank and entertained one another in discourse. . . .

As he told us of many things that were amiss in those new-discovered countries, so he reckoned up not a few things, from which patterns might be taken for correcting the errors of these nations among whom we live; of which an account may be given, as I have already promised, at some other time; for, at present, I intend only to relate those particulars that he told us, of the manners and laws of the Utopians: but I will begin with the occasion that led us to speak of that commonwealth. After Raphael had discoursed with great judgment on the many errors that were both among us and these nations, had treated of the wise institutions both here and there, and had spoken as distinctly of the customs and government of every nation through which he had passed, as if he had spent his whole life in it, Peter, being struck with admiration, said, "I wonder, Raphael, how it comes that you enter into no king's service, for I am sure there are none to whom you would not be very acceptable; for your learning and knowledge, both of men and things, is such, that you would not only entertain them very pleasantly, but be of great use to them, by the examples you could set before them, and the advices you could give them; and by this means you would both serve your own interest, and be of great use to all your friends."

"As for my friends," answered he, "I need not be much concerned, having already done for them all that was incumbent on me; for when I was not only in good health, but fresh and young, I distributed that among my kindred and friends which other people do not part with till they are old and sick: when they then unwillingly give that which they can enjoy no longer themselves. I think my friends ought to rest contented with this, and not to expect that for their sakes I should enslave myself to any king whatsoever."

"Soft and fair!" said Peter; "I do not mean that you should be a slave to any king, but only that you should assist them and be useful to them."

"The change of the word," said he, "does not alter the matter."

"But term it as you will," replied Peter, "I do not see any other way in which you can be so useful, both in private to your friends and to the public, and by which you can make your own condition happier."

"Happier?" answered Raphael, "is that to be compassed in a way so abhorrent to my genius? Now I live as I will, to which I believe, few courtiers can pretend; and there are so many that court the favor of great men, that there will be no great loss if they are not troubled either with me or with others of my temper."

Upon this, said I, "I perceive, Raphael, that you neither desire wealth nor greatness; and, indeed, I value and admire such a man much more than I do any of the great men in the world. Yet I think you would do what would well become so generous and philosophical a soul as yours is, if you would apply your time and thoughts to public affairs, even though you may happen to find it a little uneasy to yourself; and this you can never do with so much advantage as by being taken into the council of some great prince and putting him on noble and worthy actions, which I know you would do if you were in such a post; for the springs both of good and evil flow from the prince over a whole nation, as from a lasting fountain. So much learning as you have, even without practice in affairs, or so great a practice as you have had, without any other learning, would render you a very fit counselor to any king whatsoever."

"You are doubly mistaken," said he, "Mr. More, both in your opinion of me and in the judgment you make of things: for as I have not that capacity that you fancy I have, so if I had it, the public would not be one jot the better when I had sacrificed my quiet to it. For most princes apply themselves more to affairs of war than to the useful arts of peace; and in these I neither have any knowledge, nor do I much desire it; they are generally more set on acquiring new kingdoms, right or wrong, than on governing well those they possess: and, among the ministers of princes, there are none that are not so wise as to need no assistance, or at least, that do not think themselves so wise that they imagine they need none; and if they court any, it is only those for whom the prince has much personal favor, whom by their fawning and flatteries they endeavor to fix to their own interests; and, indeed, nature has so made us, that we all love to be flattered and to please ourselves with our own notions: the old crow loves his young, and the ape her cubs.

"Now if in such a court, made up of persons who envy all others and only admire themselves, a person should but propose anything that he had either read in history or observed in his travels, the rest would think that the reputation of their wisdom would sink, and that their interests would be much depressed if they could not run it down: and, if all other things failed, then they would fly to this, that such or such things pleased our ancestors, and it were well for us if we could but match them. They would set up their rest on such an answer, as a sufficient confutation of all that could be said, as if it were a great misfortune that any should be found wiser than his ancestors. But though they willingly let go all the good things that were among those of former ages, yet, if better things are proposed, they cover themselves obstinately with this excuse of reverence to past times. I have met with these proud, morose, and absurd judgments of things in many places, particularly once in England."

[He recounts his time in England and laments that courtiers did not value his counsels.]

● ● ●

"Thus, Mr. More, I have run out into a tedious story, of the length of which I had been ashamed, if (as you earnestly begged it of me) I had not observed you to hearken to it as if you had no mind to lose any part of it. I might have contracted it, but I resolved to give it you at large, that you might observe how those that despised what I had proposed, no sooner perceived that the Cardinal did not dislike it but presently approved of it, fawned so on him and flattered him to such a degree, that they in good earnest applauded those things that he only liked in jest; and from hence you may gather how little courtiers would value either me or my counsels."

To this I answered, "You have done me a great kindness in this relation; for as everything has been related by you both wisely and pleasantly, so you have made me imagine that I was in my own country and grown young again, by recalling that good Cardinal to my thoughts, in whose family I was bred from my childhood; and though you are, upon other accounts, very dear to me, yet you are the dearer because you honor his memory so much; but, after all this, I cannot change my opinion, for I still think that if you could overcome that aversion which you have to the courts of princes, you might, by the advice which it is in your power to give, do a great deal of good to mankind, and this is the chief design that every good man ought to propose to himself in living; for your friend Plato thinks that nations will be happy when either philosophers become kings or kings become philosophers. It is no wonder if we are so far from that happiness while philosophers will not think it their duty to assist kings with their counsels."

"They are not so base-minded," said he, "but that they would willingly do it; many of them have already done it by their books, if those that are in power would but hearken to their good advice. But Plato judged right, that except kings themselves became philosophers, they who from their childhood are corrupted with false notions would never fall in entirely with the counsels of philosophers, and this he himself found to be true in the person of Dionysius.

"Do not you think that if I were about any king, proposing good laws to him, and endeavoring to root out all the cursed seeds of evil that I found in him, I should either be turned out of his court, or, at least, be laughed at for my pains? For instance, what could I signify if I were about the King of France, and were called into his cabinet council, where several wise men, in his hearing, were proposing many expedients; as, by what arts and practices Milan may be kept, and Naples, that has so often slipped out of their hands, recovered; how the Venetians, and after them the rest of Italy, may be subdued; and then how Flanders, Brabant, and all Burgundy, and some other kingdoms which he has swallowed already in his designs, may be added to his empire?

"One proposes a league with the Venetians, to be kept as long as he finds his account in it, and that he ought to communicate counsels with them, and give them some share of the spoil till his success makes him need or fear them less, and then it will be easily taken out of their hands; another proposes the hiring the Germans and the securing the Switzers by pensions; another proposes the gaining the Emperor by money, which is omnipotent with him; another proposes a peace with the King of Arragon, and, in order to cement it, the yielding up the King of Navarre's pretensions; another thinks that the Prince of Castile is to be wrought on by the hope of an alliance, and that some of his courtiers are to be gained to the French faction by pensions. The hardest point of all is, what to do with England; a treaty of peace is to be set on foot, and, if their alliance is not to be depended on, yet it is to be made as firm as possible, and they are to be called friends, but suspected as enemies: therefore the Scots are to be kept in readiness to be let loose upon England on every occasion; and some banished nobleman is to be supported underhand (for by the League it cannot be done avowedly) who has a pretension to the crown, by which means that suspected prince may be kept in awe.

"Now when things are in so great a fermentation, and so many gallant men are joining counsels how to carry on the war, if so mean a man as I should stand up and wish them to change all their counsels—to let Italy alone and stay at home, since the kingdom of France was indeed greater than could be well governed by one man; that therefore he ought not to think of adding others to it; and if, after this, I should propose to them the resolutions of the Achorians, a people that lie on the southeast of Utopia, who long ago engaged in war in order to add to the dominions of their prince another kingdom, to which he had some pretensions by an ancient alliance: this they conquered, but found that the trouble of keeping it was equal to that by which it was gained; that the conquered people were always either in rebellion or exposed to foreign invasions, while they were obliged to be incessantly at war, either for or against them, and consequently could never disband their army; that in the meantime they were oppressed with taxes, their money went out of the kingdom, their blood was spilt for the glory of their king without procuring the least advantage to the people, who received not the smallest benefit from it even in time of peace; and that, their manners being corrupted by a long war, robbery and murders everywhere abounded, and their laws fell into contempt; while their king, distracted with the care of two king-doms, was the less able to apply his mind to the interest of either.

"When they saw this, and that there would be no end to these evils, they by joint counsels made a humble address to their king, desiring him to choose which of the two kingdoms he had the greatest mind to keep, since he could not hold both; for they were too great a people to be governed by a divided king, since no man would willingly have a groom that should be in common between him and another. Upon which the good prince was forced to quit his new kingdom to one of his friends (who was not long after dethroned), and to be contented with his old one. To this I would add that after all those warlike at-tempts, the vast confusions, and the consumption both of trea-sure and of people that must follow them, perhaps upon some misfortune they might be forced to throw up all at last; there-fore it seemed much more eligible that the king should improve his ancient kingdom all he could, and make it flourish as much as possible; that he should love his people, and be beloved of them; that he should live among them, govern them gently and let other kingdoms alone, since that which had fallen to his share was big enough, if not too big, for him—pray, how do you think would such a speech as this be heard?"

"I confess," said I, "I think not very well."

"But what," said he, "if I should sort with another kind of ministers, whose chief contrivances and consultations were by what art the prince's treasures might be increased? Where one proposes raising the value of specie when the king's debts are large, and lowering it when his revenues were to come in, that so he might both pay much with a little, and in a little receive a great deal. Another proposes a pretense of a war, that money might be raised in order to carry it on, and that a peace be concluded as soon as that was done; and this with such appearances of religion as might work on the people, and make them impute it to the piety of their prince, and to his tenderness for the lives of his subjects.

"A third offers some old musty laws that have been antiquated by a long disuse (and which, as they had been forgotten by all the subjects, so they had also been broken by them), and proposes the levying the penalties of these laws, that, as it would bring in a vast treasure, so there might be a very good pretense for it, since it would look like the executing a law and the doing of justice.

"A fourth proposes the prohibiting of many things under severe penalties, especially such as were against the interest of the people, and then the dispensing with these prohibitions, upon great compositions, to those who might find their advantage in breaking them. This would serve two ends, both of them acceptable to many; for as those whose avarice led them to transgress would be severely fined, so the selling licenses dear would look as if a prince were tender of his people, and would not easily, or at low rates, dispense with anything that might be against the public good.

"Another proposes that the judges must be made sure, that they may declare always in favor of the prerogative; that they must be often sent for to court, that the king may hear them argue those points in which he is concerned; since, how unjust soever any of his pretensions may be, yet still some one or other of them, either out of contradiction to others, or the pride of singularity, or to make their court, would find out some pretense or other to give the king a fair color to carry the point. For if the judges but differ in opinion, the clearest thing in the world is made by that means disputable, and truth being once brought in question, the king may then take advantage to expound the law for his own profit; while the judges that stand out will be brought over, either through fear or modesty; and they being thus gained, all of them may be sent to the Bench to give sentence boldly as the king would have it; for fair pretenses will never be wanting when sentence is to be given in the prince's favor.

"It will either be said that equity lies on his side, or some words in the law will be found sounding that way, or some forced sense will be put on them; and, when all other things fail, the king's undoubted prerogative will be pretended, as that which is above all law, and to which a religious judge ought to have a special regard. Thus all consent to that maxim of Crassus, that a prince cannot have treasure enough, since he must maintain his armies out of it; that a king, even though he would, can do nothing unjustly; that all property is in him, not excepting the very persons of his subjects; and that no man has any other property but that which the king, out of his goodness, thinks fit to leave him.

"And they think it is the prince's interest that there be as little of this left as may be, as if it were his advantage that his people should have neither riches nor liberty, since these things make them less easy and willing to submit to a cruel and unjust government. Whereas necessity and poverty blunts them, makes them patient, beats them down, and breaks that height of spirit that might otherwise dispose them to rebel.

"Now what if, after all these propositions were made, I should rise up and assert that such counsels were both unbecoming a king and mischievous to him; and that not only his honor, but his safety, consisted more in his people's wealth than in his own; if I should show that they choose a king for their own sake, and not for his; that, by his care and endeavors, they may be both easy and safe; and that, therefore, a prince ought to take more care of his people's happiness than of his own, as a shepherd is to take more care of his flock than of himself?

"It is also certain that they are much mistaken that think the poverty of a nation is a means of the public safety. Who quarrel more than beggars? Who does more earnestly long for a change than he that is uneasy in his present circumstances? And who run to create confusions with so desperate a boldness as those who, having nothing to lose, hope to gain by them? If a king should fall under such contempt or envy that he could not keep his subjects in their duty but by oppression and ill usage, and by rendering them poor and miserable, it were certainly better for him to quit his kingdom than to retain it by such methods as make him, while he keeps the name of authority, lose the majesty due to it.

"Nor is it so becoming the dignity of a king to reign over beggars as over rich and happy subjects. And therefore Fabricius, a man of a noble and exalted temper, said 'he would rather govern rich men than be rich himself; since for one man to abound in wealth and pleasure when all about him are mourning and groaning, is to be a gaoler and not a king.' He is an unskillful physician that cannot cure one disease without casting his patient into another. So he that can find no other way for correcting the errors of his people but by taking from them the conveniences of life, shows that he knows not what it is to govern a free nation. He himself ought rather to shake off his sloth, or to lay down his pride, for the contempt or hatred that his people have for him takes its rise from the vices in himself.

"Let him live upon what belongs to him without wronging others, and accommodate his expense to his revenue. Let him punish crimes, and, by his wise conduct, let him endeavor to prevent them, rather than be severe when he has suffered them to be too common. Let him not rashly revive laws that are abrogated by disuse, especially if they have been long forgotten and never wanted. And let him never take any penalty for the breach of them to which a judge would not give way in a private man, but would look on him as a crafty and unjust person for pretending to it.

"To these things I would add that law among the Macarians—a people that live not far from Utopia—by which their king, on the day on which he began to reign, is tied by an oath, confirmed by solemn sacrifices, never to have at once above a thousand pounds of gold in his treasures, or so much silver as is equal to that in value. This law, they tell us, was made by an excellent king who had more regard to the riches of his country than to his own wealth, and therefore provided against the heaping up of so much treasure as might impoverish the people. He thought that moderate sum might be sufficient for any accident, if either the king had occasion for it against the rebels, or the kingdom against the invasion of an enemy; but that it was not enough to encourage a prince to invade other men's rights—a circumstance that was the chief cause of his making that law.

"He also thought that it was a good provision for that free circulation of money so necessary for the course of commerce and exchange. And when a king must distribute all those extraordinary accessions that increase treasure beyond the due pitch, it makes him less disposed to oppress his subjects. Such a king as this will be the terror of ill men, and will be beloved by all the good.

"If, I say, I should talk of these or such-like things to men that had taken their bias another way, how deaf would they be to all I could say!"

"No doubt, very deaf," answered I; "and no wonder, for one is never to offer propositions or advice that we are certain will not be entertained. Discourses so much out of the road could not avail anything, nor have any effect on men whose minds were prepossessed with different sentiments. This philosophical way of speculation is not unpleasant among friends in a free conversation; but there is no room for it in the courts of princes, where great affairs are carried on by authority."

"That is what I was saying," replied he, "that there is no room for philosophy in the courts of princes."

"Yes, there is," said I, "but not for this speculative philosophy, that makes everything to be alike fitting at all times; but there is another philosophy that is more pliable, that knows its proper scene, accommodates itself to it, and teaches a man with propriety and decency to act that part which has fallen to his share. If when one of Plautus' comedies is upon the stage, and a company of servants are acting their parts, you should come out in the garb of a philosopher, and repeat, out of *Octavia*, a discourse of Seneca's to Nero, would it not be better for you to say nothing than by mixing things of such different natures to make an impertinent tragi-comedy? For you spoil and corrupt the play that is in hand when you mix with it things of an opposite nature, even though they are much better.

"Therefore go through with the play that is acting the best you can, and do not confound it because another that is pleasanter comes into your thoughts. It is even so in a commonwealth and in the councils of princes; if ill opinions cannot be quite rooted out, and you cannot cure some received vice according to your wishes, you must not, therefore, abandon the commonwealth, for the same reasons as you should not forsake the ship in a storm because you cannot command the winds.

"You are not obliged to assault people with discourses that are out of their road, when you see that their received notions must prevent your making an impression upon them: you ought rather to cast about and to manage things with all the dexterity in your power, so that, if you are not able to make them go well, they may be as little ill as possible; for, except all

men were good, everything cannot be right, and that is a blessing that I do not at present hope to see."

Modernity

George Washington

Farewell Address
1796 AD, United States

———————

Properly estimate the immense value of your
national Union, to your collective and individual
happiness . . . accustoming yourselves to think and
speak of it as of the Palladium of your political safety
and prosperity.

Friends & Fellow Citizens   United States 19th September 1796
The period for a new election of a Citizen, to Administer
the Executive government of the United States, being not far
distant, and the time actually arrived, when your thoughts must
be employed in designating the person, who is to be clothed
with that important trust, it appears to me proper, especially as
it may conduce to a more distinct expression of the public voice,
that I should now apprise you of the resolution I have formed,
to decline being considered among the number of those, out of
whom a choice is to be made.

I beg you, at the same time, to do me the justice to be assured, that this resolution has not been taken, without a strict regard to all the considerations appertaining to the relation, which binds a dutiful citizen to his country—and that, in withdrawing the tender of service which silence in my situation might imply, I am influenced by no diminution of zeal for your future interest; no deficiency of grateful respect for your past kindness; but am supported by a full conviction that the step is compatible with both.

The acceptance of, and continuance hitherto in, the office to which your Suffrages have twice called me, have been a uniform sacrifice of inclination to the opinion of duty, and to a deference for what appeared to be your desire. I constantly hoped, that it would have been much earlier in my power, consistently with motives, which I was not at liberty to disregard, to return to that retirement, from which I had been reluctantly drawn. The strength of my inclination to do this, previous to the last Election, had even led to the preparation of an address to declare it to you; but mature reflection on the then perplexed and critical posture of our Affairs with foreign Nations, and the unanimous advice of persons entitled to my confidence, impelled me to abandon the idea.

I rejoice, that the state of your concerns, external as well as internal, no longer renders the pursuit of inclination incompatible with the sentiment of duty, or propriety; and am persuaded whatever partiality may be retained for my services, that in the present circumstances of our country, you will not disapprove my determination to retire.

The impressions with which I first undertook the arduous trust, were explained on the proper occasion. In the discharge of this trust, I will only say, that I have with good intentions, contributed towards the Organization and administration of the government, the best exertions of which a very fallible judgment was capable. Not unconscious, in the outset, of the inferiority of my qualifications, experience in my own eyes, perhaps still more in the eyes of others, has strengthened the motives to diffidence of myself; and every day the increasing weight of years admonishes me more and more, that the shade of retirement is as necessary to me as it will be welcome. Satisfied that if any circumstances have given peculiar value to my services, they were temporary, I have the consolation to believe, that while choice and prudence invite me to quit the political scene, patriotism does not forbid it.

In looking forward to the moment, which is intended to terminate the career of my public life, my feelings do not permit me to suspend the deep acknowledgment of that debt of gratitude which I owe to my beloved country, for the many honors it has conferred upon me; still more for the steadfast confidence with which it has supported me; and for the opportunities I have thence enjoyed of manifesting my inviolable attachment, by services faithful and persevering, though in usefulness unequal to my zeal. If benefits have resulted to our country from these services, let it always be remembered to your praise, and as an instructive example in our annals, that, under circumstances in which the Passions agitated in every direction were liable to mislead, amidst appearances sometimes dubious, vicissitudes of fortune often discouraging, in situations in which not unfrequently want of Success has countenanced the spirit of criticism, the constancy of your support was the essential prop of the efforts, and a guarantee of the plans by which they were effected. Profoundly penetrated with this idea, I shall carry it with me to my grave, as a strong incitement to unceasing vows that Heaven may continue to you the choicest tokens of its beneficence—that your Union and brotherly affection may be perpetual—that the free constitution, which is the work of your hands, may be sacredly maintained—that its Administration in every department may be stamped with wisdom and virtue—that, in fine, the happiness of the people of these States, under the auspices of liberty, may be made complete, by so careful a preservation and so prudent a use of this blessing as will acquire to them the glory of recommending it to the applause, the affection—and adoption of every nation which is yet a stranger to it.

Here, perhaps, I ought to stop. But a solicitude for your welfare, which cannot end but with my life, and the apprehension of danger, natural to that solicitude, urge me on an occasion like the present, to offer to your solemn contemplation, and to recommend to your frequent review, some sentiments; which are the result of much reflection, of no inconsiderable observation, and which appear to me all important to the permanency of your felicity as a People. These will be offered to you with the more freedom, as you can only see in them the disinterested warnings of a parting friend, who can possibly have no personal motive to bias his counsel. Nor can I forget, as an encouragement to it, your indulgent reception of my sentiments on a former and not dissimilar occasion.

Interwoven as is the love of liberty with every ligament of your hearts, no recommendation of mine is necessary to fortify or confirm the attachment.

The Unity of Government which constitutes you one people is also now dear to you. It is justly so; for it is a main Pillar in the Edifice of your real independence, the support of your tranquility at home, your peace abroad; of your safety; of your prosperity; of that very Liberty which you so highly prize. But as it is easy to foresee, that from different causes and from different quarters, much pains will be taken, many artifices employed, to weaken in your minds the conviction of this truth; as this is the point in your political fortress against which the batteries of internal and external enemies will be most constantly and actively (though often covertly and insidiously) directed, it is of infinite moment, that you should properly estimate the immense value of your national Union, to your collective and individual happiness; that you should cherish a cordial, habitual and immoveable attachment to it; accustoming yourselves to think and speak of it as of the Palladium of your political safety and prosperity; watching for its preservation with jealous anxiety; discountenancing whatever may suggest even a suspicion that it can in any event be abandoned; and indignantly frowning upon the first dawning of every attempt to alienate any portion of our Country from the rest, or to enfeeble the sacred ties which now link together the various parts.

For this you have every inducement of sympathy and interest. Citizens by birth or choice, of a common country, that country has a right to concentrate your affections. The name of AMERICAN, which belongs to you, in your national capacity, must always exalt the just pride of Patriotism, more than any appellation derived from local discriminations. With slight shades of difference, you have the same Religion, Manners, Habits and political Principles. You have in a common cause fought and triumphed together—the independence and Liberty you possess are the work of joint councils, and joint efforts—of common dangers, sufferings and successes.

But these considerations, however powerfully they address themselves to your sensibility, are greatly outweighed by those which apply more immediately to your Interest. Here every portion of our country finds the most commanding motives for carefully guarding and preserving the Union of the whole.

The *North*, in an unrestrained intercourse with the *South*, protected by the equal Laws of a common government, finds in the productions of the latter, great additional resources of maritime and commercial enterprise and precious materials of manufacturing industry. The *South* in the same Intercourse, benefitting by the Agency of the *North*, sees its agriculture grow and its commerce expand. Turning partly into its own channels the seamen of the *North*, it finds its particular navigation invigorated; and while it contributes, in different ways, to nourish and increase the general mass of the national navigation, it looks forward to the protection of a maritime strength, to which itself is unequally adapted. The *East*, in a like intercourse

with the *West*, already finds, and in the progressive improvement of interior communications, by land and water, will more
and more find a valuable vent for the commodities which it
brings from abroad, or manufactures at home. The *West* derives
from the *East* supplies requisite to its growth and comfort—and
what is perhaps of still greater consequence, it must of necessity
owe the *secure* enjoyment of indispensable *outlets* for its own
productions to the weight, influence, and the future maritime
strength of the Atlantic side of the Union, directed by an indis-
soluble community of Interest as *one Nation*. Any other tenure
by which the *West* can hold this essential advantage, whether
derived from its own separate strength, or from an apostate and
unnatural connection with any foreign Power, must be intrinsi-
cally precarious.

While then every part of our country thus feels an immediate and particular Interest in Union, all the parts combined
cannot fail to find in the united mass of means and efforts
greater strength, greater resource, proportionably greater security from external danger, a less frequent interruption of their
Peace by foreign Nations; and, what is of inestimable value!
They must derive from Union an exemption from those broils
and Wars between themselves, which so frequently afflict
neighboring countries, not tied together by the same government; which their own rivalships alone would be sufficient to
produce, but which opposite foreign alliances, attachments and
intrigues would stimulate and embitter. Hence likewise they
will avoid the necessity of those overgrown military establishments, which under any form of Government are inauspicious

to liberty, and which are to be regarded as particularly hostile to Republican Liberty: In this sense it is, that your Union ought to be considered as a main prop of your liberty, and that the love of the one ought to endear to you the preservation of the other.

These considerations speak a persuasive language to every reflecting and virtuous mind, and exhibit the continuance of the UNION as a primary object of Patriotic desire. Is there a doubt, whether a common government can embrace so large a sphere? Let experience solve it. To listen to mere speculation in such a case were criminal. We are authorized to hope that a proper organization of the whole, with the auxiliary agency of governments for the respective Subdivisions, will afford a happy issue to the experiment. 'Tis well worth a fair and full experiment. With such powerful and obvious motives to Union, affecting all parts of our country, while experience shall not have demonstrated its impracticability, there will always be reason to distrust the patriotism of those, who in any quarter may endeavor to weaken its bands.

In contemplating the causes which may disturb our Union, it occurs as matter of serious concern, that any ground should have been furnished for characterizing parties by *Geographical* discriminations—*Northern* and *Southern*—*Atlantic* and *Western*; whence designing men may endeavor to excite a belief that there is a real difference of local interests and views. One of the expedients of party to acquire influence, within particular districts, is to misrepresent the opinions and aims of other Districts. You cannot shield yourselves too much against the jealousies and heart burnings which spring from these misrepresentations. They tend to render alien to each other those who ought to be bound together by fraternal affection. The Inhabitants of our Western country have lately had a useful lesson on this head. They have seen, in the Negotiation by the Executive, and in the unanimous ratification by the Senate, of the Treaty with Spain, and in the universal satisfaction at that event, throughout the United States, a decisive proof how unfounded were the suspicions propagated among them of a policy in the General Government and in the Atlantic states unfriendly to their Interests in regard to the MISSISSIPPI. They have been witnesses to the formation of two Treaties, that with G: Britain and that with Spain, which secure to them every thing they could desire, in respect to our Foreign relations, towards confirming their prosperity. Will it not be their wisdom to rely for the preservation of these advantages on the UNION by which they were procured? Will they not henceforth be deaf to those advisers, if such there are, who would sever them from their Brethren and connect them with Aliens?

To the efficacy and permanency of Your Union, a Government for the whole is indispensable. No Alliances however strict between the parts can be an adequate substitute. They must inevitably experience the infractions and interruptions which all Alliances in all times have experienced. Sensible of this momentous truth, you have improved upon your first essay, by the adoption of a Constitution of Government, better calculated than your former for an intimate Union, and for the efficacious management of your common concerns. This government, the offspring of our own choice uninfluenced and unawed, adopted upon full investigation and mature deliberation, completely free in its principles, in the distribution of its powers, uniting security with energy, and containing within itself a provision for its own amendment, has a just claim to your confidence and your support. Respect for its authority, compliance with its Laws, acquiescence in its measures, are duties enjoined by the fundamental maxims of true Liberty. The basis of our political systems is the right of the people to make and to alter their Constitutions of Government. But the Constitution which at any time exists, till changed by an explicit and authentic act of the whole People, is sacredly obligatory upon all. The very idea of the power and the right of the People to establish Government presupposes the duty of every Individual to obey the established Government.

All obstructions to the execution of the Laws, all combinations and associations, under whatever plausible character, with the real design to direct, control, counteract, or awe the regular deliberation and action of the Constituted authorities are destructive of this fundamental principle and of fatal tendency. They serve to organize faction, to give it an artificial and extraordinary force—to put in the place of the delegated will of the Nation, the will of a party; often a small but artful and enterprising minority of the Community; and, according to the alternate triumphs of different parties, to make the public administration the Mirror of the ill concerted and incongruous projects of faction, rather than the Organ of consistent and wholesome plans digested by common councils and modified by mutual interests. However combinations or Associations of the above description may now and then answer popular ends, they are likely, in the course of time and things, to become potent engines, by which cunning, ambitious and unprincipled men will be enabled to subvert the Power of the People, and to usurp for themselves the reins of Government; destroying afterwards the very engines which have lifted them to unjust dominion.

Towards the preservation of your Government and the permanency of your present happy state, it is requisite, not only that you steadily discountenance irregular oppositions to its acknowledged authority, but also that you resist with care the spirit of innovation upon its principles however specious the pretexts. One method of assault may be to effect, in the forms of the Constitution, alterations which will impair the energy of the system, and thus to undermine what cannot be directly overthrown. In all the changes to which you may be invited, remember that time and habit are at least as necessary to fix the true character of Governments, as of other human institutions—that experience is the surest standard, by which to test the real tendency of the existing Constitution of a country—that facility in changes upon the credit of mere hypotheses and opinion exposes to perpetual change, from the endless variety of hypotheses and opinion: and remember, especially, that for the efficient management of your common interests, in a country so extensive as ours, a Government of as much vigor as is consistent with the perfect security of Liberty is indispensable—Liberty itself will find in such a Government, with powers properly distributed and adjusted, its surest Guardian. It is indeed little else than a name, where the Government is too feeble to withstand the enterprises of faction, to confine each member of the Society within the limits prescribed by the laws, and to maintain all in the secure and tranquil enjoyment of the rights of person and property.

I have already intimated to you the danger of Parties in the State, with particular reference to the founding of them on Geographical discriminations. Let me now take a more comprehensive view, and warn you in the most solemn manner against the baneful effects of the Spirit of Party, generally.

This spirit, unfortunately, is inseparable from our nature, having its root in the strongest passions of the human Mind. It exists under different shapes in all Governments, more or less stifled, controlled, or repressed; but in those of the popular form it is seen in its greatest rankness and is truly their worst enemy.

The alternate domination of one faction over another, sharpened by the spirit of revenge natural to party dissension, which in different ages and countries has perpetrated the most horrid enormities, is itself a frightful despotism. But this leads at length to a more formal and permanent despotism. The disorders and miseries, which result, gradually incline the minds of men to seek security and repose in the absolute power of an Individual: and sooner or later the chief of some prevailing faction more able or more fortunate than his competitors, turns this disposition to the purposes of his own elevation, on the ruins of Public Liberty.

Without looking forward to an extremity of this kind (which nevertheless ought not to be entirely out of sight) the common and continual mischiefs of the spirit of Party are sufficient to make it the interest and the duty of a wise People to discourage and restrain it.

It serves always to distract the Public Councils and enfeeble the Public Administration. It agitates the Community with ill founded jealousies and false alarms, kindles the animosity of one part against another, foments occasionally riot and insurrection. It opens the door to foreign influence and corruption, which find a facilitated access to the government itself through the channels of party passions. Thus the policy and the will of one country, are subjected to the policy and will of another.

There is an opinion that parties in free countries are useful checks upon the Administration of the Government and serve to keep alive the spirit of Liberty. This within certain limits is probably true—and in Governments of a Monarchical cast Patriotism may look with indulgence, if not with favor, upon the spirit of party. But in those of the popular character, in Governments purely elective, it is a spirit not to be encouraged. From their natural tendency, it is certain there will always be enough of that spirit for every salutary purpose. And there being constant danger of excess, the effort ought to be, by force of public opinion, to mitigate and assuage it. A fire not to be quenched; it demands a uniform vigilance to prevent its bursting into a flame, lest instead of warming it should consume.

It is important, likewise, that the habits of thinking in a free Country should inspire caution, in those entrusted with its administration, to confine themselves within their respective Constitutional spheres, avoiding in the exercise of the Powers of one department to encroach upon another. The spirit of encroachment tends to consolidate the powers of all the departments in one, and thus to create whatever the form of government, a real despotism. A just estimate of that love of power, and proneness to abuse it, which predominates in the human heart is sufficient to satisfy us of the truth of this position. The necessity of reciprocal checks in the exercise of political power; by dividing and distributing it into different depositories, and constituting each the Guardian of the Public Weal against invasions by the others, has been evinced by experiments ancient and modern; some of them in our country and under our own eyes. To preserve them must be as necessary as to institute them. If in the opinion of the People, the distribution or modification of the Constitutional powers be in any particular wrong, let it be corrected by an amendment in the way which the Constitution designates. But let there be no change by usurpation; for though this, in one instance, may be the instrument of good, it is the customary weapon by which free governments are destroyed. The precedent must always greatly overbalance in permanent evil any partial or transient benefit which the use can at any time yield.

Of all the dispositions and habits which lead to political prosperity, Religion and morality are indispensable supports. In vain would that man claim the tribute of Patriotism, who should labor to subvert these great Pillars of human happiness, these firmest props of the duties of Men and citizens. The mere

Politician, equally with the pious man ought to respect and to cherish them. A volume could not trace all their connections with private and public felicity. Let it simply be asked where is the security for property, for reputation, for life, if the sense of religious obligation *desert* the oaths, which are the instruments of investigation in Courts of Justice? And let us with caution indulge the supposition, that morality can be maintained without religion. Whatever may be conceded to the influence of refined education on minds of peculiar structure—reason and experience both forbid us to expect that National morality can prevail in exclusion of religious principle.

'Tis substantially true, that virtue or morality is a necessary spring of popular government. The rule indeed extends with more or less force to every species of free Government. Who that is a sincere friend to it can look with indifference upon attempts to shake the foundation of the fabric?

Promote then as an object of primary importance, Institutions for the general diffusion of knowledge. In proportion as the structure of a government gives force to public opinion, it is essential that public opinion should be enlightened.

As a very important source of strength and security cherish public credit. One method of preserving it is to use it as sparingly as possible: avoiding occasions of expense by cultivating peace, but remembering also that timely disbursements to prepare for danger frequently prevent much greater disbursements to repel it—avoiding likewise the accumulation of debt, not only by shunning occasions of expense, but by vigorous exertions in time of Peace to discharge the Debts which unavoidable wars may have occasioned, not ungenerously throwing upon posterity the burden which we ourselves ought to bear. The execution of these maxims belongs to your Representatives, but it is necessary that public opinion should cooperate. To facilitate to them the performance of their duty, it is essential that you should practically bear in mind, that towards the payment of debts there must be Revenue—that to have Revenue there must be taxes—that no taxes can be devised which are not more or less inconvenient and unpleasant—that the intrinsic embarrassment inseparable from the selection of the proper objects (which is always a choice of difficulties) ought to be a decisive motive for a candid construction of the conduct of the Government in making it, and for a spirit of acquiescence in the measures for obtaining Revenue which the public exigencies may at any time dictate.

Observe good faith and justice towards all Nations; cultivate peace and harmony with all—Religion and morality enjoin this conduct; and can it be that good policy does not equally enjoin it? It will be worthy of a free, enlightened, and, at no distant period, a great Nation, to give to mankind the magnanimous and too novel example of a People always guided by an exalted justice and benevolence. Who can doubt that in the course of time and things the fruits of such a plan would richly repay any temporary advantages which might be lost by a steady adherence to it? Can it be, that Providence has not connected the permanent felicity of a Nation with its virtue? The experiment, at least, is recommended by every sentiment which ennobles human Nature. Alas! Is it rendered impossible by its vices?

In the execution of such a plan, nothing is more essential than that permanent, inveterate antipathies against particular Nations and passionate attachments for others should be excluded; and that in place of them just and amicable feelings towards all should be cultivated. The Nation, which indulges towards another a habitual hatred, or a habitual fondness, is in some degree a slave. It is a slave to its animosity or to its affection, either of which is sufficient to lead it astray from its duty and its interest. Antipathy in one Nation against another disposes each more readily to offer insult and injury, to lay hold of slight causes of umbrage, and to be haughty and intractable, when accidental or trifling occasions of dispute occur. Hence frequent collisions, obstinate envenomed and bloody contests. The Nation, prompted by ill will and resentment sometimes impels to War the Government, contrary to the best calculations of policy. The Government sometimes participates in the national propensity, and adopts through passion what reason would reject; at other times, it makes the animosity of the nation subservient to projects of hostility instigated by pride, ambition and other sinister and pernicious motives. The peace often, sometimes perhaps the Liberty, of Nations has been the victim.

So likewise, a passionate attachment of one Nation for another produces a variety of evils. Sympathy for the favorite nation, facilitating the illusion of an imaginary common interest, in cases where no real common interest exists, and infusing into one the enmities of the other, betrays the former into a participation in the quarrels and Wars of the latter, without adequate inducement or justification: It leads also to concessions to the favorite Nation of privileges denied to others, which is apt doubly to injure the Nation making the concessions—by unnecessarily parting with what ought to have been retained—and by exciting jealousy, ill will, and a disposition to retaliate, in the parties from whom equal privileges are withheld: And it gives to ambitious, corrupted, or deluded citizens (who devote themselves to the favorite Nation) facility to betray, or sacrifice the interests of their own country, without odium, sometimes even with popularity; gilding with the appearances of a virtuous sense of obligation a commendable deference for public opinion, or a laudable zeal for public good, the base or foolish compliances of ambition, corruption or infatuation.

As avenues to foreign influence in innumerable ways, such attachments are particularly alarming to the truly enlightened and independent Patriot. How many opportunities do they afford to tamper with domestic factions, to practice the arts of seduction, to mislead public opinion, to influence or awe the public Councils! Such an attachment of a small or weak, towards a great and powerful Nation, dooms the former to be the satellite of the latter.

Against the insidious wiles of foreign influence (I conjure you to believe me, fellow citizens) the jealousy of a free people ought to be *constantly* awake; since history and experience prove that foreign influence is one of the most baneful foes of Republican Government. But that jealousy to be useful must be impartial; else it becomes the instrument of the very influence to be avoided, instead of a defense against it. Excessive partiality for one foreign nation and excessive dislike of another, cause those whom they actuate to see danger only on one side, and serve to veil and even second the arts of influence on the other. Real Patriots, who may resist the intrigues of the favorite, are liable to become suspected and odious; while its tools and dupes usurp the applause and confidence of the people, to surrender their interests.

The great rule of conduct for us, in regard to foreign Nations is in extending our commercial relations to have with them as little *political* connection as possible. So far as we have already formed engagements let them be fulfilled with perfect good faith. Here let us stop.

Europe has a set of primary interests, which to us have none, or a very remote relation. Hence she must be engaged in frequent controversies, the causes of which are essentially foreign to our concerns. Hence therefore it must be unwise in us to implicate ourselves, by artificial ties, in the ordinary vicissitudes of her politics, or the ordinary combinations and collisions of her friendships, or enmities.

Our detached and distant situation invites and enables us to pursue a different course. If we remain one People, under an efficient government, the period is not far off, when we may defy material injury from external annoyance; when we may take such an attitude as will cause the neutrality we may at any time resolve upon to be scrupulously respected; when belligerent nations, under the impossibility of making acquisitions upon us, will not lightly hazard the giving us provocation; when we may choose peace or War, as our interest guided by justice shall counsel.

Why forego the advantages of so peculiar a situation? Why quit our own to stand upon foreign ground? Why, by interweaving our destiny with that of any part of Europe, entangle our peace and prosperity in the toils of European ambition, Rivalship, Interest, Humor or Caprice?

'Tis our true policy to steer clear of permanent Alliances, with any portion of the foreign world—So far, I mean, as we are now at liberty to do it—for let me not be understood as capable of patronizing infidelity to existing engagements. (I hold the maxim no less applicable to public than to private affairs, that honesty is always the best policy). I repeat it therefore, let those engagements be observed in their genuine sense. But in my opinion, it is unnecessary and would be unwise to extend them.

Taking care always to keep ourselves, by suitable establishments, on a respectably defensive posture, we may safely trust to temporary alliances for extraordinary emergencies.

Harmony, liberal intercourse with all Nations, are recommended by policy, humanity and interest. But even our Commercial policy should hold an equal and impartial hand: neither seeking nor granting exclusive favors or preferences; consulting the natural course of things; diffusing and diversifying by gentle means the streams of Commerce, but forcing nothing; establishing, with Powers so disposed—in order to give trade a stable course, to define the rights of our merchants, and to enable the Government to support them—conventional rules of intercourse, the best that present circumstances and mutual opinion will permit, but temporary, and liable to be from time to time abandoned or varied, as experience and circumstances shall dictate; constantly keeping in view; that 'tis folly in one Nation to look for disinterested favors from another—that it must pay with a portion of its Independence for whatever it may accept under that character—that by such acceptance, it may place itself in the condition of having given equivalents for nominal favors and yet of being reproached with ingratitude for not giving more. There can be no greater error than to expect, or calculate upon real favors from Nation to Nation. 'Tis an illusion which experience must cure, which a just pride ought to discard.

In offering to you, my Countrymen, these counsels of an old and affectionate friend, I dare not hope they will make the strong and lasting impression, I could wish—that they will control the usual current of the passions, or prevent our Nation from running the course which has hitherto marked the Destiny of Nations: But if I may even flatter myself, that they may be productive of some partial benefit, some occasional good, that they may now and then recur to moderate the fury of party spirit, to warn against the mischiefs of foreign Intrigue, to guard against the Impostures of pretended patriotism—this hope will be a full recompense for the solicitude for your welfare, by which they have been dictated.

How far in the discharge of my Official duties, I have been guided by the principles which have been delineated, the public Records and other evidences of my conduct must witness to You and to the world. To myself, the assurance of my own conscience is, that I have at least believed myself to be guided by them.

In relation to the still subsisting War in Europe, my Proclamation of the 22d of April 1793 is the index to my Plan. Sanctioned by your approving voice and by that of your Representatives in both Houses of Congress, the spirit of that measure has continually governed me; uninfluenced by any attempts to deter or divert me from it.

After deliberate examination with the aid of the best lights I could obtain I was well satisfied that our country, under all the circumstances of the case, had a right to take, and was bound in duty and interest, to take a Neutral position. Having taken it, I determined, as far as should depend upon me, to maintain it, with moderation, perseverance and firmness.

The considerations which respect the right to hold this conduct, it is not necessary on this occasion to detail. I will only observe, that according to my understanding of the matter, that right, so far from being denied by any of the Belligerent Powers has been virtually admitted by all.

The duty of holding a Neutral conduct may be inferred, without any thing more, from the obligation which justice and humanity impose on every Nation, in cases in which it is free to act, to maintain inviolate the relations of Peace and amity towards other Nations.

The inducements of interest for observing that conduct will best be referred to your own reflections and experience. With me, a predominant motive has been to endeavor to gain time to our country to settle and mature its yet recent institutions, and to progress without interruption, to that degree of strength and consistency, which is necessary to give it, humanly speaking, the command of its own fortunes.

Though in reviewing the incidents of my Administration, I am unconscious of intentional error—I am nevertheless too sensible of my defects not to think it probable that I may have committed many errors. Whatever they may be I fervently beseech the Almighty to avert or mitigate the evils to which they may tend. I shall also carry with me the hope that my Country will never cease to view them with indulgence; and that after forty-five years of my life dedicated to its Service, with an upright zeal, the faults of incompetent abilities will be consigned to oblivion, as myself must soon be to the mansions of rest.

Relying on its kindness in this as in other things, and actuated by that fervent love towards it, which is so natural to a man, who views in it the native soil of himself and his progenitors for several Generations; I anticipate with pleasing expectation that retreat, in which I promise myself to realize, without alloy, the sweet enjoyment of partaking, in the midst of my fellow Citizens, the benign influence of good Laws under a free Government—the ever favorite object of my heart, and the happy reward, as I trust, of our mutual cares, labors and dangers.

Theodore Roosevelt

Citizenship in a Republic
1910 AD, United States

The average citizen must be a good citizen if our republics are to succeed. The stream will not permanently rise higher than the main source; and the main source of national power and national greatness is found in the average citizenship of the nation. . . . and the average cannot be kept high unless the standard of the leaders is very much higher.

Selections

Today I shall speak to you on the subject of individual citizenship, the one subject of vital importance to you, my hearers, and to me and my countrymen, because you and we are great citizens of great democratic republics. A democratic republic such as ours—an effort to realize in its full sense government by, of, and for the people—represents the most gigantic of all

possible social experiments, the one fraught with great responsibilities alike for good and evil. The success of republics like
yours and like ours means the glory, and our failure the despair,
of mankind; and for you and for us the question of the quality
of the individual citizen is supreme.

Under other forms of government, under the rule of one
man or very few men, the quality of the leaders is all-important.
If, under such governments, the quality of the rulers is high
enough, then the nations for generations lead a brilliant career,
and add substantially to the sum of world achievement, no matter how low the quality of the average citizen; because the average citizen is an almost negligible quantity in working out the
final results of that type of national greatness. But with you and
us the case is different.

With you here, and with us in my own home, in the long run,
success or failure will be conditioned upon the way in which the
average man, the average woman, does his or her duty, first in
the ordinary, everyday affairs of life, and next in those great occasional cries which call for heroic virtues. The average citizen
must be a good citizen if our republics are to succeed. The stream
will not permanently rise higher than the main source; and the
main source of national power and national greatness is found
in the average citizenship of the nation. Therefore it behooves us
to do our best to see that the standard of the average citizen is
kept high; and the average cannot be kept high unless the standard of the leaders is very much higher.

It is well if a large proportion of the leaders in any republic,
in any democracy, are, as a matter of course, drawn from the

classes represented in this audience today; but only provided that those classes possess the gifts of sympathy with plain people and of devotion to great ideals. You and those like you have received special advantages; you have all of you had the opportunity for mental training; many of you have had leisure; most of you have had a chance for enjoyment of life far greater than comes to the majority of your fellows. To you and your kind much has been given, and from you much should be expected. Yet there are certain failings against which it is especially incumbent that both men of trained and cultivated intellect, and men of inherited wealth and position, should especially guard themselves, because to these failings they are especially liable; and if yielded to, their—your—chances of useful service are at an end.

Let the man of learning, the man of lettered leisure, beware of that queer and cheap temptation to pose to himself and to others as a cynic, as the man who has outgrown emotions and beliefs, the man to whom good and evil are as one. The poorest way to face life is to face it with a sneer. There are many men who feel a kind of twisted pride in cynicism; there are many who confine themselves to criticism of the way others do what they themselves dare not even attempt. There is no more unhealthy being, no man less worthy of respect, than he who either really holds, or feigns to hold, an attitude of sneering disbelief toward all that is great and lofty, whether in achievement or in that noble effort which, even if it fails, comes second to achievement.

A cynical habit of thought and speech, a readiness to criticize work which the critic himself never tries to perform, an intellectual aloofness which will not accept contact with life's realities—all these are marks, not as the possessor would fain to think, of superiority, but of weakness. They mark the men unfit to bear their part painfully in the stern strife of living, who seek, in the affectation of contempt for the achievement of others, to hide from others and from themselves their own weakness. The role is easy; there is none easier, save only the role of the man who sneers alike at both criticism and performance.

It is not the critic who counts; not the man who points out how the strong man stumbles or where the doer of deeds could have done them better. The credit belongs to the man who is actually in the arena, whose face is marred by dust and sweat and blood; who strives valiantly; who errs, who comes short again and again, because there is no effort without error and shortcoming; but who does actually strive to do the deeds; who knows the great enthusiasms, the great devotions; who spends himself in a worthy cause; who at the best knows in the end the triumph of high achievement, and who at the worst, if he fails, at least fails while daring greatly, so that his place shall never be with those cold and timid souls who neither know victory nor defeat.

Shame on the man of cultivated taste who permits refinement to develop into fastidiousness that unfits him for doing the rough work of a workaday world. Among the free peoples who govern themselves there is but a small field of usefulness open for the men of cloistered life who shrink from contact with their fellows. Still less room is there for those who deride or slight what is done by those who actually bear the brunt of the day; nor yet for those others who always profess that they would like to take action, if only the conditions of life were not exactly what they actually are. The man who does nothing cuts the same sordid figure in the pages of history, whether he be cynic, or fop, or voluptuary.

There is little use for the being whose tepid soul knows nothing of the great and generous emotion, of the high pride, the stern belief, the lofty enthusiasm, of the men who quell the storm and ride the thunder. Well for these men if they succeed; well also, though not so well, if they fail, given only that they have nobly ventured, and have put forth all their heart and strength. It is war-worn Hotspur, spent with hard fighting, he of the many errors and the valiant end, over whose memory we love to linger, not over the memory of the young lord who "but for the vile guns would have been a valiant soldier."

Winston Churchill

Consistency in Politics
1932 AD, United Kingdom

---

*No one can read the Burke of Liberty and the Burke
of Authority without feeling that here was the same
man pursuing the same ends, seeking the same ideals
of society and Government, and defending them from
assaults, now from one extreme, now from the other.*

No one has written more boldly on this subject than
Emerson:

Why should you keep your head over your shoulder?
Why drag about this corpse of your memory, lest you
contradict somewhat you have stated in this or that
public place? Suppose you should contradict yourself; what then? . . . A foolish consistency is the hob-
goblin of little minds, adored by little statesmen and
philosophers and divines. . . . Speak what you think
now in hard words and tomorrow speak what

tomorrow thinks in hard words again, though it contradict everything you said today.

These are considerable assertions, and they may well stimulate thought upon this well-worn topic. A distinction should
be drawn at the outset between two kinds of political inconsistency. First, a Statesman in contact with the moving current of
events and anxious to keep the ship on an even keel and steer
a steady course may lean all his weight now on one side and
now on the other. His arguments in each case when contrasted
can be shown to be not only very different in character, but
contradictory in spirit and opposite in direction: yet his object
will throughout have remained the same. His resolves, his
wishes, his outlook may have been unchanged; his methods
may be verbally irreconcilable. We cannot call this inconsistency. In fact it may be claimed to be the truest consistency. The
only way a man can remain consistent amid changing circumstances is to change with them while preserving the same dominating purpose. Lord Halifax on being derided as a trimmer
made the celebrated reply: "I trim as the temperate zone trims
between the climate in which men are roasted and the climate
in which they are frozen."

No greater example in this field can be found than Burke. His
Thoughts on the Present Discontents, his writings and speeches
on the conciliation of America, form the main and lasting ar-
mory of Liberal opinion throughout the English-speaking world.
His *Letters on a Regicide Peace*, and *Reflections on the French
Revolution*, will continue to furnish Conservatives for all time

with the most formidable array of opposing weapons. On the one hand he is revealed as a foremost apostle of Liberty, on the other as the redoubtable champion of Authority. But a charge of political inconsistency applied to this great life appears a mean and petty thing. History easily discerns the reasons and forces which actuated him, and the immense changes in the problems he was facing which evoked from the same profound mind and sincere spirit these entirely contrary manifestations.

His soul revolted against tyranny, whether it appeared in the aspect of a domineering Monarch and a corrupt Court and Parliamentary system, or whether, mouthing the watchwords of a nonexistent liberty, it towered up against him in the dictation of a brutal mob and wicked sect. No one can read the Burke of Liberty and the Burke of Authority without feeling that here was the same man pursuing the same ends, seeking the same ideals of society and Government, and defending them from assaults, now from one extreme, now from the other. The same danger approached the same man from different directions and in different forms, and the same man turned to face it with incomparable weapons, drawn from the same armory, used in a different quarter, but for the same purpose.

It is inevitable that frequent changes should take place in the region of action. A policy is pursued up to a certain point; it becomes evident at last that it can be carried no further. New facts arise which clearly render it obsolete; new difficulties, which make it impracticable. A new and possibly the opposite solution presents itself with overwhelming force. To abandon the old policy is often necessarily to adopt the new. It sometimes happens that the same men, the same Government, the same Party have to execute this *volte face*. It may be their duty to do so because it is the sole manner of discharging their responsibilities, or because they are the only combination strong enough to do what is needed in the new circumstances. In such a case the inconsistency is not merely verbal, but actual, and ought to be boldly avowed. In place of arguments for coercion, there must be arguments for conciliation; and these must come from the same lips as the former. But all this may be capable of reasonable and honorable explanation. Statesmen may say bluntly, "We have failed to coerce; we have now to conciliate," or alternatively, "We have failed to conciliate; we have now to coerce."

Ireland with its mysterious and sinister influence has been responsible for many changes of this kind in British politics. We see Mr. Gladstone in 1886 after five years of coercion, after the fiercest denunciation of Irish Nationalists "marching through rapine to the disintegration of the Empire," turn in a month to those policies of reconciliation to which the rest of his life was devoted. Mr. Gladstone in his majestic and saintly manner gave many comforting and convincing reasons for his change, and there is no doubt that his whole nature was uplifted and inspired by his new departure. But behind all the eloquence and high-sounding declamation there was a very practical reason for his change, which in private at any rate he did not conceal.

During the interval between the fall of his Government in 1885 and his resumption of power in 1886, a Conservative Government held office with the support of the Irish vote, and the people—wrongly no doubt but sincerely—thought the Conservatives were themselves meditating a solution of the Irish problem on Home Rule lines. Confronted with this supposed fact he felt it impossible for the Liberal Party to march further along the path of coercion and a denial of Irish claims. But Mr. Gladstone was wrong in his judgment of the impending Conservative action. The Conservative Party would never at that stage have been capable of a Home Rule policy. They might have coquetted with the Irish vote as a maneuver in their fierce political battle with the Liberals; but any decided advance towards Home Rule would have split them from end to end, dethroned their leaders in such a course, and destroyed the power of the Party as a governing instrument.

Mr. Gladstone gave to his opponents through this miscalculation what was virtually a twenty years' reign of power. Nevertheless the judgment of history will probably declare that Mr. Gladstone was right both in his resistance to Home Rule up to a certain point and in his espousal of it thereafter. Certainly the change which he made upon this question in 1886, for which he was so much condemned, was in every way a lesser change than that which was made by the whole Conservative Party on this same question thirty-five years later in 1921.

Apart from action in the march of events, there is an inconsistency arising from a change of mood or heart. "*Le coeur a ses raisons que la raison ne connaît pas.*" Few men avoid such changes in their lives, and few public men have been able to conceal them. Usually youth is for freedom and reform, maturity for judicious compromise, and old age for stability and repose. The normal progression is from Left to Right, and often from extreme Left to extreme Right. Mr. Gladstone's progress was by a striking exception in the opposite direction. In the immense period covered by his life he moved steadily and irresistibly from being "the rising hope of stern unbending Tories" to become the greatest Liberal statesman of the nineteenth century.

Enormous was the change of mood which this august transition represented. From the young Member of Parliament whose speech against the abolition of slavery attracted the attention of the House of Commons in 1833, from the famous Minister who supported the Confederate States against the North in the sixties, to the fiery orator who pleaded the cause of Bulgarian independence in the eighties, and the veteran Premier, the last scraps of whose matchless strength were freely offered in the nineties to the cause of Irish self-government—it was a transit almost astronomical in its scale.

It were a thankless theme to examine how far ambition to lead played its unconscious but unceasing part in such an evolution. Ideas acquire a momentum of their own. The stimulus of a vast concentration of public support is almost irresistible in its potency. The resentments engendered by the warfare of opponents, the practical responsibilities of a Party Leader—all take a hand. And in the main great numbers are at least an explanation for great changes. "I have always marched," said Napoleon, "with the opinion of four or five millions of men." To which, without risking the reproach of cynicism, we may add two other sayings: "In a democratic country possessing representative institutions it is occasionally necessary to defer to the opinions of other people"; and, "I am their leader; I must follow them." The integrity of Mr. Gladstone's career is redeemed by the fact that these two last considerations played a far smaller part in his life than in those of many lesser public men whose consistency has never been impugned.

It is evident that a political leader responsible for the direction of affairs must, even if unchanging in heart or objective, give his counsel now on the one side and now on the other of many public issues. Take for instance the strength and expense of the armed forces of a country in any particular period. This depends upon no absolute or natural law. It relates simply to the circumstances of the time and to the view that a man may hold of the probability of dangers, actual or potential, which threaten his country. Would there, for instance, be any inconsistency in a British Minister urging the most extreme and rapid naval preparations in the years preceding the outbreak of the Great War with Germany, and advocating a modest establishment and strict retrenchment in the years following the destruction of the German naval power?

He might think that the danger had passed and had carried away with it the need for intense preparation. He might believe that a long period of peace would follow the exhaustion of the World War, and that financial and economic recovery were more necessary to the country than continuous armed strength. He might think that the Air was taking the place of the Sea in military matters. And he might be right and truly consistent both in the former and in the latter advocacy. But it would be easy to show a wide discrepancy between the sets of arguments in the two periods. Questions of this kind do not depend upon the intrinsic logic of the reasoning used on the one hand or the other, but on taking a just view of the governing facts of different periods. Such changes must, however, be considered in each particular case with regard to the personal situation of the individual. If it can be shown that he swims with the current in both cases, his titles to a true consistency must be more studiously examined than if he swims against it.

A more searching scrutiny should also be applied to changes of view in relation not to events but to systems of thought and doctrine. In modern British politics no greater contrast can be found than in comparing the Free Trade speeches of the late Mr. Joseph Chamberlain as President of the Board of Trade in the early eighties, with the Protectionist speeches which he delivered during the Tariff campaign at the beginning of the nineteenth century. Here we are dealing not with the turbulent flow of events, but with precise methods of thought. Those who read Mr. Chamberlain's Free Trade speeches will find that almost every economic argument which he used in 1904 was foreseen and countered by him in 1884. Yet the sincerity of his later views was generally accepted by friends and opponents alike.

And after all, once he had come to think differently on economic subjects, was it not better that he should unhesitatingly give his country the benefit of his altered convictions? Still, it must be observed that the basis of reasoning had changed very little in the twenty years' interval, that the problem was mainly an abstract one in its character, and that it was substantially the same problem. There need be no impeachment of honesty of purpose or of a zealous and unceasing care for the public interest. But there is clearly in this case a contradiction of argument in regard to the same theory which amounts to self-stultification.

We may illustrate this distinction further. Mr. Chamberlain argued in 1884 that a tax on imports was paid by the home consumer, and in 1904 that it was paid, very largely at any rate, by the foreigner. We cannot help feeling that the reasoning processes underlying these two conclusions are fundamentally incompatible, and it is hard to understand how a man who once saw the one process so clearly should subsequently have visualized and accepted the opposite process with equal vehemence and precision. It would have been better, tactically at any rate, for Mr. Chamberlain to have relinquished the abstract argument altogether and to have relied exclusively in his advocacy upon the facts—the world facts—which were really his reasons, the importance of consolidating the British Empire by means of a Zollverein, and the necessity of rallying support for that policy among the British industrial interests and the Conservative working classes; for these considerations, in his view, overruled—whether or not they contradicted—the validity of his purely economic conviction.

A Statesman should always try to do what he believes is best in the long view for his country, and he should not be dissuaded from so acting by having to divorce himself from a great body of doctrine to which he formerly sincerely adhered. Those, however, who are forced to these gloomy choices must regard their situation in this respect as unlucky.

The great Sir Robert Peel must certainly be looked on as falling within the sweep of this shadow. Of him Lord John Russell sourly observed:

> He has twice changed his opinion on the greatest political question of his day. Once when the Protestant Church was to be defended and the Protestant Constitution rescued from the attacks of the Roman Catholics, which it was said would ruin it, the Right Honorable Gentleman undertook to lead the defense. Again, the Corn Laws were powerfully attacked in this House and out of it. He took the lead of his Party to resist a change and to defend Protection. I think, on both occasions, he has come to a wise conclusion, and to a decision most beneficial to his country; first, when he repealed the Roman Catholic disabilities, and, secondly, when he abolished Protection. But that those who followed him—men that had committed themselves to these questions, on the faith of his political wisdom, on the faith of his sagacity, led by the great eloquence and ability he displayed in debate—that when they found he had changed his opinions and proposed measures different from those on the faith of which they had followed him—that they should exhibit warmth and resentment was not only natural, but I should have been surprised if they had not displayed it.

This was a hard, yet not unjust, commentary upon the career of one of the most eminent and one of the noblest of our public men; for here not merely a change of view is in question, but the workaday good faith of a leader towards those who had depended upon his guidance and had not shared in his conversion.

A change of Party is usually considered a much more serious breach of consistency than a change of view. In fact as long as a man works with a Party he will rarely find himself accused of inconsistency, no matter how widely his opinions at one time on any subject can be shown to have altered. Yet Parties are subject to changes and inconsistencies not less glaring than those of individuals. How should it be otherwise in the fierce swirl of Parliamentary conflict and Electoral fortune? Change with a Party, however inconsistent, is at least defended by the power of numbers. To remain constant when a Party changes is to excite invidious challenge. Moreover, a separation from Party affects all manner of personal relations and sunders old comradeship. Still, a sincere conviction, in harmony with the needs of the time and upon a great issue, will be found to override all other factors; and it is right and in the public interest that it should.

Politics is a generous profession. The motives and characters of public men, though constantly criticized, are in the end broadly and fairly judged. But, anyhow, where is Consistency today? The greatest Conservative majority any modern Parliament has seen is led by the creator of the Socialist party, and dutifully cheers the very Statesman who a few years ago was one of the leaders of a General Strike which he only last year tried to make again legal. A life-long Free Trader at the Board of Trade has framed and passed amid the loudest plaudits a whole-hearted Protectionist Tariff. The Government which only yesterday took office to keep the sterling from falling, is now supported for its exertions to keep it from rising. These astonishing tergiversations could be multiplied: but they suffice. Let us quote the charitable lines of Crabbe, in the hopes of a similar measure of indulgence:

> Minutely trace man's life; year after year,
> Through all his days let all his deeds appear.
> And then, though some may in that life be strange,
> Yet there appears no vast nor sudden change;
> The links that bind those various deeds are seen.
> And no mysterious void is left between.

Charles de Gaulle

Edge of the Sword
1932 AD, France

*When the position becomes serious, when the nation
is in urgent need of leaders with initiative who can
be relied upon, and are willing to take risks, then . . .
credit goes to whom credit is due. A sort of a ground
swell brings the man of character to the surface.*

On Character (Selections)

When faced with the challenge of events, the man of character has recourse to himself. His instinctive response is to leave his mark on action, to take responsibility for it, to make it *his own business*. Far from seeking shelter behind his professional superiors, taking refuge in textbooks, or making the regulations bear the responsibility for any decision he may make, he sets his shoulders, takes a firm stand, and looks the problem straight in the face. It is not that he wishes to turn a blind eye to orders, or to sweep aside advice, but only that he is passionately anxious to exert his own will, to make up his own mind. It is not that he is unaware of the risks involved, or careless of consequences, but that he takes their measure honestly, and frankly accepts them.

Better still, he embraces action with the pride of a master; for if he takes a hand in it, it will become his, and he is ready to enjoy success on condition that it is really *his own*, and that he derives no profit from it. He is equally prepared to bear the weight of failure, though not without a bitter sense of satisfaction. In short, a fighter who finds within himself all the zest and support he needs, a gambler more intent on success than profits, a man who pays his debts with his own money lends nobility to action. Without him there is but the dreary task of the slave; thanks to him, it becomes the divine sport of the hero.

This does not mean that he carries out his purpose unaided. Others share in it who are not without the merit of self-sacrifice and obedience, and give of their best when carrying out his orders. Some there are who even contribute to his planning—technicians or advisers. But it is character that supplies the essential element, the creative touch, the divine spark; in other words, the basic fact of initiative. Just as talent gives to a work of art a special stamp of understanding and expression, character imparts its own dynamic quality to the elements of action, and gives it personality which . . . makes it live and move, just as the talent of the artist breathes life into matter.

The power to vivify an undertaking implies energy sufficient to shoulder the burden of its consequences. The man of character finds an especial attractiveness in difficulty, since it is only by coming to grips with difficulty that he can realize his potentialities. Whether or no he proves himself the stronger is a matter between it and him. He is a jealous lover and will share with no one the prizes or the pains that may be his as a result of trying to overcome obstacles. Whatever the cost to himself, he looks for no higher reward than the harsh pleasure of knowing himself to be the man responsible.

The passion of self-reliance is obviously accompanied by some roughness in method. The man of character incorporates in his own person the severity inherent in his effort. This is felt by his subordinates, and at times they groan under it. In any event, a leader of this quality is inevitably aloof, for there can be no authority without prestige, nor prestige unless he keeps his distance. Those under his command mutter in whispers about his arrogance and the demands he makes. But once action starts, criticism disappears. The man of character then draws to himself the hopes and the wills of everyone as the magnet draws iron.

When the crisis comes, it is him they follow, it is he who carries the burden on his own shoulders, even though they collapse under it. . . . The knowledge that the lesser men have confidence in him exalts the man of character. The confidence of those under him gives him a sense of obligation. It strengthens his determination but also increases his benevolence, for he is a born protector. If success attends upon his efforts, he distributes its advantages with a generous hand. If he meets with failure, he will not let the blame fall on anybody but himself. The security he offers is repaid by the esteem of his men.

In his relationship with superiors he is generally at a disadvantage. He is too sure of himself, too conscious of his strength to let his conduct be influenced by a mere wish to please. . . . All he asks is that he shall be given a task to do, and then be left alone to do it. . . .

And so it comes about that the authorities dread any officer who has the gift of making decisions and cares nothing for routine and soothing words: "Arrogant and undisciplined" is what the mediocrities say of him, treating the thoroughbred with a tender mouth as they would a donkey which refuses to move, not realizing that asperity is, more often than not, the reverse side of a strong character, that you can only lean on something that offers resistance, and that resolute and inconvenient men are to be preferred to easy-going natures without initiative.

But when the position becomes serious, when the nation is in urgent need of leaders with initiative who can be relied upon, and are willing to take risks, then matters are seen in a very different light, and credit goes to whom credit is due. A sort of a ground swell brings the man of character to the surface. His advice is listened to, his abilities are praised, and his true worth becomes apparent. To him is entrusted, as a matter of course, the difficult task, the direction of the main effort, the decisive mission. Everything he suggests is given serious consideration; all his demands are met. He . . . does not take advantage of this change in his fortunes, but shows a generous temperament and responds wholeheartedly when he is called upon. Scarcely . . .

does he taste the sweet savor of revenge, for his every faculty is brought to bear on the action he must take.

This rallying to character when danger threatens is the outward manifestation of an instinctive urge, for all men at heart realize the supreme value of self-reliance, and know that without it there can be no action of value. In the last resort, we must, to quote Cicero, "judge all conduct in the light of the best examples available," for nothing great has ever been achieved without that passion and that confidence which is to be found only in the man of character. . . .

It goes without saying that the successes achieved by great men have always depended on their possessing many different faculties. Character alone, if unsupported by other qualities, results only in rashness and obstinacy. On the other hand, purely intellectual gifts, even of the highest order, are not sufficient. History is filled with examples of men who, though they were gifted beyond the ordinary, saw their labors brought to nothing because they were lacking in character. Whether serving, or betraying, their masters in the most expert fashion, they were entirely uncreative. Notable they may have been, but famous never.

Acknowledgments

First and foremost, I would like to thank the Intercollegiate Studies Institute for the privilege of serving as its president and CEO and for allowing me the time to write and edit this book on statesmanship. I am also grateful for the education I received at Hillsdale College where my interest in the mirror-for-princes genre was born over a decade ago, thanks in no small part to Larry Arnn and Stephen Smith.

I am appreciative of Amanda Burtka, John Burtka III, Daniel McCarthy, Daniel Mahoney, Joseph Prud'homme, Tom Buchanan, Spencer Kashmanian, Yual Levin, and Joshua Mitchell for feedback on my manuscript, as well as to Francis Oakley, Harvey Mansfield, Michael Anton, and Victor Davis Hanson for input on the selection of texts.

Bibliography

Agapetus. *Advice to the Emperor Justinian*. In *Three Political Voices from the Age of Justinian: Agapetus,* Advice to the Emperor; Dialogue on Political Science; *Paul the Silentiary,* Description of Hagia Sophia, translated by Peter N. Bell, 99–123. Liverpool: Liverpool University Press, 2010.

al-Farabi, Abu Nasr Muhammad. *Alfarabi: The Political Writings; "Selected Aphorisms" and Other Texts*. Translated by Charles E. Butterworth. 10–13, 27–28, 37–38, 63–64. Ithaca and London: Cornell University Press, 2001. Internet Archive. https://archive.org/stream/AlfarabiSelectedApho rismsAndOtherTexts/Alfarabi%20-%20Selected%20 aphorisms%20and%20other%20texts_djvu.txt.

Ambler, Wayne. "Xenophon's *Education of Cyrus*." Introduction to *The Education of Cyrus*, by Xenophon, 1–18. Ithaca, New York: Cornell University Press, 2001.

Aquinas, Thomas. *De Regno: On Kingship, to the King of Cypress*. Edited by I. Th. Eschmann and Joseph Kenny. Translated by Gerald B. Phelan. Book I, chapters 2–3; 8–11; 13; 15–16. Toronto: Pontifical Institute of Mediaeval Studies, 1949.

Aristotle. *The Nicomachean Ethics of Aristotle*. Edited by J. A. Smith. Book IV, chapter 4. Project Gutenberg, 2021. Accessed June 23, 2023. https://www.gutenberg.org/cache /epub/8438/pg8438-images.html.

Aristotle. *Nicomachean Ethics: Translation, Glossary, and Introductory Essay*. Translated by Joe Sachs. Newburyport, Massachusetts: Focus Publishing, 2002.

Augustine. *The City of God*. Vol. 1. Translated by Marcus Dods. Book V, chapters 24–25. Edinburgh: T. & T. Clark, 1871; Project Gutenberg, 2014. https://www.gutenberg.org/cache /epub/45304/pg45304-images.html#Page_177.

Bell, Peter N. Introduction to *Three Political Voices from the Age of Justinian: Agapetus*, Advice to the Emperor; Dialogue on Political Science; *Paul the Silentiary*, Description of Hagia Sophia, translated by Peter N. Bell, 1–97. Liverpool: Liverpool University Press, 2010.

Butterworth, Charles E. Preface to *Alfarabi: The Political Writings; "Selected Aphorisms" and Other Texts*, ix–xiii, translated by Charles E. Butterworth. Internet Archive. Ithaca and London: Cornell University Press, 2001. https:// archive.org/stream/AlfarabiSelectedAphorismsAndOther Texts/Alfarabi%20-%20Selected%20aphorisms%20and%20 other%20texts_djvu.txt.

Churchill, Winston. "Consistency in Politics." For quotes reproduced from the speeches, works and writings of Winston S. Churchill: Reproduced with permission of Curtis Brown, London on behalf of The Estate of Winston S. Churchill © The Estate of Winston S. Churchill.

Cicero, Marcus Tullius. *Ethical Writings of Cicero: De Officiis, De Senectute, De Amicitia, and Scipio's Dream.* Translated by Andrew P. Peabody. Book I. Boston, Massachusetts: Little, Brown, and Company, 1887.

Cicero, Marcus Tullius. *On Obligations.* Translated by P. G. Walsh. Oxford: Oxford University Press, 2008.

de Gaulle, Charles. "On Character." In *The Edge of the Sword*, translated by Gerard Hopkins, 41–46. New York, New York: Faber and Faber, Ltd., 1960.

Erasmus, Desiderius. *The Education of a Christian Prince.* Translated by Lester K. Born. Chapters 3 and 6. New York, New York: Octagon Books, 1963.

Erasmus, Desiderius. *The Education of a Christian Prince.* Edited by Lisa Jardine. Cambridge, United Kingdom: Cambridge University Press, 1997.

Eusebius Pamphilus. *The Life of the Blessed Emperor Constantine, in Four Books, from 306 to 337 A.D.* Book I, chapters 43–46; book II, chapters 24, 45, and 56; book IV, chapters 18, 31, and 75. London: Samuel Bagster and Sons, 1845. Accessed August 3, 2023, https://archive.org/details/eusebius-life -of-constantine-and-orations/page/n1/mode/2up.

Han Feizi. "The Difficulties of Persuasion." In *Basic Writings*, translated by Burton Watson, 73–79. New York, New York: Columbia University Press, 2003.

Jardine, Lisa. Introduction to *Erasmus: The Education of a Christian Prince*, vii–xxiv. Edited by Lisa Jardine. Cambridge, United Kingdom: Cambridge University Press, 1997.

Kauṭilya. *Arthaśāstra*. Translated by R. Shamasastry. Book I, chapters 6–8, 19; book VI, chapter 1. Bangalore: The Government Press, 1915. https://archive.org/details/in.ernet .dli.2015.70130/page/n5/mode/2up.

Machiavelli, Niccolò. *The Prince*. Translated by Harvey C. Mansfield. Chicago, Illinois: University of Chicago Press, 1998.

Machiavelli, Niccolò. *The Prince*. Translated by W. K. Marriott. Project Gutenberg, 2022. Accessed June 23, 2023. https:// www.gutenberg.org/cache/epub/1232/pg1232-images.html.

Mahoney, Daniel J. *The Statesman as Thinker: Portraits of Greatness, Courage, and Moderation*. New York, New York: Encounter Books, 2022.

Mansfield, Harvey C. Introduction to *The Prince*, by Niccolò Machiavelli, vii–xxvii, translated by Harvey C. Mansfield. Chicago, Illinois: University of Chicago Press, 1998.

More, Thomas. *Utopia*. Edited by Henry Morely. Project Gutenberg, 2021. Accessed June 23, 2023. https://www .gutenberg.org/cache/epub/2130/pg2130-images.html #chap02.

Oakley, Francis. *Empty Bottles of Gentilism: Kingship and the Divine in Late Antiquity and the Early Middle Ages (to 1050)*.

The Emergence of Western Political Thought in the Latin Middle Ages, vol. 1. New Haven, Connecticut: Yale University Press, 2010.

Oakley, Francis. *The Mortgage of the Past: Reshaping the Ancient Political Inheritance (1050–1300)*. The Emergence of Western Political Thought in the Latin Middle Ages, vol. 2. New Haven, Connecticut: Yale University Press, 2012.

Pizan, Christine de. *The Book of the Body Politic*. Edited and translated by Kate Langdon Forhan. Cambridge, United Kingdom: Cambridge University Press, 1994. Chapters 6, 14–16, and 21.

Roosevelt, Theodore. "Citizenship in a Republic." Address at the Sorbonne in Paris, France, April 23, 1910. Edited by Gerhard Peters and John T. Woolley. The American Presidency Project. https://www.presidency.ucsb.edu /documents/address-the-sorbonne-paris-france-citizenship-republic.

The Sacred Bible, Catholic Public Domain Version, Original Edition. Translated by Ronald L. Conte Jr. http://www .sacredbible.org/catholic/OT-18_Judith.htm.

Walsh, P. G. Introduction to *On Obligations*, by Marcus Tullius Cicero, ix–xlvii. Oxford: Oxford University Press, 2008.

Washington, George. "Farewell Address." Address on September 19, 1796. In *1 April–21 September 1796*. Vol. 20 of *The Papers of George Washington*, Presidential Series, edited by David R. Hoth and William M. Ferraro. https://founders.archives .gov/documents/Washington/05-20-02-0440-0002.

Xenophon. *Cyropaedia: The Education of Cyrus.* Translated by Henry Graham Dakyns. Edited by F. M. Stawell. Project Gutenberg, 2011. Accessed June 23, 2023. https://www.gutenberg.org/cache/epub/2085/pg2085-images.html.

Xenophon. *The Education of Cyrus.* Translated by Wayne Ambler. Ithaca, New York: Cornell University Press, 2001.

Notes

Introduction

1. Emphasis mine. Wayne Ambler, "Xenophon's *Education of Cyrus*," introduction in Xenophon, *The Education of Cyrus*, trans. Wayne Ambler (Ithaca and London, New York: Cornell University Press, 2001), 2.
2. Ibid.
3. Francis Oakley, *Empty Bottles of Gentilism: Kingship and the Divine in Late Antiquity and the Early Middle Ages (to 1050)*, The Emergence of Western Political Thought in the Latin Middle Ages, vol. 1 (New Haven, Connecticut: Yale University Press, 2010).
4. Brackets Ambler's. Ambler, "Xenophon's *Education of Cyrus*," 4.
5. Xenophon, *Cyropaedia: The Education of Cyrus*, trans. Henry Graham Dakyns, rev. F. M. Stawell (Project Gutenberg: 2000).
6. P. G. Walsh, introduction to *Cicero: On Obligations* (Oxford: Oxford University Press, 2008), xxvii.
7. Marcus Tullius Cicero, *On Obligations*, trans. P. G. Walsh (Oxford: Oxford University Press, 2008), 81.
8. Han Fei, "The Difficulties of Persuasion," in *Basic Writings*, trans. Burton Watson (New York, New York: Columbia University Press, 2003), 81.
9. Han Fei, "The Five Vermin," in *Basic Writings*, trans. Burton Watson (New York, New York: Columbia University Press, 2003), 118.

10. Oakley, *Empty Bottles of Gentilism.*

11. Aurelius Augustine, *The City of God,* vol. 1, trans. Marcus Dods (Edinburgh: T. & T. Clark, 1871; Project Gutenberg, 2014), book V.

12. Thomas Aquinas, *De Regno: On Kingship, to the King of Cyprus,* ed. I. Th. Eschmann and Joseph Kenny, trans. Gerald B. Phelan (Toronto: Pontifical Institute of Mediaeval Studies, 1949), 36.

13. Kate Langdon Forhan, introduction to Christine de Pizan, *The Book of the Body Politic* (Cambridge, United Kingdom: Cambridge University Press, 1994), xiii–xxiv.

14. Peter N. Bell, Introduction to *Three Political Voices from the Age of Justinian: Agapetus—"Advice to the Emperor"; "Dialogue on Political Science"; Paul the Silentiary—"Description of Hagia Sophia,"* translated by Peter N. Bell (Liverpool: Liverpool University Press, 2010), 47.

15. John A. Burtka, "Aristopopulism: The Fusionism America Needs," The American Mind, March 7, 2019, https://americanmind.org/features /nationalism-for-the-twenty-first-century/aristopopulism-the-new -fusionism-america-needs/.

16. Agapetus, "Advice to the Emperor Justinian," in *Three Political Voices from the Age of Justinian: Agapetus—"Advice to the Emperor"; "Dialogue on Political Science"; Paul the Silentiary—"Description of Hagia Sophia,"* trans. Peter N. Bell (Liverpool: Liverpool University Press, 2010).

17. Ibid.

18. Charles E. Butterworth, Preface to *Alfarabi, The Political Writings: "Selected Aphorisms" and Other Texts* (Ithaca and London: Cornell University Press, 2001), ix–xiii, https://archive.org/stream/AlfarabiSele ctedAphorismsAndOtherTexts/Alfarabi%20-%20Selected%20 aphorisms%20and%20other%20texts_djvu.txt.

19. Francis Oakley, *The Mortgage of the Past: Reshaping the Ancient Political Inheritance (1050-1300),* The Emergence of Western Political Thought in the Latin Middle Ages, vol. 1 (New Haven, Connecticut: Yale University Press, 2012).

20. Harvey C. Mansfield, Introduction to *The Prince: Niccolo Machiavelli,* 2nd ed., trans. Harvey C. Mansfield (Chicago, Illinois: University of Chicago Press, 1998), vii.

21. Desiderius Erasmus, *Erasmus: The Education of a Christian Prince*, ed. Lisa Jardine (Cambridge, United Kingdom: Cambridge University Press, 1997), 62.

22. Lisa Jardine, Introduction to *Erasmus: The Education of a Christian Prince*, ed. Lisa Jardine (Cambridge, United Kingdom: Cambridge University Press, 1997), x.

23. Ibid., 5.

24. Thomas More, *Utopia*, ed. Henry Morely, Project Gutenberg, accessed June 23, 2023, https://www.gutenberg.org/cache/epub/2130/pg2130-images.html#chap02.

25. Ibid.

26. Ibid.

27. George Washington, "Farewell Address," address, September 19, 1796, in *1 April–21 September 1796*. Vol. 20, *The Papers of George Washington*, Presidential Series, edited by David R. Hoth and William M. Ferraro, https://founders.archives.gov/documents/Washington/05-20-02-0440-0002; George Washington, "First Annual Address to Congress," January 8, 1790, ed. Gerhard Peters and John T. Woolley, The American Presidency Project, https://www.presidency.ucsb.edu/documents/address-the-sorbonne-paris-france-citizenship-republic.

28. Theodore Roosevelt, "Citizenship in a Republic," address at the Sorbonne in Paris, France, April 23, 1910, ed. Gerhard Peters and John T. Woolley, The American Presidency Project, https://www.presidency.ucsb.edu/documents/address-the-sorbonne-paris-france-citizenship-republic.

29. Winston Churchill, "Consistency in Politics," in *Thoughts and Adventures: Churchill Reflects on Spies, Cartoons, Flying, and the Future*, ed. James W. Muller (Wilmington, Delaware: ISI Books, 2009), 35–44.

30. Ibid.

31. Daniel J. Mahoney, *The Statesman as Thinker: Portraits of Greatness, Courage, and Moderation* (New York, New York: Encounter Books, 2022).

32. Charles de Gaulle, "On Character," in *The Edge of the Sword*, trans. Gerard Hopkins (New York, New York: Criterion Books, 1960), 44, 46.

33. Ibid., 44.

34. Roosevelt, "Citizenship in a Republic."

Xenophon

Epigraph: Xenophon, *The Education of Cyrus*, trans. Wayne Ambler (Ithaca, New York: Cornell University Press, 2001), 22.

Aristotle

Epigraph: Aristotle, *Nicomachean Ethics: Translation, Glossary, and Introductory Essay*, trans. Joe Sachs (Newburyport, Massachusetts: Focus Publishing, 2002), 69.

Marcus Tullius Cicero

Epigraph: Marcus Tullius Cicero, *Ethical Writings of Cicero: De Officiis, De Senectute, De Amicitia, and Scipio's Dream*, trans. Andrew P. Peabody (Boston, Massachusetts: Little, Brown, and Company, 1887), 36.

Kauṭilya

Epigraph: Kauṭilya, *Arthaśāstra*, trans. R. Shamasastry (Bangalore: The Government Press, 1915), 12, https://archive.org/details/in.ernet.dli.2015.70130/page/n5/mode/2up.

Han Fei

Epigraph: Han Fei, "The Difficulties of Persuasion," in *Basic Writings*, trans. Burton Watson (New York, New York: Columbia University Press, 2003), 78.

King David

Epigraph: *The Sacred Bible*, Catholic Public Domain Version, Original Edition, trans. Ronald L. Conte Jr. (www.sacredbible.org, 2009), http://www.sacredbible.org/catholic/OT-21_Psalms.htm#72.

Book of Judith

Epigraph: *The Sacred Bible,* Catholic Public Domain Version, Original
 Edition, trans. Ronald L. Conte Jr. (www.sacredbible.org, 2009),
 http://www.sacredbible.org/catholic/OT-18_Judith.htm.

Eusebius

Epigraph: Eusebius Pamphilus, *The Life of the Blessed Emperor Constantine,*
 in Four Books, from 306 to 337 A.D. (London: Samuel Bagster and
 Sons, 1845), book II, chapter 56, https://archive.org/details
 /eusebius-life-of-constantine-and-orations/page/n1/mode/2up.

Saint Augustine

Epigraph: Aurelius Augustine, *The City of God,* vol. 1, trans. Marcus Dods,
 (Edinburgh: T. & T. Clark, 1871; Project Gutenberg, 2014), book
 V, accessed June 23, 2023, https://www.gutenberg.org/cache/epub
 /45304/pg45304-images.html#Page_177.

Agapetus the Deacon

Epigraph: Agapetus, *Advice to the Emperor Justinian,* in *Three Political Voices*
 from the Age of Justinian: Agapetus—Advice to the Emperor;
 Dialogue on Political Science; Paul the Silentiary—Description of
 Hagia Sophia, trans. Peter N. Bell (Liverpool: Liverpool University
 Press, 2010), 100.

Abu Nasr Muhammad al-Farabi

Epigraph: Al-Farabi, *Alfarabi, The Political Writings: "Selected Aphorisms"*
 and Other Texts, trans. Charles E. Butterworth (Ithaca and
 London: Cornell University Press, 2001), 12, https://archive.org
 /stream/AlfarabiSelectedAphorismsAndOtherTexts/Alfarabi%20
 -%20Selected%20aphorisms%20and%20other%20texts_djvu.txt.

Saint Thomas Aquinas

Epigraph: Thomas Aquinas, *De Regno: On Kingship, to the King of Cypress*, ed. I. Th. Eschmann and Joseph Kenny, trans. Gerald B. Phelan (Toronto: Pontifical Institute of Mediaeval Studies, 1949), book 1, chapter 9.

Christine de Pizan

Epigraph: Christine de Pizan, *The Book of the Body Politic*, ed. and trans. Kate Langdon Forhan (Cambridge, United Kingdom: Cambridge University Press, 1994), 38.

Machiavelli

Epigraph: Niccolò Machiavelli, *The Prince*, trans. W. K. Marriott (Project Gutenberg, 2022), accessed June 23, 2023, https://www.gutenberg.org/cache/epub/1232/pg1232-images.html.

Erasmus

Epigraph: Desiderius Erasmus, *The Education of a Christian Prince*, trans. Lester K. Born (New York, New York: Octagon Books, 1963).

Saint Thomas More

Epigraph: Thomas More, *Utopia*, ed. Henry Morely (Project Gutenberg, 2021), accessed June 23, 2023, https://www.gutenberg.org/cache/epub/2130/pg2130-images.html#chap02.

George Washington

Epigraph: George Washington, "Farewell Address," September 19, 1796, in *1 April–21 September 1796*, vol. 20, *The Papers of George Washington*, Presidential Series, ed. David R. Hoth and William M. Ferraro, https://founders.archives.gov/documents/Washington/05-20-02-0440-0002.

Theodore Roosevelt

Epigraph: Theodore Roosevelt, "Citizenship in a Republic," address at the Sorbonne in Paris, France, April 23, 1910, ed. Gerhard Peters and John T. Woolley, The American Presidency Project, https://www.presidency.ucsb.edu/documents/address-the-sorbonne-paris-france-citizenship-republic.

Winston Churchill

Epigraph: Winston Churchill, "Consistency in Politics," in *Thoughts and Adventures: Churchill Reflects on Spies, Cartoons, Flying, and the Future*, ed. James W. Muller (Wilmington, Delaware: ISI Books, 2009), 35–44.

Charles de Gaulle

Epigraph: Charles de Gaulle, "On Character," in *The Edge of the Sword*, trans. Gerard Hopkins (New York, New York: Faber and Faber, Ltd., 1960), 44.

Permissions

Han Fei, Columbia University Press

From *Basic Writings*, by Han Fei/Burton Watson. Copyright © 2003 Columbia University Press. Reprinted with permission of Columbia University Press.

Agapetus, Liverpool University Press

From *Three Political Voices from the Age of Justinian: Agapetus*, Advice to the Emperor; Dialogue on Political Science; *Paul the Silentiary*, Description of Hagia Sophia, by Agapetus/Peter N. Bell. Copyright © 1963 Peter N. Bell. Reproduced with permission of the Licensor through PLS Clear.

Alfarabi, Cornell University Press

From *Alfarabi, The Political Writings: "Selected Aphorisms" and Other Texts*, by Charles E. Butterworth. Copyright © 2001 by Cornell University. Used by permission of the publisher, Cornell University Press.

Aquinas, Pontifical Institute of Mediaeval Studies

Reprinted, with permission, from Thomas Aquinas, *On Kingship*, trans. Gerald B. Phelan; revised with an introduction and notes by I. Th. Eschmann (Toronto: Pontifical Institute of Mediaeval Studies, 1949). © Pontifical Institute of Mediaeval Studies.

Pizan, Cambridge University Press

From *The Book of the Body Politic*, by Christine de Pizan/Kate Langdon Forhan. Copyright 1994 by Cambridge University Press. Reproduced with permission of the Licensor through PLSclear.

Erasmus, Columbia University Press

From *The Education of a Christian Prince*, by Desiderius Erasmus/Lester Born. Copyright © 1963 Columbia University Press. Reprinted with permission of Columbia University Press.

Churchill, The Estate of Winston Churchill

For quotes reproduced from the speeches, works and writings of Winston S. Churchill: Reproduced with permission of Curtis Brown, London on behalf of The Estate of Winston S. Churchill © The Estate of Winston S. Churchill.

De Gaulle, Plon and Faber & Faber

From *Le Fil de l'épée*, by Charles de Gaulle. Copyright 1932 by Plon. Used by permission of the publisher, Plon.

From *The Edge of the Sword*, by Charles de Gaulle/Gerard Hopkins. Copyright 1960 by Faber & Faber Ltd. Used by permission of the publisher, Faber & Faber Ltd.

Index